D0269160

NAZI THUG
TO BRITISH MAYOR:
Bruno's Story

NAZI THUG
TO BRITISH MAYOR:
Bruno's Story

Andrew Sangster

ROBERT HALE · LONDON

ISBN 978-0-7090-9072-4

Robert Hale Limited
Clerkenwell House
Clerkenwell Green
London EC1R 0HT

www.halebooks.com

2 4 6 8 10 9 7 5 3 1

Typeset in 10/12½pt Sabon by
Derek Doyle & Associates, Shaw Heath
Printed in Great Britain by the
MPG Books Group, Bodmin and King's Lynn

Contents

Preface

Writing an account of the life of an old friend while concealing his identity has not been an easy task. However, I thought it was worth doing as he had lived an extraordinary life and was such a decent person. The fragments of his diary show that he did not want to be identified for the sake of his family. His wife did not want to know too much about his life before they met, and she certainly did not want to know anything about his life in Nazi Germany. I believe, therefore, that his children would hardly recognize him in this account. He left me an old diary and some notes, and we had many conversations which helped me pull all the strands together. I have spent time researching the history and checking its reliability; for example, it took some time to establish that Hitler had 'dropped in' to Poltava airfield, where my friend saw him. This is why I think the footnotes are important.

Bruno, as I call my old friend, was eventually deeply influenced by many good Germans – and there were many, although their memory has been tarnished in the popular mind by the Nazi culture. Bruno followed his peers and hated Jews as a young member of the Hitler Youth, but once he discovered he was a *mischling* (a half-breed under the Nuremberg laws) he discovered what it was like to be hated and to live in fear. In April 1940 Hitler ordered all *mischlings* to be expelled from the military, but Bruno, like many others, was overlooked. Later, as a prisoner of war in England, he came to understand what it was to be disliked. Nevertheless, his quiet strength of character, his slow but steady Christian development, his ability at chess and his peculiar circumstances turned him from potentially an ardent Nazi into a liberal-minded and kindly gentleman. Many of his best friends believed he was born and bred a middle-class Englishman – as did I until an incident over a chess board caused him to talk to me about what he sometimes described as 'his dangerous inheritance'.

There will be people who think they know who Bruno is, and they may well be right. But I shall never confirm or deny it; I shall always keep my own counsel.

Acknowledgements

I am very grateful to my friend for sharing his life with me, and also to the Reverend David Hubbard and the Reverend Ken Hewitt for going over the text in its first draft. Above all I am grateful to my wife, Carol, who not only encouraged me but checked and rechecked the final text to ensure that it was readable. In fact, without her guidance, this book would have been a non-starter. Robert Hale, the publisher, asked me to reveal Bruno's real name. I said that to do so would be a betrayal of our friendship, but he had the courage to publish the work regardless, for which I am grateful. He also advised me to reduce the text by 15,000 words, for which I thank him, as the revised script is more succinct.

Part 1

Hitler Youth: and Hating

Chapter 1 1933

I am an old man now, facing death with some trepidation. It's not that I fear the process of dying, as long as it means curtains, or to put it more appropriately, oblivion. I long for oblivion, I long to be in a void where there is no consciousness, no memory. I want a death without dreams, a death in which I am as oblivious as I was before I was born. The trepidation I feel is because my mother always warned me, as she did all those in our family, that one day Almighty God would hold us to account. Not for silly things like stealing the neighbour's apples or taking money out of her purse, but for living without love.

My problem started with my birth because I was born into a world without compassion, indeed a world where compassion was a crime. My diary is anonymous and will be read only after my death by my friend, Andrew. Some of the conversations I have recorded are not verbatim, but their meaning is accurate, the gist is there, imprinted in my memory. I have an English name now, and most of my neighbours believe me to be English, while the more linguistically aware have asked whether I am of Polish extraction.

My real name is Bruno Sonn, and I was born on 27 January 1919 in a place called Petershagen on the edge of Eggersdorf, in the district of Märkisch-Oderland, in Brandenburg, about thirty kilometres from the centre of Berlin. Our house was in a long road called Hermannstrasse and was opposite a busy railway line. Fair haired and blue eyed like my older brother Josef, we were the epitome of German youth. My father, Wolfgang Sonn, had been born in Berlin in the previous century, and was a train driver before the First World War. During that war he fought with a famous

Saxon Regiment and was awarded an Iron Cross (Third Class) before he was invalided out in 1918 from Flanders. After the war he was out of work for some time, but by the late 1920s he had returned to driving trains.

I adored my father; he was big and strong and laughed most of the time. Even when he came home having had a few too many beers he was always in a good mood. He was not a quarrelsome person, and the only arguments I can recall from those early days were with my mother, Inge, which were always over religion. My father was a Roman Catholic but rarely went to church except at Easter and on Ascension Day. My mother was a Lutheran and she never missed a Sunday service. On Christmas Day my father would go with my mother to the Lutheran church, dragging me, Josef and my sister Ruth with them. My mother was always trying to convince my father either to attend her church more regularly or to go to the Catholic mission church. She did not mind which he chose, but felt it to be important for him to attend one.

'Have you lost your faith, Wolfgang? You used to go every Sunday and even serve at the altar!'

'That was before the war,' he would always reply.

My mother would shake her head and drop the subject for another day. My father hardly spoke of his time in the trenches, but there, in the mud, he lost his faith. I say he lost his faith; I think he had some doubts about his loss of faith; I think he thought he may have got it wrong, that maybe, just maybe, there was a God. I once heard him telling my mother that the army chaplains spent all their time telling them to kill the Tommies because they were evil. My father found this hard to accept as he did not think the Tommies were evil; he did not like the French, but he quite liked the few English soldiers he had met. My father rarely spoke of the war, but he was bitter about the way the war ended, and the near starvation they endured after the war. He would talk of the great depression and his favourite joke was about a man who filled his wheelbarrow with 10,000 marks in order to buy a loaf of bread. He left it outside the shop and somebody stole the wheelbarrow, but left the money intact.

My father was a train driver again, and we had food to eat and money to pay our rent, but it was never easy. I used to be sent by my mother to Frau Goldblatt's grocery shop by the railway station, with coins to buy bread and potatoes. If I was very polite Frau Goldblatt would give me a sweet before I left. She had lost both her sons in the war and she reckoned that her husband had died from a broken heart. 'My heart is still bursting,' she used to say, but she always gave me a sweet and a pat on the head.

I liked Frau Goldblatt; she was small and round with silvery hair. I also liked the cash register which she kept on a shelf behind her, beside a large family photograph of her husband and herself, with their two sons in uniform. There was always a small candle burning in front of it, and my father said it was her personal shrine. She would open at six in the morning and did not close until ten at night; she even remained opened on Sundays, but the shop was always closed on Saturday mornings. I never understood why until Josef's eighteenth birthday on 1 April 1933, which was a Saturday. I remember that particular detail because it was on that day that my family started to fall apart. My mother was preparing a meal for Josef's birthday, and her sister, my Aunt Ingrid, who lived right in the centre of Berlin, had joined us for the day. My mother had asked me to pop down to Frau Goldblatt's for some treacle, which she knew was kept behind the counter.

'She'll be shut,' said my father.

'She'll be open by the time Bruno's talked his way down the street.'

But my mother was interrupted by an outburst from birthday boy Josef. 'You can't go to that shop today, the *Führer* has forbidden it. All Jewish shops and businesses are to be ignored today, they are boycotted.'[1]

'Rubbish.' My father put his paper down. 'That only applies to large Jewish businesses, which are the old war profiteers.'

'All Jews are profiteers,' Josef retorted loudly.

'Frau Goldblatt's sons died for Germany, less than a mile from the place where I was wounded, she's as German as you and me, and don't tell me she's a profiteer, that is damned silly. The *Führer* does not mean little old German ladies like Frau Goldblatt.'

---

[1] On 30 January 1933 Adolf Hitler was appointed Chancellor of Germany, on 22 March Dachau concentration camp was opened and on 1 April there was a total boycott of all Jewish shops and businesses.

15

'She's a Jew; she's shut on a Saturday morning because it's their Sabbath.'

'She never goes near the synagogue.' My father was looking cross, and I could feel the tension between them.

'She's still a Jew, and you know that the *Führer* believes that Jews lost us the war, made all the money while men like you fought at the front.' I had never heard Josef argue with my father and I stood there with my mouth open. My mother and Aunt Ingrid looked at one another, both shaking their heads. Josef was getting more and more worked up but my father was calming down, saying, 'We'll go without treacle then, it's your birthday.'

'I would like treacle,' I blurted out. Josef gave me a venomous look and left the room. It was a quiet birthday meal, without treacle.

Next day I looked into Frau Goldblatt's shop and saw her matronly figure behind the counter; she was serving an old man from down the road, and when she saw me looking in, she smiled and waved. I could not work out this Jewish question. I had been told at school and in the Hitler Youth that the Jews were subhuman, but the pictures we were shown were not of people like Frau Goldblatt.

At school we had several lessons on the unpleasant way Jewry had wangled its way into our national life and had corrupted it from top to bottom. There were posters on the wall of our classroom showing men with hooked noses corrupting our economic system because of their greed. There was one picture of a group of Jews counting up money while German women were outside begging for bread. The Jews were the war profiteers and the women were the widows of soldiers who had died at the front. If I am quite honest in this diary, I did not like the Jews; I saw them as intruders into our life, and because of the cartoons I – and all my generation – believed they were subhuman. All the problems of the day seemed to have been caused by this race.

We were told a great deal about how evil the Jews were in the Hitler Youth (*Jugland*) which was rapidly gaining popularity. I enjoyed my time in the Hitler Youth because it meant weekends away, sport, learning to march and playing war games. My leader was called Adolf Bier; he was about seventeen years of age and was a friend of my brother Josef. He was something of a bully, but because he knew I was Josef's brother I was always treated well. We would spend entire evenings round a camp fire while Adolf gave us talks on the Jewish problem. Although I now realize that he was just a boy, at the time he was a man to me and everything he said, like my teachers, had to be right.

One evening he accused a boy called Rick of being circumcised like a Jew.

'Rick has got a funny nose; let's see if he's circumcised. Rick, drop those pants.' We all started to laugh, but I could see Rick's eyes filling with tears. 'Drop them,' Adolf shouted. 'Or have you got something to hide?'

We all fell silent and looked at Rick, who had stood up. He hesitated but when Adolf shouted again he dropped his pants. We were aghast because although when Rick stood there ashamed of his nakedness we could see that he was not circumcised, he had the biggest penis I had ever seen. There was an explosion of laughter, and Rick was from that moment on known as 'Big Dick'. Years later I met him again, as I shall recount later.

It was just after Josef's birthday that my mother and Aunt Ingrid returned to their home town of Memmingen, which was part of the Bavarian administrative region of Swabia. They liked to visit it even though it was hundreds of kilometres away, and they often travelled down to see family and friends. While my mother was away my sister Ruth looked after the house and Josef went to stay in Aunt Ingrid's flat in Berlin. She had a lovely flat above a large shop in Sophienstrasse. I liked it there, as all one had to do was pop out the door, cross Münzstrasse and one was in Alexanderplatz, the best shopping area in the world. I remember visiting it, because it was there that my father spoke to me about the Jews again. He obviously thought they were bad, but he told me that some Jews were more German than Jewish. Some of his soldier friends had been Jewish, and one had saved his life when he was wounded.

'The *Führer*, Bruno, is correct; it is the capitalist Jews who have to go. Our army was never defeated in the war, it was *Dolchstoss*,[2] it was the profiteers and Jews who lost us the war. But listen, Bruno, the Frau Goldblatts of this world, they are not really Jewish.

Frau Goldblatt is harmless.'

'What about Ruth's friend?' I asked. 'Is he a Jew?'

'No, whatever makes you think that? He goes to the Lutheran church with your mother.'

'Adolf Bier said that Hans Lobb has a Jewish name.'

'Your Adolf Bier has got that wrong.'

But I was not sure that he was right. I liked Hans and had become friendly with his brother Erik, but I knew that Erik was circumcised and although Hans went to the same church as my mother, I knew he only went because he liked Ruth. Erik did not go to any church, and his father did have a hooked nose and a funny glint in his eyes. However, as I said, I liked Erik and I liked Hans; I knew they never went to any synagogue, and as they were not wealthy, I thought they were all right. Their father was a tailor, and his mother cleaned other people's houses.

Adolf Bier told us that some teachers had been sacked because they were Jews, and I found he was right,[3] because one of my father's old army friends, who worked at the university, lost his job. I could see my father struggling with this, because although he hated what he believed the Jews had done to us, he knew some of them, and knew that they were not all to blame.

On reflection I am not sure my father fully understood the political situation. Josef told me that he had joined the *Sturmabteilung*[4] in the 1920s, but my mother said it was because there was no employment, and by joining up it was easier to get food. As soon as the railways started recruiting engineers he had left, although it was not easy to resign. My father's main talking point was how Germany could prosper, how we were a great country, and the only thing holding us back were profiteering Jews and Communists.

[2]*Dolchstoss* 'a stab in the back' – the popular theory that the German army was not defeated in the First World War but was betrayed by Social Democrats, profiteers and, most ominously, the Jews.

[3] On 17 April 1933 the Laws for Re-establishment of the Civil Service barred Jews from holding civil service, university, and state positions.

[4] *Sturmabteilung* 'Storm Division' commonly known as Brownshirts, often tough ex-soldiers recruited from 1921 on to protect Nazi speakers.

It was about this time that our family life started to change. My father had been a local district train driver; there had been times when he passed right by our house in the Hermannstrasse, and would hoot so that I could wave. But suddenly he was switched to longhaul train jobs as he called them, and would be away several days at a time. My mother and aunt had come home from Memmingen, and Josef seemed to be disappearing more and more. While staying in Berlin at Aunt Ingrid's flat he had made friends with some party activists and often went to stay with them. I was not doing well at school, but I was getting on in the Hitler Youth.

Looking back, those seem balmy days. It was a warm spring and we spent a good deal of our time camping out and singing songs around the camp fire. My sister Ruth was sixteen and she would turn seventeen on 5 November. I liked her; she was beautiful and this was made apparent by the number of boys who found her attractive. She was completely indifferent to them because she was very much in love with Hans Lobb, who was a couple of years older. Hans was nearly six feet tall but as Ruth was nearly the same height they seemed made for each other. Hans was a brilliant car mechanic who was something of an expert on the Daimler-Benz engines, as he was serving his apprenticeship with that firm. I grew to know him well as my friendship with his brother Erik developed.

Erik and I spent a good deal of time together, not only because we enjoyed the same things – like swimming and collecting birds' eggs – but because it meant that my mother was happy for Ruth and Hans to be together while their two younger brothers were in tow, as Ruth was supposed to be looking after us. It never worked like that; we would all go off together into the country, and while Ruth and Hans held hands and looked into one another's eyes, Erik and I would be off bird-nesting.

I tried to get Erik to join the Hitler Youth but he was not interested. That did not detract from our friendship, however, and we spent much of our spare time together. Erik was better at his schoolwork than I was, and that may have been because he did not spend time at Hitler Youth meetings.

There was one strange event that I persuaded Erik to come to with me. Adolf Bier had told all his Hitler Youth members to be at the library one Wednesday evening. This was unusual as we never normally met on a Wednesday. I was curious to see what was going to happen, especially as Adolf had a conspiratorial edge to his voice, and told us that we had to meet on the steps of the library but not go in. Erik and I arrived together, but because the rest of us were wearing our insignia Erik kept his distance. The Brownshirts (*Sturmabteilung*) were rushing in and out of the library throwing books at our feet and we were instructed, by Adolf, to make a pile of them in the street. I started to pick them up with care because some of them looked very expensive.

'Just grab them, Sonn,' yelled Adolf. He did not use my first name, probably, I thought, because he was trying to impress the Brownshirts. 'It's all Jewish rubbish and we have orders to burn it here in public.'

I looked at the book in my hand; it was in German, not Yiddish or Hebrew. Adolf, obviously reading my thoughts, yelled at me to get a move on, saying that the Jews also wrote in German – it was all treachery. I must confess I began to enjoy the atmosphere as the crowd grew larger and larger, and because I was helping empty the library I started to feel quite important. I was pleased Erik was there watching, as he would know that I held a position within the group which might help me to persuade him to join us. One of the Brownshirts poured a whole can of petrol over the books, and when he threw a match on the pile it nearly exploded. I spent most of the evening poking the fire with a long stick because although the flames were huge the books did not burn easily. The covers burnt quite quickly, but the pages were so dense they were slow to burn unless they were prodded. It was a fast-moving and exciting event; and I could think of no better way to spend a Wednesday evening.[5] But I could not get Erik to join in the fun; he just stood in an old tailor's shop doorway watching. I left after midnight knowing that my mother would be angry with me for being so late, and her anger might be increased as I stank of smoke, and was sweating like a pig from all the heat.

'Waste of good money that,' Erik said as we hurried home together.

'Orders from above,' I said proudly. 'Anything against the State must go; and that includes all that Jewish rubbish.'

[5] 10 May 1933 – public burning of books written by Jews, political dissidents and others not approved of by the State.

'I still can't see the point of burning good books; they must have burned half the library. Anyway, what's wrong with books written by Jews? I saw one of our school atlases being burned. If it was written by a Jew, does that make it any less true?'

'They're scum, they're not human and they're a danger to our Fatherland.' I nearly shouted this, which made him go quiet. We remained silent for ten minutes and then, not wanting to lose his friendship, I changed the subject completely and talked about birds' eggs, which did the trick.

My mother was unhappy about me being home so late. I thought she was being overprotective as I was not the youngest person in my group, and I had been amongst the first to wander off. I told her all about the event, but she did not want to discuss the matter. She said it was all very silly and was just a passing fancy. I sat in my bedroom watching out for passing trains, wondering whether one would hoot, which would tell me my father was the driver. Like most of my friends I thought the Jews were fiendish, and as I put my smelly smoke-polluted clothes over the chair I believed that I had played a small part in ridding our country of their influence. I was still not sure about Frau Goldblatt, as I believed she was really more German than Jew. I knew that Adolf Bier would spit on her windows as he passed by and so did some of my group, but I distanced myself from going that far. Of one thing I was certain: Jews were a menace to our country's future.

I was not the only one in trouble with my mother that night. Ruth came in late and I heard my mother telling her off for being out after midnight and warning her about becoming too close to Hans. Ruth protested that Hans had a good job with Daimler. But my mother said they were too young and the future uncertain.

The next day Aunt Ingrid came to see us for the afternoon; she was full of the bookburning incident she had seen in the centre of Berlin. 'Inge, my dear, it went on all night, the noise was unbelievable.'

I, of course, was all ears, wanting to say that I had been part of the great process. I did not get a chance because when she and my mother got talking it was impossible to get a word in edgeways.

'They must have emptied the library, they were burning books I had read, I had no idea they were Jewish, then this morning they made some Jews clean up the mess made by the bonfires.'

21

I remember that although Aunt Ingrid and my mother passed no opinion on the book burning, my mother seemed to disapprove of making the Jews clear up the mess made by the Brownshirts. But then she rarely mentioned politics, and I think she tried to forget my father's brief association with the *Sturmabteilung*.

I shall never forget her dismay later, when Josef announced that he was going to try and join the *Schutztaffel*[6], the SS, in which he intended to make his mark. One of his friends had already started as a junior rating in the *Gestapo*[7] and Josef, when he had been living in Aunt Ingrid's flat, had gone through a series of tests to gain entry. Tall, with blond hair like me, he would look good in their uniform. He was becoming interested in politics in a big way.

'And what's wrong with the army?' my mother asked him.

'The *Wehrmacht*[8] is run by idiots and has become soft. I intend to dedicate my life to the service of the Party[9] and therefore the country. It is an honourable thing I am going to do; I believe in Germany and the *Führer*.'

My father was away, and my mother never argued with Josef, for although she did not like some of his views, she loved him. I was proud of him and promised myself that I would follow in his footsteps in a few years' time; I knew that Adolf Bier was planning to do the same. An hour after Josef's announcement he left – he just packed his bags and went.

'Mind you,' my father ruminated over his supper, 'I'm told they only select the best; they have to be fit, racially pure, truly German, so I'm pleased he passed the selection test.'

---

[6] The *Schutztaffel* – the SS, a defence unit, almost a state within the state, an army within the army.

[7] Geheimes Staats Polizei – secret state police established on 26 April 1933 which fell under the organizational control of the SS. The chief was Himmler.

[8] *Wehrmacht* – the German armed forces, literally means 'defence force' and became synonymous with the army but really referred to all three services: army, navy and *Luftwaffe*.

[9] National Socialism was anti-capitalist, anti-Semitic, extreme nationalist political ideology developed by Adolf Hitler based on a twenty-five point programme developed by Hitler and members of the German Workers' Party; the forerunner of the National Socialist German Workers' Party – NSDAP or Nazi Party.

At the Hitler *Jugend* meeting the next evening we had the juniors with us, the *Jungvolk*, which I had left earlier that year. We knew them as *pimpf* and we had to train them in the party creed, making sure they could recite the Horst Wessel song,[10] and then we tested them to see whether they could pass the running test, which if I remember correctly was doing fifty metres in under twelve seconds. Only after they had passed the tests could they receive the dagger, which I was proud to wear as it bore the motto 'Blood and Honour' and which I took everywhere. But I enjoyed the song most of all; I can still remember it to this day:

Die Fahnen hoch, die Reihe dicht geschlossen!
SA marschiert mit ruhig festem Schritt.
Kam'raden, die Rotfront und Reaktion erschossen,
Marschieren im Geist in unser Reihen mit.[11]

I must have been the best singer as Adolf Bier always asked me to lead. I felt really good that evening as I told everyone what Josef, my big brother, was doing.

We were all good friends in the Hitler Youth, and I found the comradeship on the long hikes and camps very enjoyable. I also enjoyed the military training, when we marched along the streets singing our songs.

On Sunday of that week I avoided my mother in order to avoid going to church, so that Erik and I could go out bird nesting. We were searching barns in the hope of finding an owl's nest. I tried once again to get Erik to join the Hitler Youth, but he would not. Adolf and Josef had said that one day there would be conscription and everyone would have to join up, so I argued that it would be better to volunteer now.[12] There was one stage, when we were hiding in a barn loft to avoid being seen by the farmer, when I

[10] Horst Wessel – an SA man killed in a street fight with Communists in 1930.
[11] 'The Flags held high! The ranks stand tight together! SA march on, with quiet, firm forward pace. Comrades who, though shot by Red Front or Reaction, still march with us, their spirits in our ranks.'
[12] From December 1936 all other youth organizations were banned and it was made compulsory.

thought I had convinced him. However, other matters put a halt to my efforts. Not only did I fall out of the barn loft, but I would have been badly beaten by the farmer had Erik not intervened and then, since I had a dislocated shoulder, wheeled me home in an old wheelbarrow. The doctor told my parents that if Erik had not got me home as fast as he did I could have had a permanent injury.

While I was confined to the house for nearly a fortnight Erik came each day. We were more like brothers, and Ruth and Hans felt like family. Hans brought me some chocolate and I borrowed one of his books on car engines, which stirred an interest in things mechanical, an interest that stayed with me for the rest of my life, and would one day provide me with my livelihood. My mother and father were both fond of Hans and Erik, and along with Ruth, we made a happy household in the summer of 1933.

All the joy of that summer seemed to come crashing down around me at the end of July that year. Ruth told my parents the distressing news; I was listening while polishing my Hitler Youth dagger. 'Hans's parents are Polish. I knew they had a strange accent, but I didn't realize they were Poles. Hans and Erik were born in this country, and Hans's mother is Catholic but Herr Lobb is Jewish. Not that he's in any way religious, he never goes near the synagogue.' I nearly dropped my dagger at the news. Only the night before Adolf Bier had warned us all not to associate with known Jews, especially those who had crawled in from Eastern Europe.

'That doesn't make Hans and Erik Jewish,' I said. 'They were born here and only speak German.'

'Sorry son,' my father said. 'They're Polish Jews all right, and the new law[13] applies to them like all the others.'

'So you mean that they are no longer German? How can Erik be anything else? He only speaks German, and he got the school prize for his German language skills at the end of last term.' I was now feeling really confused. Erik, my best friend, was a Jew.

'Don't let it bother you,' Ruth said, 'I shall marry Hans whatever happens, Jew or German. I hate these stupid new laws.'

[13] On 14 July 1933 July a law was passed stripping all Eastern European Jewish immigrants of German citizenship.

'Steady,' my father said. 'The law is the law, and the Party is doing this to clean up our country. I am not allowed to vote in Poland, why should they vote here?'

'Anyway,' my mother joined in, 'you should not be talking about marriage yet to anyone, you're too young.' Ruth did not reply. She just stormed out and went to her bedroom, slamming the door behind her.

'What about Erik?' I asked.

'What about him?' My father put his paper down to look at me. 'Look at my paper, Bruno.' He was reading *Der Stürmer*[14] and there was a headline that read *Raus mit den Juden*, 'Away with the Jews.' He took the paper back. 'Until we have this Jewish problem sorted out this country will never be the same again; we will not be as powerful as we used to be. The Jews are holding us back. I know Erik and Hans are nice boys, and they seem to be very German, but they are nevertheless, Jewish. I am a rational man, and your mother and I are not going to stop you being friendly with Erik or stop Ruth seeing Hans, but they are not coming to this house again, and if I were you I would distance myself from Erik and not let your friends in the Hitler Youth know you know them.'

'And don't tell Josef,' my mother added. 'It will upset him.'

To hell with Josef, I thought, but I dared not say this to my parents. I avoided Erik for a week in order to give me time to think this through, as there was no one I could really talk to except Ruth, and she did not want to talk to me about the issue; she was in a world of her own. Josef was not a problem, as we had not heard anything from him or about him since he left home in the early summer.

Then Erik turned up at my door; and my father was in for once.

'You can't come in,' I almost whispered. 'You are Jewish.' I was about to add that I would grab my raincoat and meet him in the street, but before I could get that far Erik turned and ran down the road.

I had Hitler Youth that evening but I promised myself I would call on Erik the next day. I did not have time, however, and when

[14] *Der Stürmer* (the Stormer) – a violently anti-Semitic paper edited by Julius Streicher.

25

I called on the Thursday morning it was immediately clear that the family had moved. I stood there aghast, feeling dreadful that Erik had gone before I could see him, and explain that he was not really a Jew, even if his father was. I soon heard from Ruth what she thought about me. 'You callous little bigot,' she screamed. 'He saved your life only a month ago and you tell him to go because he's Jewish. Go back to your Party friends and boast of your bravery, you little shit.'

'He didn't give me a chance,' I protested. 'He went and now they've moved. Do you know why? Do you know where they've gone?'

'I know why and where. They've moved because their neighbours have been carrying out a hate campaign. After losing their citizenship some people seemed to think they had the right to put dog shit through their letterbox, and call Frau Lobb a Jewish whore. She could not have been a better neighbour to them, but the law changed all that. So much for your Hitler Youth, because your special friend Adolf Bier, may he rot in hell, was the main instigator of this nightmare.'

I was surprised, but then I thought of the few occasions when Adolf had warned me to stay away from Erik, and said he would never accept him into the Hitler Youth, even if I could persuade him. 'Where have they gone?' I asked.

'Do you think I'm telling you? They're safe now so keep your prying nose out.' Upon which she stormed out of the room.

I hated Jews, I mean I really hated them, but Erik and Hans and Frau Goldblatt were not really Jews, they were German. I sulked by myself all evening, and could not concentrate even on my birds' eggs.

The following evening my father was home. To our astonishment the Roman Catholic priest knocked on the door. He was concerned because he had not seen my father at church for so long. Although my mother was a Lutheran, she made him welcome, but having done so she sat quietly in the corner while my father explained that his new work kept him busy on Sundays. My mother looked at me because that was not strictly true, but she said nothing.

'I feel sorry for some of our Jewish neighbours,' the priest announced suddenly. 'They're having a rough time.'

I wondered whether he had heard about Erik and me, but then I saw him looking at my father's copy of *Der Stürmer*, with its cartoons of hook-nosed Jewish profiteers. My father did not look embarrassed. Indeed, he pointed out that Jewish profiteers had brought the country to its knees.

'It wasn't us soldiers who lost the war, Padre, it was those Jewish profiteers.'

'I agree it was the profiteers, and I agree some of them were Jewish, but not all. I'm sad to say many priests agree with you but there are also many who are getting worried that we're turning good Jewish Germans into scapegoats.'

'It was the Jews who crucified Christ,' my father said, turning to theology, of all things. 'It may have been the Romans who hammered in the nails, but they did it under pressure from the Jews.'

'Wolfgang, I am glad you think upon our Lord, but may I remind you that Jesus himself and the Blessed Virgin Mary were Jewish, really Jewish.'

For a moment I thought my father was stumped, but he was soon back saying that Jews were all right if they were in Palestine.

'So you wouldn't want Jesus in your home because he was a Jew?' the priest countered.

I saw my mother smiling; I wish I knew where she stood on this important national issue which seemed to be destroying the lives of so many people around us.

'I will not argue religion with you, Padre,' said my father. I thought that rich since he had started it. 'But I believe the Party is right, and the more I think about it, and talk about it with my friends the more I agree that even part Jews, half Jews, call them what you like, should not corrupt our nation.'

'But what if a person who is a Jew by birth worships as a Christian, kneels at the same altar rail as you, and fought alongside you for his country, is suddenly denounced. Would you still condemn him?'

'If you had asked me that a few weeks ago I might have agreed. I fought with some good German Jewish soldiers, but many of my best mates on the railway, and intelligent writers in *Der Stürmer* point out that the Jewish blood pollutes good German blood and makes us weak.'

'I can't agree with the stand you are taking because I believe you are being brainwashed. I know half of my congregation feel the same way you do, and when I preached against this attitude towards the Jews, some even got up and left. But remember, Wolfgang, Jesus was a Jew.' And he pointed to a crucifix up on the wall.

The next day I noticed my father had taken the crucifix down. I agreed with him. The Jews had no part in the new Germany. I was a little concerned about Frau Goldblatt and Hans and Erik, but I did not think that they were real Jews.

That night Adolf Bier read us an article from *Der Stürmer* which convinced us that Jews were not really human, more subhuman, and that they were not only polluting German blood but ruining our country, as they had done in the war. Adolf never mentioned Erik to me but he looked at me several times when in the second article he read that true Germans should not be seen to associate with Jews at any level. After that meeting we went out into the field and lit a bonfire. We were all delighted when an effigy of a Jew was placed on top of the flames to burn. It was cleverly made, and whoever had done it had modelled a gigantic hooked nose for the face. I think it was Big Dick's creation because he was smirking with pride. I then led the singing of the Horst Wessel song.

There was still no news of Josef, and Ruth had become very independent in her ways. Had it not been for the Hitler Youth I would have felt quite lonely. My mother seemed to be more involved than ever in her church, Aunt Ingrid had gone on a long holiday to France, my father was away with his work, and Erik had simply disappeared. Some evenings I had the house to myself and would sit in my father's armchair, drinking one of his beers and reading *Der Stürmer*. It struck me as a brilliant newspaper. I loved the cartoons of the Jews and some of the pictures were what I would describe as saucy but interesting. I felt that Germany was alive with new ideas and with the firmer control of the *Führer* it would one day be a great country once more.

Ruth puzzled me, however. I could not work out where she kept disappearing to, and then one evening, whilst sitting in the armchair, I worked it out – she was visiting Hans in their new home. I resolved to follow her one evening to find out where it was. I missed the opportunity, because just before her seventeenth birthday, on 5 November, she started training as a nurse and left home. Despite this I promised myself that one day I would track her down and find out more.

Christmas 1933 was the strangest I had ever had; there was no sign of Joscf, Ruth was at the hospital, my father was away and my mother took me to Memmingen, her home town. We stayed with another aunt, my mother's sister Marie, where I was bored beyond belief. I seemed to be attending more church services than I had ever done before. Aunt Marie was incredibly religious, and my mother seemed to be more 'churchy' by the day. However, I did like Pastor von Jan; he talked to me as an adult and he took the time to show me all around the church. One afternoon he even took me out for tea and showed me the interesting parts of the town. He was much more human than my father's priest, and I was pleased that he never mentioned the Jewish problem to me. He did ask a list of questions about the Hitler Youth, what we did and what we thought.

Despite all the food and presents I was glad to return home and rejoin the activities of my Hitler Youth group. We had a great time staying up to see in the New Year. It was 1934 and we were confident that Germany and we young followers of the party, were making history. Adolf Bier said that as the years went by our generation would never be forgotten; now, as I reflect on all this from my Bromley flat, I can truly see the irony in that statement.

Chapter 2

1934

Sitting here in south London reflecting on my youth I realize that all my attitudes have changed completely, and part of my reason for writing this reflective account is to prove to myself that I have changed enough for me to be redeemed, either by God, if he exists, or by myself when I leave this life, which according to my local doctor is not that long. Having lived in Bromley for nearly thirty years, pre-war Germany seems like another world, but I know it is not, because I was there.

I started 1934 with the realization that Erik had gone from my life; as he never appeared at school again I knew his absence was more permanent than I had feared. From that point on I ceased to be interested in birds' eggs. School was also changing. There was a picture of the *Führer* in every classroom and our new teacher always started the day with the Party salute and the singing of the Horst Wessel song. I actually started to do better at school than in previous years. Several teachers had left and the new ones were all Party members. History was the dominant subject in the school[1] and I won a prize for writing an essay on Horst Wessel and other Party martyrs. I also enjoyed, for the first time in my life, mathematics. It was as if a veil had lifted from my mind in a subject that I had hitherto had serious problems concentrating on.

[1] On 9 May 1933 the *Reich* Minister of the Interior, Wilhelm Frick, insisted that history had to take a leading role in the curriculum, underlining that life was dominated by strife and race and blood.

School changed in 1934 in more ways than the improvement in my own progress. The teaching was very much based on the political values of the Party[2] and I did well in this because it was just a case of repeating what we had been taught in the Hitler Youth. I remember one occasion, when we were having a lesson on the dangerous effect the Jews had on our country, when one of the girls mentioned that lots of Jews had died in the German army in the war. There was total silence in the room until I blurted out 'Yes, they died from fright.' There were roars of laughter and after that I could do nothing wrong. My teacher obviously mentioned it to other teachers because at least two of them stopped me to congratulate me on my wit. I told my father about this, and he smiled, but he did not find it quite as funny as my teacher.

'I was there, son,' he said, 'I don't like Jews any more than your teachers do, but I did meet some brave ones in that war.' I did not reply as, at fifteen, I was the youngest in the family and I held my father in the highest esteem and loved him dearly. When we were asked to write an essay about our family and their attitudes to the new Germany, I wrote mainly about my father's war in the trenches, and did not mention the fact that my mother went to church regularly; I also pointed out that my father hated Jews and all profiteers. Rick, whom we had nicknamed Big Dick, wrote about his father in an entirely different way. He had told Adolf and me around a camp fire one night that his father thought the state was taking over the family. He objected to his son going off on fifty kilometre hikes on Sundays, coming back tired and missing church, and then being out every evening, and he also thought the school was teaching too much about politics. Rick also mentioned that he suspected that his father had once been a Communist. When Big Dick told me this later I asked him if he loved his father.

'Not really,' he replied. 'He's weak, he hasn't worked for years, and he keeps complaining about the Party. He objects to me going out for our Hitler Youth activities.'

'If your essay falls into the wrong hands your father could be in trouble,' I said. I did not really believe this, but I wanted Big Dick

---

[2] In January 1934 a directive was issued making it compulsory for schools to teach the spirit of National Socialism.

to feel worried; he was more of an acquaintance than a friend, more another chap in the group than a comrade. When I told my father what Big Dick had written his face became very dark. 'Listen, Bruno, you be very careful what you say about our family. On the railways I hear all sorts of things. One of my mates was accused of being a Communist,[3] I knew he wasn't, but he just disappeared.'

'It's only school, Dad.'

'It was only the ex-Kaiser's birthday[4] which those army officers were celebrating, but the Brownshirts still beat them all up. School is part of national life these days.'

'Yes, I heard that on the wireless,' I said.

'Some of those Brownshirts are just big bullies,' my father said. 'There are more of them than the whole army put together[5].' He looked at me for a moment, and taking my arm looked me in the eyes. 'And don't repeat what I tell you. I am proud of what you do for the *Führer*, but always keep your own counsel.'

I looked puzzled for a moment, and he stood me right in front of his chair. 'Bruno, we live in a difficult world. The *Führer* is doing great things for our country; look at the *autobahns*, they're magnificent, everyone who wants work gets work, he's putting profiteering Jews in their place, but Bruno, he's surrounded by men who are sycophants, creeps, who would do anything he asked. My foreman is nothing, but because he has rank in the Brownshirts, he acts as if he's second to the *Führer*, and sometimes I feel as if I am back in the army when he starts bossing us about. We can't quarrel with him because he is a Party member. I think it was him who told the authorities my friend was a Communist. He wasn't a Communist; he just had the guts to stand up over our long hours. But he's gone now.'

[3] There was unnecessary alarmist propaganda in 1933 about the resurgence of the Communist Party.

[4] In January 1934 some ex-army officers were celebrating the ex-Kaiser's birthday in the Hotel Kaiserhof when Brownshirts broke in and broke up the party.

[5] The German Army at this stage was limited to 100,000 whereas Brownshirts numbered, at a conservative count, at least two million.

I only nodded. I was not sure whether to believe him or not, but home was home, school was school, and I had always managed to keep them apart. A week later I realized the truth of what my father had said because I heard that Big Dick's father had been arrested and sent to Dachau.[6]

'What did his mother say?' I asked Adolf Bier.

'There's not much she can say, her old man was a Communist.'

'How's Big Dick feel?'

Adolf looked at me and grinned. 'He's as pleased as punch, he's got the weakling out of the house, he's helped cleanse the new Germany and now he's the man of the house. When his sister cried Big Dick thumped her and that was that.'

I never spoke to Big Dick about the matter until we shared a tent at the Nuremberg Rally later that year. Adolf was right, he was still boasting about what he had achieved.

My own mother was really upset, and I think she had tears in her eyes when I told her, which I found rather strange given she had never met Big Dick or his family. 'I find that the most terrible thing I've ever heard,' she said. 'I hope my son would never do a thing like that.'

'Of course I wouldn't.' And I meant what I said; I really loved my parents. I even loved Ruth, although I had not seen her for months. None of us had heard anything from Josef, but I loved him too.

'I don't like your Hitler Youth,' she said. 'I see them in the street and they are nothing but a bunch of loud-mouthed bullies; they even taunted a pastor the other day, and in public, I hope you never do that Bruno.'

'Never, Mum,' I lied.

I had not taunted her pastor, but we had teased another clergyman who walked by our field. I remember feeling uncomfortable about it to start with, but when we all joined in, it was fun. I even started to gain the impression that we scared some adults. I had not attended church for some time because the Hitler Youth used to meet nearly every Sunday for hikes or for military drill. I remember that in February 1934 I won the prize for

---

[6] Dachau concentration camp was opened on 22 March 1934.

marksmanship with a rifle. I was so proud of my new badge I wore my uniform nearly every day. My mother, despite her views on the Hitler Youth, paid for a new uniform and sewed the badge on. I can still recall her paying 135 reichsmarks for it, which was a great deal of money for us as a family.

So Sunday became a Hitler Youth day, and church started to become more of a distant memory. One night we attacked a small church because it had some Hebrew over its door. We smashed the windows and took pot shots at the cross on the roof, then daubed the doors with yellow paint and 'Juden'. In fact, it became quite a popular pastime to tease clerics and their congregations.[7] I always tried to keep out of the way of such activities in my own area, and twice even persuaded my comrades to move to other districts for the fun.

We were having more and more lectures in the evenings from guest speakers,[8] which meant some of the younger ones wanted to stay away because they were getting bored. I was very pleased when Adolf Bier appointed me to chase up some of these malingerers. One evening this led to an unfortunate incident. I knocked on one boy's front door and his father came to the door. He told me that he was in charge of his family, not some boy scout. I protested, 'We are not boy scouts, we work for the *Führer*, and Günther is expected there now.'

'Damnation on your *Führer*,' he shouted. 'I run my family, not you petty thugs.' Then he hit me so hard I fell over the small wall at the front of their house. I told Adolf Bier what had happened and we all marched around to Günther's house and threw stones through the front window. When we saw Günther's father looking at us from an upstairs window we threw stones at him, which smashed more windows. Then two policemen appeared and told us to clear off. I remember being surprised that they only told us to clear off; they ignored the broken glass. Adolf stood up to them and said we were following orders in finding defaulters. The

---

[7] There had always been radical anti-clerical groups (*Pfaffenfresseren*), but some Hitler Youth eclipsed this in their behaviour.

[8] A regulation in January 1934 gave Hitler Youth groups the same status as schools as educational institutions.

argument had hardly begun when a group of Brownshirts came and asked what had happened. One of them took a policeman aside, after which the police simply withdrew. Then, to my further astonishment, two of the Brownshirts went to the front door and when it was not opened they kicked it open. It all happened so fast I could hardly believe it, but Günther's father suddenly flew through the downstairs front window and lay motionless across the very wall I had fallen over. Then they dragged Günther out with them and we marched him off, Big Dick holding him by his ear. I looked back and saw Günther's father still motionless. I wondered whether he were still alive. I felt good about the fact we had taken our revenge, and even better when Günther was given a public dressing down.

As I walked home that night I realized how powerful our Hitler Youth was but I never told my parents, and the next day I was not entirely sure that what had happened was right. Günther came the next week and I was pleased to hear that his father was only bruised, but after that we never saw him again, and I heard later that the family had moved to Memmingen of all places, my mother's birthplace. That night, outside a local church was a poster asking people to pray 'for the children of Abraham'. I knew that would not stay up long, and nor did it, because two days later I painted the board with black paint in the middle of the night. My mother was furious, my father was ambivalent, but they never knew it was me.

It was an adventurous year for my Hitler Youth group because we went off to a grand Nuremberg Rally. There were thousands of us and we were camped in a huge tent city, which was marked off in streets and lines. All the tents were the same and we really had to remember our line number in order to find our tent. I shared mine with Big Dick, Adolf and another comrade called Wilhelm. We had a great time, running around setting up chairs, helping with the banners and practising drills. I also helped with the floodlighting and with Wilhelm acted as a runner for a famous film maker.[9] We saw all the top men including the *Führer* himself. We

[9] The 1934 Nuremberg Rally was the subject of Leni Riefenstahl's film *The Triumph of the Will*.

were really inspired by the whole occasion; we felt powerful and important. I admired the uniforms of the SS; their very blackness with the silver insignia made them stand out. They looked very smart compared to the Brownshirts, who, after they had beaten up Günther's father, went down in my estimation.

As I started coming home later and later in the evening, I saw many Brownshirts who always seemed to be drunk. It had started to occur to me that the Brownshirts spent most of their time in the taverns. My father said their day was over now that the Party was established; they were no longer needed for street fighting or breaking up opposition groups, because opposition was no longer viable in public. I heard rumours that the Brownshirts were going to take over the army, and then suddenly we were told that they had rebelled against the *Führer* and that Röhm, the head of the SA had been executed.[10] When I look back on all this I think how inconceivable it would be to hear that a Prime Minister had ordered the execution of seventy-seven men he did not trust. It would be world-breaking news and change the nature of this society overnight. Yet in 1934 in Germany we were surprised, but the *Führer* was praised by one and all for reacting with such decisive firmness.

After a month the whole business was forgotten when we heard the news of Hindenburg's death;[11] it was a Thursday and I remember it well, because I was at home in bed recovering from a bout of food poisoning. In future, we were told by the wireless, the *Führer* would be known as the *Führer* and *Reich* Chancellor. He had all the armed forces swear an oath, which we repeated in our Hitler Youth. I wrote it all down and can still remember it to this day. It ran:

> I swear by God this holy oath, that I will render unconditional obedience to the Leader of the German Reich and people, Adolf Hitler, the supreme commander of the

---

[10] In June 1934 occurred the Night of the Long Knives, when Hitler purged the SA. It was claimed that seventy-seven had died but the figure is probably closer to a thousand.

[11] At 9 a.m. on 2 August 1934.

armed forces, and as a brave soldier am willingly prepared to risk my life for this oath at any time.

I can recall the two thoughts that passed through my mind. First, I would obey it to the end of my life. We had had it instilled in us that a man's word was his bond, but with an oath his soul and life depended on keeping it. Secondly, however, I was perplexed about swearing an oath before God. Adolf Bier had spent most of that year denigrating any belief in God, and molesting clergy. Did Adolf Hitler, I wondered, believe in God?

I cannot remember exactly when we heard news of Josef. All I do know is that it happened some time in the middle of 1934 and that Ruth was home after several months' absence. We were all sitting round the table having some tea and cake, talking about how Ruth was getting along in her training. She was obviously enjoying her work at the hospital.

'What happened to Hans and Erik?' I asked.

'I'm surprised you want to know,' she said. 'They're only Jews to you.' I felt the sting, and whilst my mother looked away my father just winked at me.

'Are they all right?' I persisted, but before Ruth had a chance to answer there was a sudden heavy hammering at the front door. My father looked surprised – we were not used to visitors – and when he came back into the room there was an SS officer with him, and a man in a long black leather coat. They looked very stern, but upon seeing me in my Hitler Youth uniform they immediately saluted. I jumped to my feet and returned the salute with a '*Heil Hitler*' and clipped my heels, as I had seen officers do when they visited us at camp.

'We are here about Josef Sonn – your son I believe?' The leather-coated man asked.

'Is he all right?' my mother asked, obviously worried that they were the bearers of bad news.

'He's fine,' the SS officer smiled. 'He's passed all his fitness training, and he gained excellent results in his military exams and was first in his group in weapon training, but before he joins the SS we want to check his pedigree.'

'His pedigree? Makes him sound like a dog.' Ruth said.

'Any member of the SS,' the leather-clad man replied, 'must have a pure Aryan background. We think he has, but I am doing a final check before I sign his forms.'

'Ruth, go and check the fire in the kitchen, please, dear.' My mother could see, as I could, that Ruth was becoming agitated at their presence.

'I don't know much about my own background,' my father said. 'We're just working people and have lived in Berlin and its environs all our lives.'

'Any Jewish blood?' The man in black leather asked.

'Certainly not,' my father snapped back. 'My father was also called Wolfgang Sonn and I think his father was called Wolfgang before him, as all eldest sons were back then. None of us has ever been near a synagogue except to walk by. I fought in the war and my father was also a soldier.'

'What about your mother?' the man persisted.

'She was called Ruth. I have no idea what her maiden name was because all our birth certificates were burned in a fire at our last house, back in 1920.'

I had no idea that we had had a fire, but then I was just a baby.

'And your parents?' they asked my mother.

'My father was called Wilhelm and my mother had the same name as my sister Ingrid, and we all came from Memmingen. I remember my grandfather on my father's side was called Josef Dorf, and on my father's side Walter Buch. Good German names and we were all Lutherans, not Jews.'

'That tallies with our own research; we just needed to check with you. It is an honour to belong to the SS and we only want the best.'[12] The SS officer smiled at me and asked what I would do when school finished. I replied I would like to follow my brother. They then left as abruptly as they came, both of them patting me on the head as they went. For a brief moment we all sat in silence, though Ruth had stayed in the kitchen.

---

[12] During the period 1933–5 Himmler purged many of the ranks of the SS in order to find the best and most pure in racial terms. In 1935 in order to be an SS officer proof of pure Aryan ancestry had to be traced back as far as 1750, and to 1800 for non-officers.

'At least we know Josef's well,' my mother said. 'But I do wish he'd write; we are silly, we should have asked for his address. Didn't one of them mention the barracks in Potsdam?'

'That would not do, Inge, there are hundreds of them, and he'll come home as soon as he's finished. He seems to have done well.' My father was obviously pleased. Ruth, when she returned to the room, could hardly hide her contempt – her attitude could pose a problem. Some of my comrades in the Hitler Youth would have reported her, but my family still came first, even in those heady days. My parents quizzed her about Hans, who had lost his job because he was Jewish, which my father found puzzling because it was 'essential work'. Ruth exploded claiming that Jews were being thrown out of all essential work.

Despite my mother's appeals Ruth walked out of the house and it was another year before I saw her again. After she had gone we said nothing, my father read aloud from the latest *Stürmer* an entertaining article by Herr Streicher.[13] My mother went out to her church.

In the autumn of 1934 a rather strange thing happened. I was doing my homework for once, in the hope that I might be able to get an apprenticeship with Daimler-Benz, as Hans Lobb once had. I had just finished reading the Party newspaper[14] and my father was reading about someone he once knew who had been promoted from being Commandant of Dachau to become Inspector of all concentration camps.[15] I never knew how he knew such an important person, but I guess it was from his early days either during the war or immediately afterwards. He was drinking coffee and my mother was at some church do when there was a knock at the door. I looked up from my work to see that my father had let in a man who looked as skinny as a half-starved peasant.

'My God,' my father said. 'What's happened to you, Otto? You look as sick as a dog.'

This Otto, whom I had never met before, half smiled at me and seemed to take in my Hitler Youth uniform. 'I was hoping to catch

[13] Julius Streicher, the editor, was hanged at Nuremberg in 1946.

[14] The Nazi newspaper was called *The Racial Observer*.

[15] Theodore Eicke was appointed by Himmler to this post on 4 July 1934.

up with you, Wolfgang, alone,' he said.

'Bruno, this is Otto, we used to be train drivers together, and Otto was also in my old regiment. You do your work in the kitchen, while I pour Otto some coffee and we have a chat.'

I obeyed but I was very curious; my father hardly had any visitors and I had never met any old war friends of his. So, to say the least, I was disappointed. I am ashamed to say that although I pulled the door to behind me I did not close it fully, and I sat on a stool by the door so I could listen to what was being said.

I heard Otto explain he had been arrested by the *Gestapo* because of a criminal offence several years before,[16] and that he had spent a brief time in Dachau for cracking jokes about Adolf Hitler.[17]

'You know they're allowed to open your mail and can listen in on your phone?'[18]

'I didn't think you had a phone; we haven't got one,' my father said.

'No, of course I haven't got a phone, but even the damned walls have ears.'

'Otto, you're not getting paranoid are you?'

'The point is I only told my jokes to a select few, I'm not stupid, I know people report you for any criticism of the Government. But when I was coming to the end of my sentence, and hoping to get out I suddenly realized who it was that reported me. It was unquestionably Max Brett my block warden,[19] and I reckon yours as well.'

---

[16] In the early 1930s the *Gestapo* did have a crackdown on what they called 'community aliens', and arrested professional criminals, vagrants and mendicants. They were classified as 'a-socials'.

[17] There were 'malicious gossip' laws whereby anyone denigrating the party was liable to arrest.

[18] The Reichstag Fire Decree of 28 February 1933 allowed *Gestapo* to open mail and tap phones.

[19] Every group of houses or flats had a block warden, a low-ranked Party member who ensured that people cooperated by hanging out flags on special occasions and attending rallies, and who kept their ears to the ground for any dissidents or malicious scandal-mongering about the Party. By 1935 there were over 200,000 such appointments, and the numbers were increasing rapidly.

'You mean our golden pheasant?'[20]

'Wolfgang, that's why I'm here as an old friend. Beware of him.'

'I hardly ever see him unless we've forgotten to hang bunting out, but young Bruno always does that in good time.'

When he had gone I asked my father whether it was true. 'He's not a Communist is he?' I asked.

'No he's not a closet Communist or anything like that. If he had been I would not have invited him in – that would have severed all our past friendship. He may have been a Social Democrat, but even that I'm not sure about.'

'But surely he didn't go to prison for telling jokes?'

My father paused to put his slippers on and sat down in his chair before he spoke again. He told me that it was not the first time he had heard how serious it was to laugh at the *Führer*. One of his railway friends had entertained his work mates by imitating him in their canteen. The next day he had been arrested by the *Gestapo*.

'What happened to him?' I asked.

'He wasn't sent to Dachau because he was back at work a week later, but he had a black eye and one of his hands was damaged. We asked him what had happened but he simply refused to speak; to be honest he was a changed man.'

The following year my resolution was to be tested but for the time being I glowed at father's approval. My father was also pleased with my work. I had stayed on at school and passed my examinations; I surprised myself because until this last year I had been a poor pupil. I was interviewed for an apprenticeship with Daimler-Benz on 10 December 1934, if my memory serves me correctly. I travelled by train into Berlin, a short journey, and spent the morning with four others. We were shown around the work areas, as well as the design centre, and then we were interviewed several times before sitting a written test, which included some easy mathematics – more like arithmetic. There was a Party member there, who asked us whether we had any Jewish or foreign blood in the family. Apparently the firm supported the Party[21] and had

[20] They were called golden pheasants because of their brown uniforms and red tabs.

[21] Daimler-Benz made several contributions to Party funds.

expelled all Jews and anyone who was not thoroughly German. We were told that they dealt with sensitive military matters and they wanted only the best of German youth to work for them.

The following week I was told I would start work at a Daimler-Benz garage near the Berlin aerodrome,[22] I was so excited, and my parents were thrilled. My first day started with a shock, however, because I was shown a locker that was to be mine, and when I opened the door I discovered an old label that indicated it had once belonged to Hans Lobb, the Jew my sister still loved. It stopped me dead because it also made me reflect on my old friend Erik, and I wondered where on earth he was these days.

My father had warned me that for my first year I would just be a 'grease-monkey' making cups of coffee and cleaning up oil, but he was wrong. I was put under a qualified mechanic, who was to look after me, and who was called Bruno just like me. He was a man in his late fifties and my job that month was to hand him the right tools and listen to what he was doing and why. He took my apprenticeship very seriously, and as he worked he talked all the time about what he was doing and why each component was important to the huge lorry engines he was working on. Even during breaks he made me explain all the parts of the engine, and tested me on the tools by making me select and name the right ones. I enjoyed the work from the very start and was pleased I had already studied engines, both petrol and diesel, and the different systems of combustion and how they worked in Hans Lobb's book. When I look back I realize now how important big Bruno's training was to my life, because he gave me a love for my work, as well as a lifetime's occupation. He equipped me with skills that would serve me all my life and one day make me fairly well off given all that happened in my youth.

We did not see Ruth that Christmas, but to my mother's delight Josef at last turned up at our front door. I was very impressed by his smart black SS uniform with the silver bolts of lightning on his collar. My father did not get home until mid-morning that Christmas but he was also delighted. I pestered my big brother about all his training, but all he would tell me was that it was very

[22] Probably Tempelhof.

tough and the SS were only choosing the best. Apparently he had been admitted at a special ceremony the previous November,[23] but there were still some tests to do and some parades to attend before he was given his rank. I found it all a little confusing. I still hankered after doing the same thing myself, but the mechanic's job seemed more interesting to me.

'What do you do at the moment?' my father asked him.

'I'm not fully fledged yet, so we have to do a good deal of physical training. We also study history and the question of race and plenty of military exercises. I have formed a junior guard at some parades because our marching has to be the best in the world. Last month I did three weeks on guard duty at Dachau concentration camp.'

I watched my mother's jaw drop and for a moment she just sat with her mouth open; my father's face remained expressionless.

'Anyway,' Josef added as an afterthought, 'that's finished now because I am back on military exercises in January and parade duties in April.'[24]

'Who are the prisoners?' I looked at my father. He knew the answer so I wondered about the reason behind his question, and I almost wondered whether he was going to ask about Otto.

'Complete range of traitors, criminals, and those who oppose the *Führer* and his holy work.'

'Holy!' my mother said. 'Holy belongs to God, not governments.'

Josef looked at her and I could see him weighing up the situation. He told her that religion no longer meant anything to him, that the most sacred thing in his life was his country and his *Führer*. My father changed the subject almost at once, using my new job to start a new conversation.

Josef only stayed for the day because he had to report to his

---

[23] New candidates were accepted in a mass parade on the anniversary of the Munich Beer Hall Putsch in November 1923. They were then expected to take an oath on Hitler's birthday in April and entered the service of the SS at a ceremonial parade in October, during which they were awarded their ceremonial engraved daggers.

[24] This would be the oath-taking ceremony on Hitler's birthday.

barracks in Potsdam by midnight. I noticed during his time with us that my mother had become unusually quiet. She took the Church very seriously and I think Josef had really upset her with his remarks. I knew from my Hitler Youth lectures that the clergy were not generally trusted and that only weak people and dissidents went to church, but my mother had always been to church and I shelved the issue in my mind, keeping off the subject whenever possible.

We had a two-day break and I enjoyed that Christmas time at home. As I have said there was no sign of Ruth, and Josef came and went like the flash of lightning on his lapels. I played cards with my father and also a few games of chess. Because I had made some money I also bought some beer and I really started to feel grown up. My father said that I ought to join a chess club and although I was tempted, having won the school championship three years in a row, I was too busy working all day and staying in touch with my Hitler Youth group. There was a light smattering of snow which added to the festive atmosphere and it was a truly comfortable time at home. Christmas that year was on a Tuesday and I did not have to report to work until Friday. Then we had the weekend. It was a completely relaxed time and I was sorry for my parents that Ruth made no contact. I know my father tried to see her on the Thursday but she was not at the hospital and they had no idea where she was spending her time off. I think he was more concerned than my mother which surprised me, although the following year I was to find out why.

Chapter 3

1935

In 1935 I completed my first year of employment, working five or six days a week with big Bruno on all kinds of engines as well as gear boxes, until I had a very good idea of the fundamentals. Occasionally I would go to another workshop, which broadened my knowledge, but my main apprenticeship was to understand the function and components of engines and gear boxes. I was kept very busy and big Bruno treated me well, never neglecting to test me to ensure that I knew everything he could possibly teach me. He used to tell me that if in three years I could do all he could do I would never be out of work, 'because engines are the future'. I saw less and less of my original Hitler Youth friends, but following another apprentice's advice, I attached myself to a specialist Hitler Youth section that dealt with engineering, which still involved me with long Sunday hikes and military training. That said, I became infatuated with my work and was often too tired to join in all the expected activities of my new *Jugland*.

When I mentioned to big Bruno that I played chess, he immediately brought out his own chess set in the lunch breaks and we played daily. He was very serious about his chess, which meant I did not beat him for months. He taught me that it was not simply a matter of pushing pieces around the board, waiting for your opponent to make a mistake; you needed to think ahead. He taught me openings such as the Sicilian and the French and how, as white, to play the Ruy Lopez.

His lessons in this wonderful game not only gave me a hobby for the rest of my life, but in later years chess was to turn my life around completely. I even went to his chess club, which met on a Monday night, in a down-and-out tavern near Tempelhof station. I loved the chess club and slowly but surely my game improved by playing more experienced players.

One of the best players there was an elderly man called Johann Epp, who like big Bruno was happy to give me lessons in the openings and also in the end game where, through lack of knowledge, I often lost an otherwise good game. I kept losing. He was a very kind, gentle man, who never laughed at my blunders, and even in serious games would let me take a move back, which big Bruno certainly never allowed. Johann gave me some tuition in games played by Capablanca and Alekhine and spent hours going through their games with me so that I could understand the thinking behind these great chess minds. He had a small book on the Ruy Lopez opening, and one evening he gave it to me as a present, signing the front cover with his name, 'to Bruno Sonn, my youngest friend!'

I have to say some of my happiest evenings were spent in the company of big Bruno and Johann, which seemed strange because big Bruno must have been over fifty years of age and Johann at least seventy, and I was only sixteen. My birthday that year was on a Sunday, and my parents bought me a new chess set. When I attended big Bruno's club as usual that Monday evening, Johann had brought me a cake and everyone made such a fuss of me it felt as if I had a second family. On becoming sixteen I had to sign some forms for the firm, thus making my apprenticeship formal. I felt good about life.

I also gathered from big Bruno that he had a weakness for the cinema; he was always getting his leg pulled by his mates on the next bench because of his love of Mickey Mouse. I have to admit I was surprised that big Bruno, who could build a diesel engine with his eyes shut and beat me at chess, enjoyed Mickey Mouse. I told him about the time I had acted as a runner for the film *Triumph of the Will* when I had attended the Nuremberg Rally the previous year.

'The trouble, little Bruno,' he said, 'is that all the films today are home made and are too serious. They're always pushing the Party line; they should be there, like Mickey Mouse, to entertain us. I haven't seen a good American film for months; I think they've been banned.'[1]

I was not sure how to respond; big Bruno was like a second father to me, but he seemed to be criticizing the Party. I said nothing and he noted my silence.

'Well, little Bruno, you like the German films do you?'

'I haven't seen many,' I confessed. 'But I see a few Party ones with my unit of the Hitler Youth.'

'Yes, of course, I suppose you are obliged to watch them.'

Again I felt that he was wandering into the dangerous area of politics, and I wanted to keep him as my god of the workbench and friend at chess. 'Well,' I paused, I wanted to express myself cautiously, 'we're taught to admire what the Party is doing for our country and not to criticize.'

Big Bruno looked at me over the engine block for several moments, as if trying to understand what I had said. He put his screwdriver down and, taking off his funny round glasses, wiped his forehead with his pocket rag. 'I can see that with your generation the era of individualism is dying,' he said.

'What do you mean?' I asked. I instantly wished that I hadn't as it became clear that big Bruno thought the Party was depriving us of personal freedom.

'Shush,' I said, 'you don't know who may be listening.'

'So you'll not report me?'

I shook my head, big Bruno was like my father. He was close to me even after a few months, and I liked him.

'I didn't think you would, you're a good boy at heart.'

'Someone else might,' I said.

'Who?' he asked, casting his eyes at his nearest work mate, who

---

[1] On 12 November 1934 the German government quadrupled import duties on films so there was no profit for the distributors. Some Nazi papers saw Mickey Mouse as decadent, but Goebbels gave Adolf Hitler eighteen Mickey Mouse films as a birthday present in 1937, so obviously he must have known that Hitler enjoyed this bit of American culture.

was grinning at our conversation. The workplace was a different place from the Hitler Youth, and it dawned on me that not everyone there was in the Party. I told big Bruno about our block warden and what my father's friend Otto had said. He said that the block warden needed sorting out.

'I had a good apprentice before you, like you a clever lad and willing to learn, and a hard worker. He'd only just finished his apprenticeship and they got rid of him because he was Jewish. He'd never spoken Yiddish in his life, he went to church on a regular basis, more than I do even now, and they got rid of him because he was circumcised. Stupid, just plain stupid, did not even make economic sense, they trained him up to deal with the most complex engines then threw him on the scrap heap because he didn't have a foreskin.'

Suddenly big Bruno was working himself up into a frenzy, and I was really worried that some Party member would take issue with him or even report him. I looked nervously at his work mate who had been grinning, and he winked at me. I was not sure whether it was a wink to say 'that's big Bruno' or a knowing wink to say that he had heard everything. I tried to change the subject, but big Bruno rumbled on and then he dropped his bombshell, namely, he had no problems with Jews. I started to protest but he interrupted me saying, 'in your locker you have a gift from a Jew, Johann Epp.'

If ever there was a knock-out blow that was it. I was stunned into silence and also plunged into inner turmoil. Here was a man whom I admired, criticizing the Party in public, and then announcing that the old man who had befriended me, given me presents and was patiently teaching me chess, was a Jew. I could not dislike Johann if I tried, but I felt I was betraying my country: fortunately work came to a halt and I travelled home thinking of all I had been obliged to digest.

At work next day big Bruno did not mention the subject of our conversation the day before, but very quickly began to give me a lecture on the importance of clean piston heads and chambers, as we de-carbonized the heads of a large lorry engine. When I went to chess club the following Monday Johann was there, as always, and he offered to play me, an offer I accepted. He was such a brilliant player I always deemed myself lucky if he offered me a game; there were much better players who wanted to play him. As I was playing with him, big Bruno came up behind me and rubbed the top of my head with his huge hands. I looked up and saw that his eyes were smiling, and I guess it was because I was still playing chess with a Jew: but inside I felt very uncertain.

My doubts were increased in the early spring of 1935. The shoulder, which had been dislocated a couple of years before, caused me pain when I had to lift heavy objects, which I often had to do at work. I went along the road to see the doctor who had first attended me; he was a lovely old man who had looked after our family for years. When I arrived at his house, however, there was a notice pinned over his brass plaque saying he was a Jew and could only treat Jews. I was angry, because I thought he was only going to look after his own. Fires of rage built up within me, but when I exploded at home my mother showed me a notice in the local newspaper which I had missed. It said that Jewish doctors could treat only Jews; they had been forbidden to treat Aryans.

Later that week the notice was taken down so I attended his surgery. He gave me some pain killers and told me how to pick up objects without straining my shoulder too much. I gathered that it was the local Party in our area that had decided on this restriction, but it was not official. I was pleased that the Party seemed to be better balanced than big Bruno thought.[2] My father was also pleased but he pointed out another article in the Party paper which said that the armed forces had lost a number of officers and men because Jews had been banned from serving.

At this juncture I was very involved in the Hitler Youth, and a great supporter of the *Führer* and all that was happening in Germany. I understood the Party creed and I had all the credentials because as a member of my local Hitler Youth group I was also attached to the Mechanical Unit in Berlin. I felt very grown up and confident about the future; Germany was going places and I was

[2] This policy must have been peculiar to that area because it was not until 3 March 1936 that Jewish doctors were barred from practising in German institutions.

playing my part, even as a young boy. Nevertheless, I had moments of doubt when I saw Frau Goldblatt or played a game of chess with Johann: I shared these doubts less and less with my father and would never have mentioned them to Josef – not that we saw much of him.

My father had bought a new wireless set[3] because his old 'people's receiver' had only a limited range. The new set, however, could receive many stations, some of which were foreign. If he was in by 7.00 p.m. he would listen to a programme called *The Hour of the Nation*, which was always a Party political broadcast. I did not enjoy the wireless as much as he did and I was seldom in during the evenings. The Hitler Youth and chess kept me more than busy after a day's work. When there were no political broadcasts or speeches by the *Führer*, the output was mainly music and I have to confess that even to this day I have never been a great lover of music. I loved the marching songs and quite enjoyed what today we would call light classical music, but as a young boy I could not sit still listening to music for entertainment.

Sometimes at work there would be an announcement system telling us to down tools and we would gather around to listen to a broadcast about some important development or a speech by the *Führer*. Not everyone was happy with this because sometimes it meant stopping when you were in the middle of a complex procedure.

During lunch breaks Bruno and I would play chess but in the coffee breaks everyone read a newspaper; there is no doubt that, whatever else is said about this period in German history, we were well informed, and with the benefit of hindsight, well indoctrinated. The most popular paper was the *Racial Observer*[4] which my father had at home. Big Bruno, who I soon realized was self taught and well educated, read an unusual paper called the *Frankfurter*

---

[3] In 1934 over 6 million radio sets were is use in Germany. Seventy per cent of households owned a wireless, which was the highest percentage in the world, including the USA.

[4] Rosenberg was the editor in chief.

Zeitung.[5] I got into the habit of reading parts of it. It was certainly different from the *Racial Observer* and the other Party papers. It gave world news, but more to the point – and this astonished me – it was sometimes critical of the Party and even of the *Führer*.

Big Bruno also read the *Berliner Tageblatt* but seldom looked at the *Racial Observer* unless he wanted to point out an article to me that was either patently untrue or ridiculous. One day people had signed a petition in the *Racial Observer* requesting that all Jewish businesses be closed down, and I remember big Bruno saying that if that happened commercial life in Germany would shudder to a halt. On the other hand, I would sometimes point out articles in the *Frankfurter Zeitung* saying that some foreigners admired the way the *Führer* was turning Germany around. I even found an article that said that some English readers – our old enemies – thought the Versailles Treaty was wrong and they hoped, indeed anticipated, that the *Führer* would put right some of its iniquities. At least he agreed with that; he said the French and Americans had been appallingly greedy.

I asked my father about the *Frankfurter Zietung* and he said it was a good paper but Party members should avoid it because it sometimes spoke against the Party's policy.

One thing big Bruno had no personal freedom over was where he worked, and at the beginning of April 1935 he announced that we were being transferred to the other end of the factory right by the aerodrome itself. We were to be working on aircraft engines by special directive; eight of us left our workbenches and took a long walk to an area of the factory I did not know existed.

'Will it be different?' I asked Bruno.

'More care will be needed,' he said, 'but I have spent time on

---

[5] The *Franfurter Zeitung* was renowned for its objective reporting; during the Weimar Republic it had been taken over by I.G. Farben, which dictated some of its policy, especially regarding economic matters. In 1933 some Stormtroopers had invaded the newspaper offices because it seemed anti-Party. Because I.G. Farben, which owned 98 per cent of the paper, was needed by the Nazis, the editorial staff had more freedom for longer than any other German newspaper of the day. It was also widely read by people outside Germany. From 1936 the Party took a stronger line with the editorial staff.

these engines before. They're more powerful and more refined.'

'They will be bigger?'

'Yes, they're high-performance, supercharged and turbocharged, twelve cylindered engines; put them in a car and the wheels would come off.'

'Will it be more difficult?'

'Not really, but we will get paid more.'

I was excited about the change, and pleased with the increment in my pay, but I did not realize that this change would have a major effect on my early manhood. I was to become an expert mechanical engineer on an engine called the DB600 and later the DB601, known to us as an inverted V-12 series. For three years big Bruno and I were to work together on these engines. Others fitted them in the planes, but we helped make and repair them. As I watched my engines being put into all sorts of planes, saw my engines tested by experts to their limit, I felt grateful to Bruno who had taught me well. There was not an engine I would one day be unable to fix, so long as it was of the DB600 series. I built, fixed and mended these great engines in the best of planes, including later in my youth in Messerschmitt Me109s as well as various Dorniers. I had to learn to use a new set of tools and to achieve new standards in a new environment. Unlike the lorry garage I had started in, the aircraft engine room felt like a hospital ward, surgically clean with everything in its place.

Over the years we also became used to having some very important people from the Party and the military prowling around watching the work we were doing. We were also surrounded by top engineers, who kept experimenting with the engine in order to refine its tuning. Unlike the main garage we were given identity cards with our photographs on, and when we came to work we had to show our cards to the security guards. Later these security guards were replaced by SS men and we knew then that the work we were doing was important. We also had to sign an agreement not to talk to anyone about the engines that we built or that were being developed. The threat of Dachau loomed if we breached these rules, and we were told there would be no coming back if we disobeyed our instructions. Even big Bruno had no problem with this because he said it was for the sake of national security.

My father was pleased about my move, but I had to stress to him and my mother that my work, although not secret, was not to be talked about: the authorities were very sensitive about the engines we were building. I was not a fool, even though I was very young, and Bruno explained to me early on that these very powerful engines were not just for transport planes, but would be for fighter aircraft as well. It was obvious to me from the amount of work passing through the workshops that the military machine was itself being fine tuned. The new engine I was working on was a fantastic size. It displaced 33.8 litres, had roller bearing connector rods, used dry cylinder liners and had a unique system of attaching the cylinders to the crankcase. All in all, I was given a thorough training by big Bruno, and courtesy of Daimler-Benz AG, and my expertise in all types of engine was going to save my skin in a way I could never have anticipated. And this love of engines started for me because of the book Hans Lobb had given me a year or so before. I actually saw him in the distance one evening when I was strolling to the chess club. I called out to him; he looked around and I think he saw me, but as I looked right and left in order to cross the road he disappeared. It was a total mystery.

I had a brief holiday during the Nuremberg Rally that year, and although I enjoyed being useful with the rest of my contingent I actually missed the workshop, the chess club and home. I almost felt guilty about it, but although I found the marches and ceremony impressive and uplifting, at other times I was bored to tears; it was only out of a sense of duty that I stayed. I attended a lecture one evening about the new Nuremberg Laws[6] that were to be enforced in September. I soon gathered that there were two types of person in Germany: the *Reichsbürger*, who was a citizen of pure German blood – that was me; and the *Staatsangehörige*, who was merely a subject of the State. The two were never to inter-marry. The latter were mainly Jews but the question of half-Jews was also addressed and I remember finding these classifications complicated. If one's mother was Jewish that made a person a half-breed, a *mischling* of

---

[6] The first of many anti-Jewish laws drafted by Wilhelm Stukart.

the first degree (a *mischling* of the second degree was when one had a Jewish grandparent). These could only marry a full Aryan. Full Jews were not allowed to marry *mischlings* of the second degree or Aryan Germans. The theory was that this would eventually breed Jewish blood out of the nation, and for the sake of German blood and honour these rules were to be enforced straight away. The lecture finished with everyone cheering loudly.

Big Bruno laughed when I told him about it on my return to the workshops. 'I wouldn't be surprised if half of Germany isn't *mischling*,' he said, 'even our great leaders would have trouble proving pure German blood.'

'But Bruno—' I started.

'Don't Bruno me,' he snapped. 'I'm all German, but I have no idea who my grandparents were, they had all died before I was ten. Only the aristocrats, the vons this and that would have any idea.'

I did not argue because I detected that big Bruno was in a bad mood. I think, on reflection, that he was unhappy about me getting time off to attend the rally in Nuremberg. During lunch we played a game of chess and I never raised the subject again. He had just checkmated me when a *Luftwaffe* officer paused and asked for a game. Bruno needed to go to the lavatory so I played him, and soon we were surrounded by several work mates and other *Luftwaffe* officers. He was not difficult to beat, and after the game he shook my hand and my work mates cheered. I returned to my workbench feeling a little conceited.

'You played well,' big Bruno said. 'I came back just as he fell for that back row trap, the one that Jew Johann taught you.'

I looked up at him but he just winked at me and we got on with the task of fitting pistons into the block we were working on. My father was pleased when I told him about the game. I noticed that he was reading a different paper, one called the *Schwarze Korps*, which I gather Josef had sent him; it was the official paper of the SS. Inside was an article which stated that if any Jews harmed Germans abroad then German Jews would be punished in a systematic way. My father thought this was a good warning, and I agreed, but I wondered what big Bruno would have to say; not that I would mention it to him – he was always in a better mood when not discussing politics.

In the August I had a complete week's holiday. I spent a few days with my mother back in her home town of Memmingen, and it was more interesting for me this time because I discovered that her pastor, J. von Jan was a keen chess player. He was good but I managed to get the better of him once I recognized his cautious style of play. Although he was a pastor I really liked him, and he was interested in my views. He was similar to big Bruno in his thinking, and so I steered clear of the Jewish problem, even though it was difficult at times. He was more concerned about the way the country was heading, as he felt this indicated the possibility of another major war. He also challenged me on the whole question of the existence of God and gave me considerable pause for thought.

Later that holiday, back in Berlin, I spotted Hans Lobb again. He was on the other side of the Alexanderplatz, and this time I did not call out, but quickly crossed the road to catch up with him before he could disappear, because I felt that last time he had avoided me. I was about 100 metres behind him when he moved into Münzstrasse. I had nearly closed the gap when I lost him in Sophienstrasse, a major street where my Aunt Ingrid lived. I did not want to meet my aunt because I was trying to have a few days to myself, so I looked once more before heading back in the afternoon sun to the Tiergarten. One day, I vowed, I would track Hans down, if only to see what had happened to Erik, Jew or no Jew.

Back at the works I told big Bruno about my games of chess with the pastor in Memmingen.

'You are a strange Hitler youngster if you play with clergy, little Bruno, what would your political superiors have to say? Pass me the oil can.'

'Do you go to church, Bruno?'

'None of your business.'

'I was only asking. I go when my mother begs me to.'

He paused and looked at me over the engine block, 'Yes, I do go, but not as often as I used to. My pastor has taken to wearing his Nazi uniform when he's preaching, and I object to party politics and the Bible being mixed up.'

'But the Party is trying its best to unify the different churches,'[7] I said proudly.

'All the Party is trying to do is make sure the churches tow the Party line, there's nothing Godly in their intentions.'

I did not respond for a moment because I had heard my mother express similar sentiments. She had found her local church difficult because they had carved a swastika above the cross on the new pulpit. I saw nothing wrong in this but my mother was in some distress, saying that German politics had nothing to do with Jesus Christ.

'You come with me to a church I know,' continued big Bruno, ignoring my silence, or taking advantage of it. 'It's in Dahlem.'[8]

'That's a posh area, Bruno; I didn't think you'd go there!'

'I don't live there you dumb-cluck. My sister's in domestic service there, bless her, so I go with her sometimes.'

'When I go, I go to please my mother.'

'You come and listen to this pastor. He was a submariner in the war, greatly respected, and he used to support your *Führer*, but now he tells the truth. He's called Martin Niemöller and he's against the Party attacking Christians who were born Jews. He's not frightened of the police or any of the big-wigs, and I guarantee he'll give you something to think about.'

I really did not take in the implications of what big Bruno was saying because I was more caught up with the fact that he said your *Führer* and not our *Führer*. I looked around to see if anyone had heard him, but I should not have worried; he really did not care one bit who heard him, and the country needed men like him, so why should I worry?

At home I mentioned this man Niemöller to my mother, but she had never heard of him. Later that evening she showed me one of

---

[7] The Nazis did in fact attempt to do this, using first *Reich* Bishop Ludwig Muller. In July 1935, the year Bruno raised this question, a new Ministry for Church Affairs was created under Hanns Kerrl; this movement was strongly opposed by those clergy who disagreed with the Nazis. It was known as the Confessing Church.

[8] A suburb of expensive villas.

her church papers, which had an article by a Dietrich Bonhoeffer,[9] which she said I should read but not share with my father. That surprised me because, although my parents sometimes argued about the difference between Catholics, Lutherans, Calvinists and Evangelicals, they were always open about the issues in front of me and Ruth, when she was home.

If you had asked me in 1944 who Niemöller and Bonhoeffer were I would not have remembered. It was much later in my life, and through my general reading, that the memory of these discussions came back to me. I never saw these men, never went with big Bruno to his fancy church. I took the paper to bed and it was obvious, even to my sixteen-year-old mind that the churches were beginning to oppose the *Führer*. A Roman Catholic cardinal[10] had objected to the Party's attacks on non-Aryan Christians and a bishop[11] had attacked the book called *The Myth of the Twentieth Century*[12] because it denied the validity of Christianity. There was also an article on how many churches had been banned from putting on musicals or plays, including Christmas nativity plays,[13] which I had once so enjoyed myself. I have to admit I was puzzled by the latter prohibition: the rest bemused me because in those days I knew that the *Führer* and the Party were doing their best to unify Germany. I returned the paper next day to my mother with a manly grunt, but I did not pursue the issues because I had already decided I would always put family first; that was something my father had drilled into me from my earliest days. I could understand why my mother did not want my father to hear of this because he was a Party member and very anti-Jewish with just a few reservations for the few Jews he actually knew. He continued, I noted, to buy his small cigars and papers from Frau Goldblatt without any twist of conscience.

[9] Today recognized as an important theologian, who was to die in a concentration camp in 1945.
[10] Probably Cardinal Michael Faulhaber.
[11] Unquestionably Clemens von Galen Bishop of Münster who launched a vociferous attack on this book on 19 March 1935.
[12] Author was the notorious Alfred Rosenberg.
[13] From 1935 the *Reich* Theatre Chamber placed a ban on all Church productions outside of church services.

Looking back, I realize that 1935 was the year when there was conflict between the different churches and the Party. I was probably more aware of this than many of my contemporaries in the Hitler Youth because my mother still went to church, my father had not thrown his Catholicism out of the window, and big Bruno obviously raised the subject, along with a hundred others, as we worked on our engines. Some time before I had attended a mass rally of the Hitler Youth of Berlin and heard our leader, Baldur von Schirach,[14] condemn Catholic youth organizations because they were detrimental to the unity of the state; he even encouraged us to pick fights with Catholic clubs as a matter of policy. I remember joining in the fun, but the local club we attacked was mainly girls so it only lasted a few weeks, and most of the boys there joined the Hitler Youth fairly speedily. We were taught a quasi-hymn; I can no longer recall the words, except the line 'the swastika is our redemption on earth', but I do remember that when I sang it at home both my parents were upset, so I dropped the habit at once. I heard from big Bruno that many soldiers still went to church but the *Gestapo* had started taking note of who went and what was said from the pulpit, and members of the SS never attended.

Big Bruno also raised the question of why the Party should attack Jews who had been Christians for years, and he quoted my old friend Hans Lobb as an example. The Party papers were now full of the definition of what constituted a Jew. According to a simple view a Jew was defined as anyone with three Jewish grandparents or even two Jewish grandparents. Others were designated as *mischlings* of various degrees. I have touched on this before, but by the end of 1935[15] it was impossible to read any newspaper without an article on this subject.

That year is carved in my memory for another reason: in early December big Bruno and his boss passed me as a junior qualified mechanic. I was very proud, knowing that in two years I would be fully qualified. Later I went with Bruno and some others to have a

---

[14] Von Shirach condemned these church youth groups and demanded street fights on 15 March 1934.

[15] Nov 15 1935 the Nuremberg Race Laws came into effect.

celebratory drink in central Berlin, a good start to our Christmas holiday.

On the way home I saw Hans Lobb again; he was with my sister Ruth walking along hand in hand. I had been sure that Ruth would not have lost sight of him. I did not have my Hitler Youth uniform on because I had been at work, and so instead of shouting out I merged in amongst the crowd and followed them as carefully as I could. They followed the same route that I had tracked him on last time, through the Alexanderplatz, then into Münzstrasse. It was there that I realized I was not the only one following them. In front of me but behind them a man in a long coat paused when they paused, slowed down when they slowed down, and it suddenly dawned on me that the man was *Gestapo*. I wondered what Ruth could have done to raise the interest of the *Gestapo*, then, just as they disappeared into Sophienstrasse, I realized that it was the race laws. Hans had already been sacked because although he was a Christian he had Jewish parents, and Ruth was a full bodied Aryan like me. I had very mixed emotions about all this; it might bring suspicion on the family, but on the other hand I was annoyed that my sister's friendship should provoke such interest. Also, I liked Hans Lobb and I had always regretted the manner in which I had treated Erik.

I say that Hans and Ruth 'disappeared' because, just as I had lost sight of Hans there once before, so I lost him again. The *Gestapo* man had the same problem because he was now frantically dashing around looking into various doorways. I stood beside a pavement news-stand and watched him walk up and down the street and then he too went back towards Alexanderplatz. On an impulse I decided to visit my Aunt Ingrid and crossed the street, through the alley and up the stairs to her spacious flat. I knocked on the door and was taken aback when Ruth opened it. It was not exactly a warm welcome. 'What do you want?' she said.

'Well,' I stuttered, 'I had decided to visit Aunty, but I saw you and Hans just now as well.'

'You followed us?'

'The *Gestapo* followed you,' I snapped. Her facial muscles grew taut but she just looked at me.

'Are you going to let me in?'

'Aunty is not here, go away.'

But then Aunt Ingrid appeared behind her and smiled and invited me in. I was so surprised by what I saw that I just sat down at the table and stared at everyone. Sitting by the window were Hans Lobb and Erik.

'It's good to see you both,' I eventually managed to say, 'especially you Erik. I wondered where you'd gone.'

The strained atmosphere relaxed slightly.

'Bruno,' Aunt Ingrid put her hand on my shoulder. 'We are family and neither your mother nor I would want you to tell anyone that Hans and Erik are staying here.'

'Why's it such a secret?' I asked.

'Either you are still a nasty, twisted little bigot or you're stupidly naïve.' Ruth's attitude was far from warm.

'Mum knows?' I asked.

'Of course she does,' Aunt Ingrid replied. 'But we felt it best not to say anything to your father.'

'Why?'

'He's like you,' Ruth answered, 'a member of the Party, and we wouldn't want to embarrass you with your high nationalistic ideals.'

'Ruth,' Aunt Ingrid interrupted her outburst, 'let Bruno speak. He is family.'

She had said the right thing. I was confused; I hated Jews but I liked Frau Goldblatt, Johann, Hans and Erik. But above all Ruth and Aunt Ingrid were family, and my father had always said family comes first.

I was forced into making an instant decision; there was no time to weigh up the consequences, no time to consult friends. I could not speak to my father and I knew what big Bruno would have said. For a brief moment there was a palpable silence in the room whilst they waited for me to pronounce where I stood. Erik looked thinner than usual and Hans was looking at Ruth. It dawned on me that my sister appeared to hate me, my best friend was frightened of me and my aunty was nervous.

'Of course I won't say anything; your secret is safe with me. Why it has to be safe you will have to explain, but I won't let you down.' I then apologized to Erik for the way we had parted and like a gentleman I stood up and shook his hand. To my astonishment Ruth hugged me and Aunt Ingrid and Hans clapped.

'You're still normal,' Ruth said, 'I thought your *Führer* had turned you into an automaton.'

I learnt so much that evening as we sat down to a pleasant collation of cold meats and salad. Erik's parents had returned to Poland but as he and Hans spoke no Polish they had been staying with Aunt Ingrid. When Erik's parents had left Germany they had done so through an organization called *Reichsvertretung der Deutschen Juden*,[16] 'Reich Representation of German Jews', and Hans and Erik, sometimes with Ruth, had acted as 'runners' for the organization because they feared their post would be opened and their telephones tapped. I had no real idea how early the persecution of the Jews had started and what shape it was taking. I am sure my father was just as ignorant and would not have liked ordinary Jews to be treated in this way. During that evening I experienced a sort of inner turmoil. For three years I had played an active part in Jew hating and sometimes Jew baiting, but to a young boy it was just fun, it was what one's mates did with the encouragement of adults. Suddenly I was being confronted with the other side of the coin. Playing chess with Johann had made me think, as had big Bruno, but Ruth's determination to enter into an illegal marriage to a Jew stopped me in my tracks. I asked how she proposed to marry Hans since it was illegal, and she dropped a further bombshell: they were making a determined effort to leave Germany.

'Poland?' I asked.

'England or America,' Hans said. 'The Poles can be just as anti-Semitic as the Nazis. In England you may not, as a Jew, be able to join their posh golf clubs, but they are not violent or abusive in their prejudice. So I'm told. We do have distant relations in a place called Darlington,' he added.

England, the old enemy, I thought, but at least the English were civilized and more like us, even if their language was strange. I was

[16] Founded by a well respected liberal Rabbi called Leo Baeck, later in 1939 to be renamed Reichsvereinigung den Juden in Deutschland and under command of the *Gestapo*.

disappointed that they were keeping my father out of the picture, but I agreed to say nothing on the grounds that he could lose his job if he got caught up in all this. Then I thought that I could also be in trouble, and I remembered the *Gestapo* officer and mentioned it again.

'How did you know he was *Gestapo*?' Erik asked.

I did know the *Gestapo*. In the May of that year the *Führer* had held his May Day parade at Tempelhof and for a week before the *Gestapo* had been in and out of the works and in and out of our lives. Bruno said that they were recognizable not only because their coats were always the same but because they looked and behaved like water rats. I disagreed with him of course, but they were easily identifiable in their hats and coats – it was almost a civilian uniform.

I explained the way I had followed them and how I had spotted him. It was decided that it must be because they had done some work for the Jewish body, or even because they had been queuing outside the British Consulate in Tiergartenstrasse. They were not having much luck there because of the red tape involved in gaining a visa and departure tickets. They had even considered trying to go to England or America via China because the Chinese Embassy was, so they were told, quite liberal in giving out visas.[17]

It was clear that Hans was very keen on England or America, and he and Erik had been trying to learn English. I told him all about my work and he seemed genuinely pleased that I had been befriended by big Bruno. I gathered that Bruno had been something of a hero in the war, and, to my surprise had won a chess competition in Frankfurt. When I told Hans I played chess with a Jew called Johann it brought a relieved smile to his face; he also knew Johann from when he once visited the chess club. Apparently Johann had been a well known museum director, but had been sacked because he was Jewish. It became crystal clear they were relieved that I was telling the truth about not betraying them. They

---

[17] A Dr Ho at the Chinese Embassy saved thousands of German Jews by granting tickets and visas with little fuss and few questions. Many of these Jews ended up in Shanghai during the Japanese invasion; many others made their way to Palestine and America.

felt they could trust me because I already had a new Jewish friend in Johann. The whole evening (and it was late now) became even more relaxed. I promised them, as I left, that they could trust me, and that I would be back in the New Year.

'Then you must learn how to disappear like us.' Hans explained that they always entered the clothes store and went into the ground floor toilets before taking the exit from there, which enabled them to get a good view of anyone following them, and also placed them right by the staircase up to Aunt Ingrid's flat. I was not surprised I had lost them. The next year I would need to be aware of this information, because the *Gestapo* were on their tails for reasons unknown to us all at that time.

Part 2

Mischling: and Being Hated

Chapter 4

1936

It was a strange Christmas and an even stranger New Year; in some ways with the benefit of hindsight, it was what we would nowadays call a defining time in the development of my life. We were a family of secrets, and divided. I knew something that I could not share with my father. Moreover, if he had known what my mother, Ruth and I knew, he in turn would not have been able to share this knowledge with Josef. It detracted from our usual happy Christmas because I was suddenly conscious of what I said, and to whom. I was used to this way of life outside the family, but not within the four walls of our house in Hermannstrasse. I would, of course, never have told Big Dick or Adolf Bier that I played chess with a Jew and that my sister intended to marry one. Had Josef come home (and we saw no sign of him over the holiday, apart from a card), we would all have been committed to silence. It somehow did not feel right; we had been a close and loving family, and now we had secrets from one another.

I now realize of course that the State and the Party had entered into our domestic life, and we were not the only family to be in this situation. I had only to think of Erik's parents literally fleeing to Poland and Erik and Hans trying to flee west to put my home into a better perspective, but it did not feel like that at the time. I kept wondering what my father's reactions would be if my mother told him about Ruth, but my mother, according to Ruth, was keeping her own counsel for my father's sake more than anything else. Jews all over the railway network were losing their jobs and even people who sympathized with them were being demoted or having to find work as labourers on the new *autobahns*. I had been taught not to like Jews, but there were some I did like.

I wanted to discuss this with big Bruno but when I returned to work after the holidays I discovered that he was ill. I had to help on another bench with an apprentice I did not like very much. After some pleading and pestering I managed to get hold of his address, which happened to be in the posh suburb of Dahlem. On the first Sunday of the New Year, which was 5 January, I managed to find my way to his house. He lived with his sister, who was housekeeper to a very well-to-do family. She seemed really pleased to be able to show me to his room where he was propped up in bed.

'Well, well.' Bruno looked up from his newspaper. 'If it's not little Bruno checking up on me.'

'I'm not checking up on you, I've come to see how you are.'

'That's kind of you. Marie, can we have some coffee?' His sister left the room and big Bruno explained to me that he had gall stones, but that they had been removed by a surgeon who did it all free of charge because he was the brother of the owners of the house.

'They have looked after me as if I were a member of the family. I even went to a private clinic and they gave me the care and attention the Kaiser would have had in the old days. Game of chess?'

I spent most of the afternoon there playing chess and even joined them for an evening meal. Marie, big Bruno's sister, was a matronly woman who obviously loved her brother and cared for him all the time. Later, just as we were putting the pieces away, Bruno suddenly said, 'You realize that this time next year you will be eighteen?'

'Yes.' There was not much else I could say to such an obvious question, apart from wondering where his mind was travelling.

'That's the new conscription age.'[1]

---

[1] From May 1935 military conscription was introduced for one year, plus six months working in the *Reich* Labour Service usually building motorways or working on farms.

That thought had never crossed my mind.

'The point is,' continued big Bruno, 'that you will not be able to finish your apprenticeship. You will only have done two years instead of the necessary three.'

'I hadn't thought about that either.' I said. I was also deeply concerned, because I was looking forward to being qualified.

'In the old days we could have gone to the union, but they've all gone.'[2]

'Can't I do my time and come back?' I asked.

'You couldn't in the old days. But listen, I've been thinking about this but needed to speak to you first.'

'Well, what do you suggest?'

'I know one of the big bosses at Daimler, he was my officer in the war, and I also know that *Luftwaffe* officer who keeps hanging around these days, the one you played chess with.'

'Go on.'

'Well, the reality is, there are thousands employed in the aircraft industry,[3] but few of these are competent in engine repair. They can do body work, put in guns, do the wheels, flaps and instrumentation, but when it comes to knowledge of the big engine there are few experts.'

'Meaning?' I pestered.

'Well there's no point in you going off to do labour when you are already employed, and if you joined the *Luftwaffe*, as potential ground crew, they might wave the magic wand.'

I nearly hugged him as he promised to look into all this as soon as he returned to work, which was only another week away. As I caught the tram that evening I felt better about life again.

That year my birthday on 27 January fell on a Monday which was chess club night, and once again Johann had remembered. Not only did he give me a large cake to share around, but there were drinks all round and Johann gave me a book written by an Englishman about clever chess traps. Before I made my way home, big Bruno whispered that he had started talking about my situation

[2] By 1933 the Nazis had eliminated most of the trade union movement.
[3] By 1935 72,000 workers were employed in aircraft construction now that the *Luftwaffe* had been formed and was growing rapidly.

to the boss and the *Luftwaffe* officer, and they had not thrown his idea out, but needed time to consult with others. Suddenly life seemed full of promise; maybe I had a future.

The weekend after my birthday I called at Aunt Ingrid's flat. Both Ruth and Hans were out doing some running around for what he called the *Gemeinde*,[4] a Jewish group trying to help Jews who had no work or money to live on. Aunt Ingrid was busy with Saturday shopping but Erik and I were able to share a coffee together. He told me that my information about Ruth being followed by the *Gestapo*[5] had been accurate.

'It's happened several times,' he said, 'usually when they leave the rabbi's office,[6] but they are now splitting up when they are some distance from here and becoming adept at losing the fellow in the shopping crowds.'

'They're not stupid, Erik, they must know Ruth is staying here.'

'But she doesn't, she lives at the hospital, and they never seem bothered by her on her own.'

'So it's Hans they're interested in?'

As I walked back along Münzstrasse I noticed some Brownshirts outside a large department store with notices in their hands saying that it was owned by Jews and should be boycotted. When people ignored them, and still went through the doors, the Brownshirts swore at them and called them Jew-lovers. I remembered what big Bruno had said: that if all the Jewish businesses closed down commerce would judder to a halt. I was not sure that he was right, but I did wonder as I stood there what it would be like if Berlin were *Judenrein*.[7] I stood there for quite some time, fascinated by what was happening. The people who ignored the Brownshirts were not Jews but ordinary Germans, but I reckoned that they

---

[4] *Jüdische Kultusgemeinde zu Berlin* – the Jewish Community Organization.

[5] In February 1936 the *Gestapo* was granted national status with Heydrich as their head.

[6] Leo Baeck (1873–1956) mentioned earlier. He was a well known liberal rabbi, a philosopher and community leader. He was eventually sent to Terezin (Therensientadt), where he survived, then emigrated to England after the liberation of the ghetto.

[7] Cleansed of Jews.

were managing to turn away more than half of the potential cust-omers.

Then, to my considerable interest I noticed two Wermacht officers heading towards the doors. One the Brownshirts held his 'Jew-Free Shopping' notice in front of them. One of the officers hesitated, but the other pushed the Brownshirt back and walked by, followed cautiously by the other. One of the Brownshirts shouted at them – I think I heard the word traitor – and the first *Wehrmacht* officer returned and said something to them. What it was I do not know, but whatever it was the Brownshirts fell silent and moved to another entrance to carry on their work

January and February were busy months at work. We were making a lot of engines, as well as making changes to some and repairing others, mainly those that had been removed from aircraft. The experts were always around, trying to work out how to get more power from the engine, as well as using less fuel.

One afternoon one of the 'big-wigs' came to our section of the workshop with the same *Luftwaffe* officer with whom I had played chess. I was somewhat surprised, when everyone was doffing their caps, that he walked over to big Bruno, and put his arm around his shoulders. Others like me were snapping out our '*Heil Hitlers*' and here was big Bruno getting a hug. In fact, he held him so tightly that his funny round spectacles had to be readjusted on his nose. He asked a machinist to collect together all the apprentices in the work rooms and soon we were all gathered around big Bruno's bench, wondering what was happening.

'I gather that many of you have received your conscription papers. Now we have little or no control over this, but *Oberstleutnant*[8] Kleine has actually managed to talk to the *Reichmarschall* and special orders have been issued which suggest that you may avoid conscription by becoming full members of the *Luftwaffe*, as ground crew. *Oberstleutnant* Kleine, will you please explain?'

As the officer came to the front to address us, big Bruno winked at me. Even in that brief moment I remember marvelling at the fact that because he knew a 'big-wig' at Daimler, changes could be made in national matters, and yet I also knew what a great critic of the Party he was.

[8] The British equivalent is Wing Commander or Lieutenant Colonel.

'Comrades,' the officer said in a sophisticated voice, but in a manner that was not aloof, or even authoritative, 'if you join the army, you lose your apprenticeship indenture, because you have to serve three consecutive years to gain your first major qualification. If you are prepared to join the *Luftwaffe* full time on your eighteenth birthday, it will mean eight weeks' training in the ways of the *Luftwaffe*. Daimler-Benz has agreed to this, if you are prepared to sacrifice your annual holiday as part of this trial exercise. For most of you, this will mean that you have only a month to make up your minds, and I'm afraid there's nothing I can do about that, so it is decision time now. Any questions?'

I was surprised that only five of us went over to give our names. I gathered that many of the others were keen to join the SS, like my brother Josef. I had once had the same idea, but working on engines had filled me with awe. I was the last in the queue since I was the most junior, probably the youngest one there. In fact, they queried me when I said I was seventeen and already in my second year. Big Bruno had been hovering around the edges and so he was able to explain that I signed on at sixteen because my maths and other results had been so good.

'So you were only sixteen when you checkmated me?' asked *Oberstleutnant* Kleine.

'Yes, sir.'

'If we meet again over the chessboard, I shall take you much more seriously.'

As I strolled back to the workbenches I could hardly believe that in less than a year I would be a fully enlisted member of the *Luftwaffe*. Big Bruno grumbled about the fact that I would still be on Daimler's poor pay rates[9] but I was not as worried about that as he was. Prior to working at Daimler I had only received pocket money, so I felt quite wealthy. The hours were long,[10] but since I had known nothing different that did not worry me.

---

[9] Germany's sudden rearmament entailed a large financial sacrifice for ordinary citizens.

[10] Workers at Daimler-Benz averaged fifty-four hours a week by the late 1930s as against forty-eight in the last pre-Depression years. Richard J. Evans, *The Third Reich in Power*, (Penguin, 2005) page 480.

A couple of days later, during lunch break, big Bruno set me an interesting exercise on his chess board. He set up a position and made me work out how the game had arrived at this point by working backwards. He then explained that this was the best way to look at engines and life in general.

My mother seemed really pleased I had opted for the *Luftwaffe*, as was my father, but he also asked me whether I had given up the idea of following Josef into the SS. I liked the idea of being one of the elite in the black uniform, but I loved my work, and I would never have been able to face big Bruno if I had gone back on his suggestion. Also, after what he had said about Himmler's private army[11] and the *Gestapo*, I doubted whether he would have been as friendly as in the past. He was my instructor, and therefore my boss, but he had become a real friend, and despite the age gap we shared a very strong feeling of comradeship.

My mother was very upset that our local doctor had left the area; no one knew where he had gone but I suspected, as did my parents, that he had fled the country. Some time in March Jewish doctors, along with many other Jewish professionals, had been denied work or workplaces, or had simply been sacked.[12] I was beginning to detect a subtle but real problem at home. My father was still very supportive of the *Führer*, but my mother less so; in fact, she was becoming quite critical, especially when she thought I could not hear them. My father would argue that Germany had more cars than any other country,[13] and my mother would retort that he only said that because he believed everything he read in the Party papers. She might believe him when he owned one – which of course was impossible for even a good working-class family like us. Then my father would argue that unemployment was falling fast compared with the bad old days,[14] and my mother would retort that this was because women were being discouraged from working

[11] The SS has often been described as a 'state within a state'.
[12] On 3 March 1936 Jewish doctors were banned from practising medicine in German Institutions.
[13] Untrue, but in 1933 there were an estimated half million cars and just under one million in 1936.
[14] By 1937 unemployment had dropped below a million.

or being replaced by men, who did not do such a good job.[15] Despite this slight rift, my father was too good-natured to take it to heart, and either fell silent or agreed with my mother. This was a relief to me because I knew of families of colleagues in the Hitler Youth which had split apart because of differing political views. The day would come when my father would be very pleased that he and my mother did not fall out in a serious way.

I can recall finishing work one Saturday afternoon in March when we were called to listen to a national broadcast. We listened with joy as we heard that the *Wehrmacht* had marched into the Rhineland, which had previously been demilitarized by the unfair Versailles Treaty.[16] There was a good deal of clapping and shouting and a sense of real joy in the factory. Even big Bruno said that we should never have been in this position in the first place and that the post-war treaties were totally unjust. But as we travelled home together (as he had invited me to his home for a meal and game of chess), he did not seem as jubilant as the others.

'But even you said the treaty was unfair,' I said, trying in my juvenile way to probe what was actually on his mind.

'Don't get me wrong, little Bruno, it's not that it's wrong to take back what is ours, but this country cannot afford another war; too many died in the last war for absolutely nothing – thousands, probably millions, died for nothing.'

I could not argue with an old soldier; my father was also there and also thought the war was a waste. 'No one wants war,' I said lamely.

'Think about Daimler,' he said. 'We were happily working on lorry and car engines when suddenly everyone was transferred to aero engines. And in other factories men are now working on large marine diesels for submarines. I also gather that one of the factories is now making Mauser rifles by the thousand.'

'I expect the *Führer* knows what he's doing.'

---

[15] Hitler believed the woman's place was at home producing healthy Aryan children for the *Reich* and the party actively encouraged this theory.

[16] On 7 March 1936, thus renouncing the Locarno Treaty. The Saar had already been reoccupied following a plebiscite in 1935. Plebiscites were a popular tool with the Nazis because people could be bullied into voting the way the Party intended.

He stopped me and opened his favourite newspaper. 'Look at this quotation from your *Führer*, it reads "I go the way that providence dictates with the assurance of a sleepwalker."[17] I don't find that very encouraging.'

I looked over my shoulder as he read this aloud, anxious that no one was eavesdropping.

That night I went home with him to the posh house where Marie, big Bruno's sister, was housekeeper. I was surprised when she opened the front door and we went into the main house. It was magnificent; the furniture was old fashioned and beautiful, and there were original paintings on the walls, and some expensive china on a large oak dresser. Big Bruno went upstairs to wash and Marie gave me a small beer.

'It was strange watching you two walk up the road,' Marie said, 'big and little Bruno. I never thought I would see my brother make a friend of someone as young as you.'

'It's the chess,' I said, feeling a little embarrassed.

'Possibly' she replied, 'but I think my brother is very fond of you. He lost his wife in childbirth and his son died a few days later.'

She said this almost to herself, so I did not reply, but I had to admit that I really liked big Bruno and he seemed like a second father. He looked like the British comedian I came to enjoy in later years, Ronnie Barker, especially in *Porridge*, dressed in his overalls.

Marie had produced a tasty stew, but I just had to ask where the owners were; I felt almost like a trespasser.

'It's a sad story, my dear boy; just like your local doctor, they have fled. Do you remember the man who operated on me at the beginning of this year? He's Jewish, as are the real owners of this house.'

Bruno went on to explain that the owners of the house were in business and the law, and their brother was a surgeon; they had all either lost their jobs or had it made clear that their work was no longer needed. Apparently they had given Marie and big Bruno some money, with which Marie had purchased their house.

'So they gave you money in order to buy their home? Why?' I asked.

---

[17] Said by Hitler after the reoccupation of the Rhineland.

'As soon as things return to normal we shall give it back to them.'

'Supposing Jews are always banned from business?' I persisted.

'Then the house is ours for as long as we live.' big Bruno put his spoon down and looked at me closely. 'I am still working on the assumption that you will keep this to yourself, little Bruno.'

'Of course he will.' Marie said, and I confirmed it with a nod.

'They left the house as if they were going on holiday, but in fact they should be halfway to America now on a French liner.'

'Why America? Were they happy to go?' I asked.

Bruno pointed out that these Jews were German through and through; they had lived in Germany for several generations. He also told me that the Nazi Party was chasing out some formidable intellects and those with business acumen, and the country would be weaker as a result. 'Look at your own doctor,' he said, pointing his spoon at me. 'What are you going to do for a doctor now?' I did not answer, and Bruno, now in full flight, told me that when Herr Streicher wrote in *Der Stürmer* that Jews were subhuman, he was a maniac. They are human beings, exactly as we were. Moreover, all the remaining European royal families were a total mix of different cultures and races. I did not make any contribution to this highly dangerous conversation.

A few days later Adolf Bier was talking about the same subject because of the coming Olympics, which were to be held in Berlin. The Hitler Youth were being asked to help, but because I worked for Daimler-Benz I was not obliged to be involved, which was something of a disappointment. I had tired of the rallies, but the international aspect of the Olympics would have been more interesting.

'You know,' Adolf said, 'that the Americans have got Jews and monkeys in their team?'

'Monkeys?'

'Black men, they call them niggers. But we shall thrash them all and show the Aryan people are the top race.'

I had been reading about the black men but had not heard them called monkeys. I had also read that German teams were going to take all the top medals, and I believed that would be the case. I walked towards my house with Adolf Bier and we talked about the lecture we had listened to that evening. It was about the *Kampfzeit*[18] given by a very fat and sweaty Brownshirt who had arrived drunk and had not sobered up before he left. According to his account, he had led the fighting on the streets of Berlin, and knew the *Führer* personally. I was not sure whether I believed him on either count, even in those days, but some members of the group stood in awe of him. What I found puzzling was that Adolf Bier, who was about to start his training for the SS, believed the man to be a real hero. Certainly my father had never heard of him, and he had been up to his armpits in those early struggles.

I called at Aunt Ingrid's flat several more times that spring, mainly to see Erik. I never saw Ruth because her nursing training was keeping her at the hospital nearly all the time. Erik and Hans were still running errands for the rabbi, and Hans said that the attacks on the Jews seemed to be petering out.[19] I was pleased to hear this because it would allay some of my personal concerns, and it might also resolve the difficulties between Ruth and my father.

I wanted to share my problems with someone and had almost plucked up the courage to mention my problem to big Bruno in a 'what if' or 'a friend of mine' way when I changed my mind, because we heard that the Italian leader, Mussolini had annexed Abyssinia.[20] Big Bruno, true to form, let everyone within hearing understand that he thought Mussolini was an old-fashioned bully.

'Those Ethiopians are an ancient culture but all they had to fight with were spears and arrows and a few daggers. What's that against machine-guns and aircraft? I ask you,' he continued, 'what good will miles of ancient desert do for Italy? These are dangerous times, little Bruno, these are dangerous times.'

They certainly were dangerous; at the Hitler Youth meetings I

[18] *Kampfzeit* 'Time of Struggle', carefully created and instant mythology of the Nazi Party's heroic struggle against great odds.

[19] In the build-up to the Olympics the anti-Semitism was calmed down for the sake of the foreign press.

[20] On 9 May 1936.

often heard how vocal people like big Bruno were frequently in trouble having been reported by their work mates. Some members of the Hitler Youth gained credit for reporting men like him and I looked around nervously to see who might be listening. I was right in my suspicions; a few days later a particular apprentice, a fat boy with spots all over his face, met me after work and asked me about big Bruno.

'What about him?' I asked with a coldness that surprised me.

'I think he's against the *Führer*.'

'Rubbish. He's not fond of Italians and he's just got a sense of humour.'

'I think we should report him.'

'We!' I shot back.

'We're both members of the Hitler Youth, it's our duty.'

'Three things,' I said. 'If you do you'll be in trouble because you're wrong and big Bruno knows people in high places; secondly you will make your place in Daimler unpleasant; and thirdly, I'll give you such a thrashing you'll be lucky to wake up this side of next year.'

It seemed to do the trick because the fat slob said nothing but walked away quickly. I warned big Bruno next day but he brushed it aside, though he did thank me for warning the slob off. Later in the day I saw the slob again, but I met his look with a steady gaze and he scurried away. I hoped that had done the trick but felt it would be a waiting game. On reflection, it seems strange that as a seventeen-year-old boy I could be perplexed as to where I stood in my own country, living in a society surrounded by people all too happy to report you to the state authority.

Unfortunately, big Bruno paid no heed to the danger lurking in the background in the person of the fat slob. Two days later he was roaring with laughter over something the *Führer* had said about the white race being ordained to rule and dominate the rest of the world.[21] 'I would be interested to know what all the Chinese and Africans have to say about that.' He almost roared it out across the

---

[21] Stated in a speech at the National Socialist Student Union at Munich 1936 25 January.

machine room. In a vote earlier that year the *Führer* had won nearly 100 per cent of the national vote,[22] and no one, not even big Bruno, could doubt the his popularity. The night before this, at a Hitler Youth meeting, I had listened to one of his speeches, addressing the youth of Germany, whom he wished to be 'an ideal youth, not a generation of mother's boys and spoiled children.'[23] I guessed that the fat slob had heard the same speech, because he seemed to be taking more and more interest in big Bruno's outbursts. I was sure that it would not take long for him to report him. Sure enough, two days later, as big Bruno and I were working on the final part of one of our engines, two *Gestapo* agents approached us and ordered me in one direction and big Bruno in another.

I have to confess I was frightened – in fact, more than frightened. I could feel the sense of dread crawling all over my skin. They took me out to a car, sat me in the back in order to ask me questions about who I was and my membership of the Hitler Youth. I decided that whatever happened I had to play this calmly. As I looked out of the windows of the large Mercedes I saw big Bruno in another Mercedes being questioned like me, by another *Gestapo* officer.

Eventually they arrived at the questions I most dreaded. 'Your friend Bruno, I hear he laughs at our *Führer*! Is this true? We do not expect a Hitler Youth to tell us lies, you may know what happens if they do.'

'Not in my hearing he doesn't, he was not happy about Mussolini invading that North African country; he said the *Führer* would have done it more quickly.'

'We hear he says more than that!'

'He sometimes says things just to wind up the fat boy who works on the bench behind us, but he only does it in fun, because we all enjoy watching the boy go red; it's only a joke.' I hoped big Bruno was saying the same thing. I had suggested it to him once over coffee, in case this scenario were to arise, as it would be the only

[22] 1936 March 29 he received 98.8 per cent of approval for his policies in a national referendum.
[23] 1 May 1936 speaking in Berlin on Labour Day.

way out, but I was not convinced he was taking me seriously at the time. They seemed a little less tense at my calm reply, but I felt under enormous pressure as I tried not to show how petrified I really was. The man questioning me left me in the car and walked over to the other car in which big Bruno was sitting. When he returned I told him it was only workshop fun and big Bruno was as much an admirer of the *Führer* as I was.

'The boy who reported him was doing his duty.' He lit a strange-smelling cigarette as he spoke.

'He may have been doing his duty from your point of view, but it's only because he does not like Bruno, because Bruno criticizes his work sometimes.'

There was a tap on the window and I looked out to see *Oberstleutnant* Kleine standing there. The *Gestapo* agent got out of the car and I could hear raised voices but not what was being said. They then walked over to the other car while I waited. Eventually the man who had been speaking to me returned and told me to get back to my work, and to warn big Bruno to stop his joking. I walked back to my bench and was very relieved when big Bruno turned up a few minutes later.

'You were right, little Bruno, but I did what you said and said that we were winding up that fat peasant. I was lucky though, I owe you and that officer for getting me out of a tricky situation. I also owe Ruddie a big thank you; when he saw what was happening he went and got a senior *Luftwaffe* officer, who is our best defence against these *Gestapo* types: he gave them a dressing down for taking workshop banter seriously.'

'What did *Oberstleutnant* Kleine say to you?' I asked.

'Nothing, I found that strange, he almost seemed apologetic that I should have been disturbed!'

Later that afternoon I walked by the fat slob and whispered that before summer he would suffer. I did not have to pursue my threat, because the next day he caught his hand in a lathe which smashed several of his fingers and we never saw him again.

I heard Ruddie, whom I only knew by sight, telling big Bruno that the government was really an unruly mob gaining power, holding all the adolescents in a trance, and that all the Nazis were anti-intellectual. I resented these views, but I knew my place on the shop floor, and I owed big Bruno too much to make any comment. They also spent some of that particular lunch break criticizing the 'Strength through Joy' cruises[24] and laughing at the hypocrisy of the leaders. Apparently big Bruno had read somewhere that although we were being told not to buy in Jewish shops Goering had visited a large one for one of his shopping sprees.[25] Once again I knew that it was necessary for me to keep quiet, to watch and listen in order to try to understand, before I should participate. I remember thinking during that lunch break that I would rather not meet the *Gestapo* again, but I did not realize then that I would be coming into close contact with them very soon – indeed in a very unpleasant and shocking way that would change everything for the rest of my life.

That August I resented the fact that Daimler would not allow me time off to attend the opening of the Olympics with others in the Hitler Youth.[26] I read about it in the papers and recall big Bruno enjoying the fact that a black man had won all the major running events.[27] I also remembered not to say to Adolf Bier that an American monkey, as he called them, had beaten the German Aryans. Hans Lobb and Erik commented on these races, by quickly pointing out that God had made all men the same except for the colour of their hair, skin and eyes. They, like me, felt that there had been fewer attacks on the Jews, because of the Olympics, but we were very wrong.

I was not at home when the *Gestapo* called, so I have no idea what was said, but my parents, especially my mother, told me all that had happened that Saturday morning. I knew the instant I walked through the door that something serious had occurred, because my parents were sitting side by side at the table, my mother was holding my father's hand as if to comfort him.

They asked me to sit down and my mother told me what had

---

[24] A Nazi scheme whereby it was claimed that all workers could go on cruise ships: it never had any effect on the working classes whose pay remained very low.

[25] In 1936 Hermann Goering paid a visit to Bernheimer's carpet store.

[26] Held in Berlin in the first two weeks of August.

[27] Jesse Owens.

happened. My mind still reels when I reflect upon that hour's revelation. I was suddenly transported from the world I lived in to another; it was like going from heaven to hell in seconds, from a position of self-assuredness to total confusion, utterly lost in a world unfamiliar and alien. I was a Jew or a half-Jew, a *mischling*. The cause of that devastating change in my life was Josef, a brother I was never to speak to again. In his bid to become an SS officer, rather than stay a mere foot soldier, he had plunged the whole family into turmoil owing to the closer scrutiny of our hereditary background. My father's mother's maiden name, the investigators had discovered, was Ruth Cohen; and she was Jewish. They could not prove but suspected that my father's father had also been Jewish. My father's protestations that they had all been Roman Catholics made no difference; his mother was a Jew. This made my father either a Jew or a *mischling* of the first degree, which meant Josef, Ruth and I were *mischlings* of the second degree. They had pointed out with unpleasant forcefulness that Ruth and Cohen were Jewish names, and that my sister was intending to marry a Jew called Hans Lobb. My father had no idea about this.

As they were unable to prove without a doubt that my grandfather was a Jew, they had assigned him as a *mischling*, with a star for further investigation. Josef would not be allowed to become an SS officer, but he could remain a guard unless my father was proved to be fully Jewish. Whether my father could continue to work on the railways depended on the investigation, or on whether an Aryan could do his work. 'You are only necessary to the state if we have need of you,' he was told.

'I am not a Jew,' he kept repeating as my mother was telling me all that had happened. I just sat there with my mouth open.

'Do you feel ashamed of us?' my mother asked me.

'Why should I? I'm just totally shocked,' I replied.

'You're a good boy, Bruno, you are our son, that's all you need to know.'

I wanted to go upstairs to my room and be alone, but that, even to my juvenile mind, would have been seen as a rebuff by my father. I have never seen my father cry, but his eyes were red, and my mother kept giving him coffee and telling him that she loved him as much today as when they had first met. He then started to turn his resentment on Ruth and Hans Lobb, but my mother was quite firm with him, and pointed out she would still love him even if his father turned out to be a war-profiteering rabbi, and so by the same token Ruth and Hans should be free to love each other. She reminded him that Ruth was their daughter and her love for my father was not in question, which she would prove one day in early 1943.

The same cannot be said of Josef; a letter arrived from him two days later in which he said he was ashamed of his father. He now felt unclean, and his future was in doubt because of my father's unhealthy past. My mother showed me the letter and I felt disgusted. He was now being posted as a guard to the new Sachsenhausen concentration camp[28] and he would not be able to return to see my mother (who was truly Aryan) if my father happened to be at home. I remember my mother sitting in the kitchen quoting a poem she knew, *Ich hatte einst schönes Vaterland*,[29] 'I once had a beautiful Fatherland'. Then she penned a one-line letter to Josef which simply read, 'Dear Josef, please do not come home, for if you disown your father you are no longer our son.' I posted it for her, and she then spent most of the day in tears.

My father went to work and nothing seemed to have changed. I rushed off to tell Ruth, carrying a letter from my mother. I did not speak to Hans and Erik because I knew that Ruth would tell them. When I did see them a month later they said nothing, but I detected a genuine sense of warmth in their reaction to me. Aunt Ingrid simply gave me a big hug which said it all.

A few days later I asked big Bruno if I could spend an evening with him, in order to explain all that had happened. He said nothing while I told him all, which was extremely unusual for him. I simply had to tell someone and big Bruno was the obvious – and as it turned out the right – choice.

'Are you circumcised?' He asked me in front of Marie, who quickly passed me a white bread roll as if she had not heard a thing.

[28] Opened in July 1936.
[29] The poet Heine.

'No.'

'Do you feel as if you are now a different person?'

'No.'

'Can you still remember the way the fuel injection system works?'

'Of course!'

'Is your chess improving?'

'I hope so.'

'Do you love your father?'

'As always.'

'Do you think I am still your friend?'

'Yes.' He was firing questions at me like the *Gestapo* officers.

'Then,' he said, picking up his beer, 'nothing's changed. There's a strange illness in our world, brought about by the Nazis, that Jews are not human. You've heard me on this many times, but they, and you, and me are all the same, the only difference is in their heads.'

'Life will be more dangerous for my father now.'

'Keep your heads down, it will pass.'

Big Bruno was right about most things, but not this. Once the Olympics had finished the Jew-baiting started again with a vengeance. I realized that the Party had only reduced the attacks because Berlin was full of foreigners, and young as I was it dawned on me that other countries might find the attacks on Jews unacceptable. Now that I was a second-degree *mischling* I was beginning to view contemporary life from a very different perspective.

I used my work at Daimler-Benz as an excuse for quickly leaving the Hitler Youth. However, my problems continued during August. I received call-up papers from the *Wehrmacht* not for one year but for two,[30] with instructions to report on my eighteenth birthday, in six months' time, to some barracks near Potsdam. My sense of panic increased: I wanted to keep my apprenticeship and hoped by joining the *Luftwaffe* I could do so, but I did not want my *mischling* status exposed. I turned once again to big Bruno for advice, which

---

[30] On 24 August 1936 Hitler issued a five line directive at Obersalberg raising conscription to two years.

I followed to the letter. It changed both big Bruno's life and mine for the rest of 1936. I made an appointment to see *Oberstleutnant* Kleine, in whom I had a certain trust, because he seemed human. He did not let me down. I was invited into his office on the aerodrome, where I showed him the papers from the *Wehrmacht*. He was obviously annoyed, claiming they were gathering in as many men as they could, ignoring both the *Luftwaffe* and the *Kriegsmarine*. I felt so confident in him that I mentioned that I was a *mischling*, feeling that I would rather face the consequences then and there, not later.

'A *mischling*?' He looked at me from the other side of his desk, his sharp blue eyes examining me from top to bottom. 'You are as fair haired and blue eyed as I am, you look as much a typical Aryan as the *Führer* could want. Let me give you some advice. The *Luftwaffe* is growing fast and we need competent ground crew; I could not care less whether you are Aryan, *mischling* or any other sort, as long as you are a good mechanic, and German. Tell no one else, that is your business.' I simply nodded, but felt very relieved.

'I shall follow this up personally, but in the meantime I am going to do some thinking about all this.'

He kept his word and pursued his plan, making life difficult for the *Wehrmacht*. Meanwhile big Bruno and I were packed off to Rechlin aerodrome, which was in Mecklenburg, Pomerania, and was one of the *Luftwaffe*'s main testing sites. We stayed there until the end of the year, living in some barracks before being lodged in a small hotel. It was a new research establishment, where they conducted final trials, and we had the job of looking after our own Daimler engines, as well as learning about those from other firms. The work was not difficult or tedious; indeed we found it fascinating, especially watching the pilots test the planes after we had refined the engines to the specifications of the experts, who were there in great numbers.

Big Bruno reckoned that when the *Wehrmacht* asked for my whereabouts the *Luftwaffe* officer would state we were already in a specialist field. I had been right to put my trust in big Bruno and the officer. Our absence also provided me with the ideal opportunity to drop out of sight, as far as the Hitler Youth was concerned, and with big Bruno as my sole company for nearly six months, not only did my chess improve but I started to listen to his political views more attentively. He was not a fan of the Nazis, but was patriotic, and because of the way my father had been treated I was more inclined to lend a sympathetic ear. When I look back I owe big Bruno a great deal.

His main concern was that he believed we were heading for war. He argued that the build-up of the military was self-evident. Even at Rechlin everything had been arranged for the testing of military transport planes as well as fast fighters. During autumn and winter, we also heard that the *Führer* was joining forces with Italy and Japan and that some *Luftwaffe* squadrons had been sent to fight in the Spanish Civil War.[31] Bruno said it was obvious we were gearing up for war.

One night I contemplated what he had said, and for the first time questioned my use of the pronoun 'we'. According to the Nuremberg laws I was not truly German, yet I knew I was: I looked German, I felt German, I spoke German, I had been born in Germany and I was about to join the German *Luftwaffe*. I decided there and then, that I would not raise this question again; I was German. I wrote to my parents and they replied, but because we knew that mail could be read, we were all very cautious. Reading between the lines I gathered all was well and that my father was still busy at his work. We never heard from Josef, and my mother never mentioned Ruth, so I guessed, and hoped, that all was reasonably normal. The year ended with big Bruno and me celebrating Christmas and New Year at work before packing up to return to Berlin. It was a year in which I moved from boyhood and started to become a man.

[31] On 25 October 1936 Hitler and Mussolini formed the Rome–Berlin Axis, on 25 November there was the German–Japanese Anti-Comintern-Pact, and during the same month the German Condor Legion was sent to Spain.

Chapter 5

1937

In 1937 on my eighteenth birthday I reported to a *Flak-Artillerie Schule* (Anti-Aircraft School) as part of my *Luftwaffe* training. I do not want to go into unnecessary detail, because my account is more about what happened to me and my family, not the military background of those years, though, of course, they are inevitably intertwined. Having done my basic mechanical training, I needed to take a course on elementary military training, which after years in the Hitler Youth was not demanding. We were taught guard duties, and as ground crew we were expected to be able to man *fliergerabwehrkanone* ('AA guns'), which I confess I found highly exhilarating. The *Luftwaffe* officers who trained us really seemed a good deal more gentlemanly and pleasant than some of the *Werhmacht* officers we encountered. There was a small contingent of SS guards at the camp, and whilst some people were in awe of them, I found them arrogant, but this was because I kept reflecting on the way Josef had treated my father.

We were at an airfield where a *zerstorergeswader* ('twin-engine fighter unit') was stationed, and at the end of our induction course a few of us had the exciting experience of a flight with some of the pilots. I think it was an attempt by those in command to impress on us the fact that we were a unit that would work together but might also have to fight together at a later date. Several of us returned to work in our aero firms and we did not have to report again until we had finished our apprenticeships, which in my case took another year. We were told, however, that we were to wear our uniforms to and from work and be responsible for the way we conducted ourselves during this time, as part of our military discipline.

I did not make any particular friends during this course because we came from all over Germany. Moreover, all of the recruits, like me, had Hitler Youth backgrounds, and because I was a *mischling*, I was beginning to find the ardour of some them distasteful. I found it ironic that in a matter of a few months the revelation of my father's Semitic breeding, and big Bruno's distaste of anti-Semitism, had started to change my views. The year before I had hated Jews, but now I was more than a little disturbed in my mind about the Party's way of thinking. While on the course I played a few games of chess but no one could beat me amongst the new recruits, though a junior officer called Werner did hold me to a draw. I enjoyed being there and found that big Bruno had taught me well as my work impressed some of the instructors. I also learned a good deal about other types of aero-power units.

Only once during that period did I reflect upon my personal future with any sense of foreboding. I had taken a stroll during some time off around the perimeter of the aerodrome and I came upon a group of men working on extending an old runway. Some of our bigger transport planes needed more space to land, and several thousand metres were being laid to accommodate the obvious growth of aircraft. What caught my eye was that the men were doing manual work, and under the supervision of SS guards. I walked over to the group as casually as I could, only to be confronted by an SS guard, who told me I was in a forbidden area. I pointed at my uniform and said I was walking about the base where I worked.

'Listen, friend,' he said, 'whether you work here or not is beside the point. It is strictly forbidden to come near the prisoners.'

As I walked away I could see, even from a distance, that they were a sickly looking group, and that one of them was being pushed over and beaten by another SS guard.

I did not mention this incident to big Bruno when I caught up with him again in late February. I was so sensitive about my father's plight and my own situation I learned the art of keeping a low profile, excelling at my work and losing myself in chess. I knew how big Bruno and his friend Ruddie felt, and I guessed that there were many others, but no one spoke of these matters. I even wondered what a senior officer like *Oberstleutnant* Kleine thought – but I would never dare ask him, or anyone else. I still felt patriotic towards my country, a feeling that was entrenched by the *Luftwaffe* training and the fact that we were world leaders in aviation and engines. When I read that a butcher had tried to assassinate the *Führer*[1] I recall feeling angry that someone should try to kill the head of state, but for the first time I also reflected that if the Nazis fell from power life might be a little more gentle, and Germany might be a better place for *mischlings* like myself and my father.

When I eventually returned to my home in Hermannstrasse I found that my father was still working for the *Reichsbahn* ('National Railways'), but he was a changed man. He was quieter, he did not go out after work, and he was attending his Catholic church more often. I wondered whether this was because he was trying to impress neighbours, who might know what was happening (since Jews and half-Jews did not normally go to church), or because he was seeking to return to those early days when he never doubted that he was a German soldier of the Aryan race. My mother, despite being a solid Lutheran, sometimes went with him, and it was very clear to me that she was making every effort to keep him happy and safe. It was not easy.

I gathered much later that the *Führer* had decided to talk to delegates from the *Reichsbahn*[2] and that my father's work mates had elected him to represent the train drivers. He had, however, been turned down by top management because he was *reichsangehörigen*, a subject of the state still under investigation, not a full citizen. This clearly indicated that although he had kept his job, his suspected Jewish background and his status as a *mischling* was known. The problem had not gone away, it had been placed on hold, and only time would tell whether his status would become a problem for him and the family. My heart bled for him,

---

[1] On 14 February 1937 Franz Kroll a 33-year-old butcher made an attempt on Hitler's life but was thwarted by the bodyguards; he was executed.

[2] On 4 February 1937 Hitler did address a delegation of the *Reichsbahn* in the *Reich* Chancellery.

and for my mother, struggling with his issues, and I worried for myself as well. No one amongst his closest work mates ever mentioned his lack of status. He himself never raised it, and was therefore ignorant as to whether their silence on the issue was because they did not know or did not care. He stopped going to Frau Goldblatt's shop to avoid the area warden and other nosey neighbours thinking him a Jew-lover; once he could not have cared less, but now he too was scared. My mother, of course, did go, and more frequently than normal. My father continued to read the Party publications, but he never read them aloud any more, and I also wondered whether he kept the papers on his stool to impress anyone who came into our house.

One Sunday near the end of February, my parents had gone to church so I took myself off to central Berlin. It was the *Heldengedenktag* ('War Heroes Memorial Day') and I stood in my *Luftwaffe* uniform watching the *Führer* review the troops on Unter den Linden. The only reason I remember the occasion so clearly is that I saw Big Dick marching in the *Werhmacht* ranks.

Later that morning I worked out how to find my way to Aunt Ingrid's front door. When she opened it there was initially a look of horror on her face, because she saw the uniform before she saw who was wearing it. I had hoped to see Erik and Ruth but discovered I had missed them by a day. They had left Germany on the previous Saturday. At first Aunt Ingrid was reluctant to tell me much of what had happened, but I encouraged her to do so by pointing out my own status as a *mischling*.

'You're not intending to leave are you? It would break your mother's heart.'

I confirmed that I was now an enlisted member of the *Luftwaffe*, and if I left the country, even if I could or wanted to, that would be seen as desertion, and I would never be able to return to Germany again. Slowly but surely I coaxed the details from her. All three of them, Ruth, Hans and Erik, had at last found a sympathetic ear at the British Embassy. It was all very clandestine, because although the British passport officer had been extremely helpful and issued the necessary visas, the German authorities would not issue travel tickets. Technically visas could not be issued without tickets and travel permits. Ruth had been able to obtain everything but Hans and Erik had been turned down. The passport officer had been extremely helpful, and it was soon clear that he also had a great distaste for the German regime. He had moved heaven and earth to facilitate their safe departure but the German regulations seemed to remain firm at every turn. He had tried to encourage Ruth to travel alone but she had refused to go without Hans. They had visited the Embassy many times, and sometimes they had acted as couriers for the passport officer, who was obviously in contact with Benno Cohn of the Jewish Council. Hans was under the impression that the Englishman was something more than a passport officer[3] because he had also made several trips himself to speak to different Jewish people all over the city. Apparently, it would have been easier for them if they had been given a precious Palestine Certificate, but it was clear that someone on the German side did not want Hans or Erik to leave Germany at all.

The Englishman arranged for a colleague to travel with them to the French border, where they would cross at a point where papers were not too carefully scrutinized. Then they were to cross France alone; they had tickets for the ferry to Britain, where their papers would be in order. They had distant relatives there, and had been promised accommodation with them, though they intended to try to make it to America eventually. Hans argued that the further away from Germany they managed to go, the safer they would all be. Aunt Ingrid believed that once their disappearance had been noted she would have a knock on her door, hence her fright when she saw my uniform. Everything was done with the utmost secrecy; even my parents had not been told. Aunt Ingrid asked me to tell them, which of course I agreed to do, but with some reluctance.

I was surprised by my mother's reaction when told her. She seemed delighted; I had thought she would miss her only daughter, especially after losing Josef. 'If I know she's safe, and she's happy then I am happy too,' she explained to me. My father, after being kept in the dark, had eventually been informed of their plans, and he just nodded his head, but I could detect real sadness in his eyes.

[3] This was probably Captain Frank Foley, a British Passport Officer (1936–39) who saved over 10,000 Jewish people, especially after 1938; he was in reality an undercover agent.

A few months later we received a letter from an apparent stranger in England, but I recognized Ruth's handwriting. Everything was written in double talk in case the letters were being read. They had arrived safely and within a few weeks of their arrival they had been married in a Protestant church in Darlington. I remembered Erik telling me about his wish to visit Darlington in our birds'-nesting days. They had all been made very welcome in this northern English town and they were making good progress in speaking English. We received several more letters over the next two years but then, with the outbreak of war in 1939, we heard no more.

I bumped into Big Dick again when I was on my way home one evening; that was not too surprising given that we lived in the same area.

'*Heil Hitler*,' he barked. 'I see you've joined a minor service of the *Werhmacht*.' He fingered my uniform.

'They needed my expertise,' I boasted.

'Never did have any fire in your belly.' He was even more unpleasant than usual. Despite my coldness and curt replies to his questions, he insisted on walking with me and telling how well he was doing. He did not mention that I was a *mischling*, so I presumed that he did not know, for had he known he most certainly would have sneered at me. I peeled away from him as I neared home and as I passed by Frau Goldblatt's shop I could see that she was still busy behind her counter. Her shop did not seem quite as full as usual, but when she looked up she gave me a cheerful wave which I returned, this time quite happily.

At home my mother was in an unusually talkative mood. Apparently her church was putting on a performance of Beethoven, and the pastor had been told that the notice was to contain the line that Jews were not allowed to attend any Beethoven concert.[4] I remember my mother's annoyance at what she called 'childish stupidity'.

Work was going well, and big Bruno and I worked on more advanced versions of what we called the Big Engine. I had to

[4] In 1937 Jews were forbidden to listen to any public performances of Beethoven.

undergo various tests with different inspectors, but thanks to big Bruno's training I passed with flying colours. I did notice that big Bruno was less vociferous with his opinions than he had been in my early training and I suspected – wrongly as it transpired – that he no longer felt he needed to challenge my way of thinking.

Some time in April there was a problem in the chess club. I had been playing a rather good game of the Queen's Gambit Declined with Johann when a brick came through the window. Along with big Bruno and two others I rushed out of the room to the front of the tavern, and found a group of Hitler Youth shouting abuse because Jews were playing chess. They had painted along the wall, 'Jews not wanted here.' The tavern keeper also came out, and the level of abuse increased. One of them spotted my *Luftwaffe* uniform which, according to instructions, I had to wear all the time. More politely, he asked me whether I knew that some of the chess players were Jews. I walked up to him quietly and said, 'Bring us proof, otherwise you are damaging good Aryan property.'

He talked to his friends – there were only four or five of them – and they said they would bring proof the following week. Fortunately they then wandered off; my uniform had helped. We did not see them the following week because the proprietor of the tavern banned us, not because of the Jewish members, but because he could not afford broken windows every week. He was also scared, and I realized that the anti-Jewish programme was increasing in its vehemence. I never thought I would see the day when ordinary innkeepers, usually a tough breed, were made to tow the Party line. On being told the club was to close we had a brief meeting. The normal chairman was not there that week, so big Bruno took the chair and the rest of us sat around in a circle, fifteen in all.

'How many Jews or *mischlings* do we have?' big Bruno asked.

I did not put my hand up, nor did big Bruno look at me as if he expected me to do so. Only Johann Epp raised his hand. 'I am a Jew, a German Jew, as all of you know, and I am prepared to leave the club, so that you can continue to use the tavern as club premises,' he said.

'Johann is prepared to leave the club,' big Bruno continued. Then taking off his round glasses he looked at us one by one, and asked, 'How many of us think that is a good idea?' No one put their hands up.

'Meet at my place. I have a large front room and my house is not far from here.' This quick and positive reply came from a man I only remember as Paul, an old man who played brilliantly with the white pieces, but could never win if he played black.

'What about your wife?' big Bruno asked.

'She knows Johann well, there'll be no problem.'

Ten minutes later it was all settled. Because of the nature of the evening big Bruno and I decided to walk home with Johann, about half an hour away. It was fortunate that big Bruno had thought of this because the Hitler Youth contingent was at the end of Johann's street. There was a notice strung across the road which read, 'Jews enter this locality at their peril.' It reminded me of one near my road, the Hermannstrasse which read, 'The Jew's Father is the Devil.'

At work the next day I asked after Johann. It transpired that he had stayed with big Bruno because the district in which he lived had too many Brownshirts and Hitler Youth living there, and as Johann had once held an important post they were all well aware of his existence.

'I trust you, little Bruno,' he said, 'but I am learning to keep a low profile. Johann often stays with us, but for Marie's sake, we come and go only when it's dark.'

That was the reason why big Bruno was suddenly less vociferous in his views; to all outward appearances he was towing the Party line, which would not allow him to shelter elderly Jewish chess players. Once again, I recall those German chess players who never batted an eyelid, who would not accept Johann's resignation, and who quietly stood by their Jewish friend. I have no doubt in my mind that they too were frightened about the possible ramifications. Even big Bruno was learning discretion, but he was a brave and just man, and he stood by Johann in his hour of need.

I spent a Sunday with big Bruno and went with him and Marie to his local church, where I was surprised to see several *Werhmacht* officers.

'There are a large number of the military who are still Christian,' big Bruno said. 'They'll never be able to close the churches, but they will get rid of those clergy who protest too much. Look at the man sitting at the back, near the door.'

'He looks like *Gestapo*,' I said.

'You're right. He's here every week just to ensure that the pastor and his colleagues say nothing against the Party.'

We played chess in the afternoon, but we also talked about the Church. I had told big Bruno that my mother went to church, and my father was now attending more often. I had also told him about my conversation with the pastor in Memmingen. 'Do you really believe in God?' I asked.

'I wouldn't waste my Sundays otherwise,' he retorted.

'Supposing you're wrong, supposing it's a medieval hangover?'

Big Bruno paused and stopped the chess clock. He took off his glasses, and with his characteristic flourish wiped them on the table cloth, 'If I'm wrong then the worst I fear is oblivion, and that's nothing to fear; if I'm right then I'll be glad not to have denied Him. "The fool hath said in his heart, there is no God" – that's what the psalmist says, and I am no fool.'

Big Bruno was deeply religious.

I pondered the religious aspect of my friend as I made my way home that night. God or no God, I had a feeling that all that we did, and said and thought, was somehow being catalogued, but I really could not have the same belief as big Bruno and my mother.

At home I discovered that my mother was trying to stop my father spending the family savings on a genealogist to prove he was not fully Jewish (*Geltüngsjuden*). She argued that this was a new industry the Nazis had spawned, and that most of them were charlatans who charged extortionate prices. Moreover, if it turned out that he was fully Jewish then he stood a good chance of being reported.

'Even approaching one could cause problems,' she said.

'What do you think, Bruno?'

It was the first time my father had asked for my opinion, and I found myself agreeing with my mother. Fortunately, my father listened to us and we heard no more of this issue, because I agreed that it was a dangerous area to start dabbling in.

The state was also intruding into the Daimler-Benz works. *Luftwaffe* officers dominated the scene more and more, and the civilian management appeared only to do the bidding of the military. There was no doubt that the engines we were making in large numbers were for fast-flying planes, and no amount of double talk could prevent us realizing that these were fighters, many of which were sent as the German contribution to the Spanish Civil War.

In the early summer of that year the newspapers were alive with yet another plot against the *Führer* and there were further attacks against Jews because the main plotter was a German Jew.[5] Notices were placed all over our work area that read 'No Jews Work Here.' I kept my head down and both big Bruno and I stopped talking about politics when at work. I think we both realized that there were dangers, but it had taken big Bruno a little longer.

Just after the attempt on the *Führer*'s life we felt justified in staying silent because big Bruno's friend Ruddie was in trouble. He had been taken away by the *Gestapo* and only the direct interference of the *Luftwaffe* had enabled him to return a week later.

At lunch time big Bruno and I sat with Ruddie out on a patch of grass and talked about what had happened. It transpired that all he had done was tell a joke about the *Gestapo* themselves. Big Bruno asked what the joke was and for a moment Ruddie hesitated but he then decided he could trust me. I was an unknown factor, although I had worked with Ruddie for nearly three years. He said that hundreds of rabbits had appeared at the Swiss border seeking political asylum. When asked by the Swiss soldiers why they were there they had explained that the *Gestapo* were rounding up all the elephants.

'But you're not elephants!' the soldiers said.

'You try explaining that to the *Gestapo*,' the rabbits replied.

We both roared with laughter.

'Was that all?' big Bruno asked.

'That's all they asked me,' Ruddie replied. 'They had nothing else.'

'And they took you away for telling a joke?' I said.

[5] On 4 June 1937 a German Jew called Helmut Hirsch was executed for being involved in a plot to kill Hitler.

'They didn't find it funny. They locked me in a cell with no food, light or water for thirty-six hours; I don't mind telling you I was scared stiff by the time they brought me out.'

'They kept you there all that time?' big Bruno asked.

'They threatened me with Dachau and with torture but I readily confessed to telling the joke. Then that *Luftwaffe* officer stormed in. They locked me up for another twenty-four hours, and then they just threw me out on the Albertstrasse without another word.'

Big Bruno asked him who had reported him; that was the most sinister twist in that whole sorry saga. He had only just heard the joke and retold it at his daughter's wedding to a few guests, whilst they were drinking beer in the garden. It could only have been a member of his own family, or his son-in-law's family, or some close family friends. He suspected one man whom he had crossed years before over a dispute about money. This sent a cold chill down my spine. It was dawning on me that we had become a society in which one's own neighbours, even a family member, could use the paranoia of the State to seek revenge for a personal matter. Big Bruno was thinking the same thing, and wondered aloud whether a beaten chess opponent might seek his revenge by reporting him for not starting the match with a '*Heil Hitler.*' Ruddie and I laughed, but it was a shallow laugh, because there was an element of truth in what he said. We knew most of the men we worked with very closely, but we decided it was safer to talk only about engines, chess and the weather if anyone else was in the vicinity.

As I went home that night I reflected that Josef had shown the same callousness by rejecting my father.

My mother told me later that Josef had written asking her to meet him, but that she had not replied because she was deeply upset by Josef's rejection of his father, and she always put my father first, even before her own life – as I was to see a few years later. Josef's letter said that he was being moved as a guard to a new concentration camp called Buchenwald.[6]

Our work of building and repairing engines was moving at a frenetic pace, and we seemed to see the new fighters, the Bf109s,

[6] Opened on 15 July 1937.

leaving the factory nearly every day.[7] They were being sent off to Spain for the Condor Legion, which we read about in the papers daily. According to the news German pilots were winning the war for General Franco, but when we were alone big Bruno told me that any war could only be won when the ground troops were sitting in enemy territory and that the planes only made that easier. 'Ground troops win wars,' he said. 'Aircraft just make it easier for them.' When we heard that Japan had invaded China[8] we wondered whether the *Luftwaffe* would be involved in that war as well, but big Bruno said that was too far, and he was right.

Germany certainly seemed to be the focus of international interest, and I can remember one occasion when some British airmen were entertained at the works by officers of the *Luftwaffe*; to all appearances they seemed the greatest of friends, and from what we saw from our workbenches they were always laughing and joking together. It seemed strange that these military men could be so friendly when a few years before they had been at war. We were also visited by the British royal family – or rather Berlin was visited by the ex-King[9] – not that we ever saw them, or indeed Mussolini when he came.[10]

Big Bruno told me that his pastor had once preached a sermon to the effect that there would be no wars if ordinary people were in control, because ordinary people had to fight the wars and most ordinary people got on with their neighbours, even if they spoke a different language. At the time I was always bemused that big Bruno took his Church so seriously, but later in life I was to understand why. He had once seen into the depths of hell in the trenches, now he sought the alternative, or the hope of the alternative. He once told me that he had come upon a French soldier who had just fallen from a burst of machine-gun fire which had opened his stomach like a tin opener. The man was

[7] New Me109 fighters as well as He 111 and Do17 bombers were in high demand.

[8] On 7 July 1937 Japan invaded China on a large scale.

[9] On 22 1937 the Duke of Windsor and his wife visited Hitler at the Berghof.

[10] On 28 September 1937 Mussolini had a sight-seeing tour of Berlin and Potsdam.

clearly dead, but his stomach still seemed to be working, and as big Bruno looked at the insides of this human being he wanted to believe that all this incredible anatomical complexity had a Creator who would not leave His creation in the mud like a rotting cabbage on a rubbish dump. He used to say that however well built our engines were they were not as good as the human heart that pumped away on average for seventy years without needing servicing or spare parts, and never stopped. 'No engine,' he said, 'can hold a candle to God's creation of the human engine.'

At the end of the year I went with my father to his Roman Catholic church for the Christmas service and, much to my surprise, my mother came as well. I think she was making a point to my father that, whatever happened, she would always be with him. I have to confess I found the church very strange, but also peaceful. I found the incense unusual and could not understand why the Holy Communion was still said in Latin. This aspect aside, there was a sense of mystery about the service, almost a sense of the holy and the awesome. There were statues everywhere, as well as boys holding candles and thuribles, processional crosses and banners, and the altar seemed to be shrouded in a cloud because of the incense. I have to admit, looking back, that I had more of a sense of God in that place than I ever felt in the pews of the Lutheran church. My mother did not comment on the way home; she had gone there to be with my father, and during the following years he would realize the depth of her dedication and commitment to him.

Chapter 6

1938

The previous two years had been a turning point for me because I had been declared a *mischling* and my father possibly a Jew, but in 1938 my thinking changed dramatically. During 1937 I had travelled some way from my Hitler Youth days but not as far as I would travel in 1938. The year started well enough but ended with horror. On reflection I consider 1936 to be the first of what I call my 'hallmark' years, and 1938 was the next. These years formulated my thinking and, therefore, my life.

During 1937, all Jews had their ration books marked with a large 'J' and my mother was pleased that my father's ration book remained unmarked. We started 1938 hoping that the misery of the previous two years would soon pass, and all our concerns would be forgotten. Perhaps my father was just a *mischling*, and too insignificant to provoke any further research. Working at Daimler, and as a member of the *Luftwaffe*, my status was never mentioned. My birthday that year was on a Thursday and, with typical Germanic efficiency, I completed the major part of my apprenticeship on that very day and was awarded my certification. At lunch time a senior manager invited me and four others to the offices to receive our paperwork. It was clear that I had excelled, thanks to big Bruno. The *Luftwaffe* officer, who was present, told me to report to him for my duties the next day. I was both thrilled and sad: thrilled to be a fully recognized mechanic, but sad that I would be leaving big Bruno. This was not entirely true because although I came and went from Berlin over the next few years, I always managed to stay in touch with him. Sometimes I would find him at the aerodrome and sometimes at the chess club. We also played postal chess, and therefore managed to communicate in our own code, which eluded possible censors.

The next day the *Luftwaffe* officer presented me with my *Hoheitsabzeichen*,[1] which according to my rank was a cloth eagle badge, to be sown onto my now not so junior uniform. I was curious that the other four apprentices had not appeared. He explained that he was seeing me on my own because I was to be attached to a special unit. I knew that the *Luftwaffe* had ten air districts (*Luftgaue*) each with its own established airfield staffing. Owing to my high marks, I was to be attached to a rapid mobility staff support unit. The concept was that in an emergency *Luftwaffe* units would move swiftly to take over a civil airfield, occupy an enemy site or even establish a temporary one, so that the pilots and planes would be closer to any ground action. We would be flown as a unit to the new site, to establish a fully manned airfield ready for the planes to come and go. Within the unit there would be expert mechanics in various fields, who would be ready to share with others the specialist knowledge of the engines that we knew so well.

As I have said, the Daimler engine I worked on was the DB series, and that was the power unit for the Heinkel III and the Messerschmitt Bf109 and 110. The Bf109 was to keep me busy for the next seven years. This fighter plane is better known as the Me109.[2] I was to spend most of 1938 being flown between Berlin and Munich. Sometimes I was in Berlin for a month, and then we would receive a sudden order to move in six hours back to Munich. Whenever I was in Berlin I managed to make contact with big

[1] Metal for senior ranks and gold for generals and similar ranks. It was widely used on letter headings and had a sinister connotation for those in occupied territories.

[2] The Me109 was properly known as the Bf109 since it came from the *Bayerisch Flugzeugwerke* and only later was known as the Messerschmitt. It entered into full production in 1938 and saw service throughout the coming war.

Bruno and my parents. At the aerodrome we were a unit of twenty ground-crew who were expected to cover all kinds of work, from manning guns, checking airstrips, armouring planes and doing emergency checks.

My section of the unit was more elite, because as engine mechanics our work was clearly defined and essential. There were four dedicated mechanics; the chief was called Friedrich Milch. He was a pleasant man and a good superior, as he was always patient when we came across difficult problems. Next in command was Franz Schmidt. He was also easy to work with, but as a strong Nazi Party member was always expounding his views, there was sometimes tension. Finally there was Albert Koch who was, over the next few years, to become a good friend. Like me, he came from the Berlin area, so we had much in common, and to my immense pleasure he too was an avid chess player. We learned a great deal from one another as we worked together on the different engines and the problems that we encountered. I often recall with great pleasure repairing a faulty DB engine that big Bruno had once worked on. I knew this because big Bruno always marked an oil cap with a small 'B'. When I sent my chess move and a brief letter to big Bruno that night I took great pleasure in telling him I had found one of his engines; his return letter also indicated that he had been pleased at the news.

For the first few months of 1938, I was busy acquiring new skills with engines I had not worked on before, as well as learning what makes an aerodrome function. The main problem was spares; they were heavy and not easily transported, but we had all the essential tools and main parts that were always ready to be packed up at a moment's notice. There were moments when we worked all day and all night, but on other occasions I can remember pleasant days when the planes were away on some exercise, and Albert and I whiled away our time playing chess. We even managed to set up a chess competition, as it was quite a popular pastime in those days. At the end of January there was a national holiday,[3] which that year fell on a Sunday, and so we were given a long weekend but were

[3] 30 January, Day of Power, the day on which Hitler became Chancellor in 1933.

not allowed to leave the aerodrome. We organized a chess competition called 'speed chess' (called *blitzkrieg* today, ironically); every game had to be finished within ten minutes. It was good fun.

I was in Munich at that time, and during the lazy week that followed we heard that major events were happening in the hierarchy of the State. At first we only heard rumours about generals being sacked, and then we heard officially that all the armed forces, the *Luftwaffe* included, were to come under a single command, the *Oberkommando der Wehrmacht* (OKW 'Armed Forces High Command'), under the *Führer*.[4] It did not mean much to us in our hangars, but we did notice that senior officers kept moving into huddles, and we had no doubt about the subject of their discussions.

Several times Franz made me shudder when he mentioned the 'Jew problem'. 'Get rid of the lot, make Germany Jew free,' he said on one occasion. None of us replied to this statement. We were working on a Heinkel at the time, and my head was buried in the cowling. 'And furthermore,' Franz reminded me of Adolf Bier's ranting voice, 'I'd send all *mischlings* back to Poland.'

'Why Poland?' Albert asked.

'That's where they all come from.'

'A *mischling* can be half or even three-quarters Aryan,' Albert persisted.

'That wouldn't worry the *Führer*.'

'It would worry the *mischlings*,' Friedrich said. 'Now let's get this Heinkel finished and back out of the hangar.'

I froze with my spanner on the cowling bolts while this conversation took place. I said nothing, but I experienced a strange fear because without knowing it they were discussing me and my father. Friedrich's interruption caused a moment of laughter, and I was grateful that the subject of *mischlings* and their future was dropped.

---

[4] On 4 February 1938 Hitler struck at dissenting Generals Blomberg and Fritsch. He abolished the War Ministry and appointed himself in Blomberg's place and set up the OKW with General Wilhelm Keitel as its chief. There was a widespread purge of other senior officers at this time.

Albert had just had a few days in Berlin, where he had attended the International Automobile Exhibition[5] and was keen on the *Führer*'s claim that 'all Germans would soon own a people's car', the Volkswagen. He reckoned the *Führer* was taking Germany in the right direction; previously I would have agreed with him, but my *mischling* status was causing me to doubt more and more where I stood regarding the State in general. Even with Albert I kept my own counsel, but I noted that he was not as definite about the *mischlings* question as Franz. None of us in those days considered the international situation; we were pleased to be in work, and the thought of owning a car appealed to our youthful dreams. Many others wanted to go on the cruises the Nazis were offering, but no one among my acquaintances knew of anyone who had managed it. Some of the pilots had been, but that transpired to be a convenient way of transporting them to the Condor Legion involved in the Spanish Civil War. Our main concern was repairing and servicing aircraft and listening carefully to what the pilots said about how their machines and engines handled. None of us wanted to send a plane out of the hangar that could prove to be dangerous.

By the end of February I was back in Templehof, Berlin, and had only just managed to catch up with big Bruno when we were ordered to return to Munich at once. This time the order seemed to have a degree of real urgency about it, and I noted that our fighter pilots were already back when we reported to our transport plane, a specially converted Dornier. It was, as I remember, Friday 11 March, because that evening I had been due to stay with big Bruno and Marie to have a game of chess. Instead I sat in the Dornier listening to Franz, who was full of the fact that no more government contracts would be awarded to Jewish-owned or Jewish-managed firms.[6] 'That will send a clear message to the Jews,' he said. No one answered him, not out of principle but because the plane had reached the speed when it either took off or crashed: most mechanics I know, keep quiet at this stage of the take-off.

---

[5] Hitler had opened this exhibition on 18 February 1937 with the claim that the Volkswagen would break down class barriers.
[6] A decree to this effect was issued in the early part of March 1938.

The next day the reason for our move was clear; the Munich airfield was packed tight with planes of every shape and size. We were up at 6 a.m. checking the fighter planes, whilst other crews were working their way through the transport aircrafts. When I look back, I realize what a political simpleton I was: I was so involved in engines and chess, I had no idea what was happening in the wider world. At 9.30 a.m. we were all hurriedly lined up in formation and told that the *Führer* himself was arriving. I actually had quite a good view because Albert stood in front of me, and he was far shorter than I was. The *Führer*'s plane arrived, and when the music struck up all the senior officers stubbed out their cigarettes, and we stood with our eyes fixed on the passenger door. I had seen the *Führer* before, but this time he seemed somewhat smaller, and was closely surrounded not only by other dignitaries, but also by armed SS guards. I almost wondered whether Josef would be there, but then I remembered that he only held ordinary rank because of his *mischling* status. I looked back to see the *Führer* again but he was already in his car and driving away.

'Lot of fuss just for that!' Friedrich grumbled, as we went back to our hangars where planes were coming and going faster than I had ever experienced before.

'What's going on?' I asked in my naïvety.

'Read the papers, Bruno,' Albert said. 'The *Führer*'s bringing Austria back into the Fatherland.'[7]

We read about it a few days later in the papers, and also watched a film in which we saw the *Führer* driving into Austria in the very same car that had met him at the aerodrome. We all felt then that we had become part of an historic moment. Even with my doubts, I thought that this was a good time for Germany, especially when I saw all the cheering crowds. Years later I would read that the Nazis were not quite as welcome as we were led to believe, but at that time it all seemed the best thing for both countries, as Austria and Germany had so much in common.

For most of April that year we were back in Berlin; we had had a very busy time in Munich during the *Anschluss*, but Berlin in April was sunny, relaxing and pleasant. My parents were pleased I

---

[7] The *Anschluss* when Austria was annexed.

was back and could go home during my free time. The interesting news that month was that Hans and Ruth had found their way to America. Apparently, Hans also had distant relations in Ohio, and they had left in the January of that year. Erik had decided to stay, but there was no news of what he was going to do with his life. I thought I might write to him but my parents decided I should keep a distance while I was serving in the military. My father had heard nothing more from those who were interested in his background, and like me he was keeping himself to himself. I went with him to his church again, not just to keep him company but because I found a real sense of peace during the mass, even though I was not able to take communion. I also spent some time with big Bruno and Marie, and once made it to the chess club. I recall it was 17 April because the *Führer*'s birthday was on the 20th, and we had been given four days off. I played with Johann and even though my skills had improved I still could not beat him. He was getting old prematurely; his grey hair had turned white and his face was gaunt. I knew this was because of the attacks on the Jews, as a consequence of which he was spending more and more time seeking shelter with big Bruno. I gathered later that he was in big Bruno's house virtually all the time, then in hiding.

When I stayed with big Bruno one weekend he was roaring with laughter because the *Führer* had invoked God himself in an election speech in Vienna.[8] 'I ask you,' he roared, 'what has God got to do with the *Führer*? Does God want the children of Abraham punished, has God got it in for people like Johann Epp?'

I was glad that all this was said in the privacy of big Bruno's home. I noticed that the more unhappy the anti-Semitism made his old friend Johann, the more vociferous big Bruno's views were becoming. I only hoped he had not reverted to his old habit of letting the rest of the factory know where he stood. There had also been problems over his buying a home from a Jewish family. Two officials had called to see the deeds of purchase, but fortunately everything was in order, and according to big Bruno, the Jewish family had been careful to ensure that an Aryan firm organized the

[8] In Hitler's last election speech in Vienna (9 April 1938) he said: 'I believe that it was God's will to send a boy from here into the *Reich*. . . .'

legal side. Johann had to register the fact that he owned his property[9] and it was becoming more than clear that the State was trying to drive all Jews out of Germany.

There was a great deal of chatter about whether another war would start, and this was further fuelled when the *Führer* was reported in the paper as having said that the statement 'Never war again' was not enough; the watchword had to be 'Never again civil war! Never again class war! Never again domestic strife and discord!'[10] The fact that he had defined war so carefully made me wonder whether big Bruno could be right, but Franz, and even Friedrich, said that the *Führer* was simply demanding peace.

At the end of May we were back in Munich, and were given a weekend off because the *Führer* was in the city to open the new underground transport system.[11] We were supposed to attend the events and so I wandered along with Friedrich and Franz but the crowds were so dense, the guards so numerous, that I did not see the *Führer* once. Albert was missing that day and he told me he had gone to church.

'You go to church?' I asked.

'When I can. I'm not ashamed of it; I just don't want Franz lecturing me on the Party ideals supplanting the outmoded Christian faith.' He was right, because Franz had held forth on this subject several times.

'Do you ever go?' he asked me.

'Sometimes.' I said no more, and we worked on quietly on the Dornier engine, which Albert knew well. Later he raised church-going again when we were by ourselves, and I told him about my father being a Roman Catholic, and my mother being a Lutheran. Albert was a Catholic and he was interested that I sometimes found a spiritual solace in the mystery of the mass. He suggested that perhaps we might go together and I agreed, just as long as we kept

[9] On 26 April 1938 registration of all property owned or held by Jewish people inside the *Reich* became mandatory.

[10] On 1 May 1938 Hitler stated this at the Berlin May Day celebrations in Berlin.

[11] On 22 May 1938 Hitler opened the new underground system in Munich.

our outings to ourselves. He was more than happy with this, but noted that although some Party members frowned on the Church and occasionally derided it, there was always *Luftwaffe* as well as *Werhmacht* personnel at his church.

'The Nazis may want us to worship them, but they will never be able to close the real churches.'

'The real churches?' I questioned.

'Well,' he answered, 'some of those evangelical churches have become like a political wing of the Party – not all, but some.'

This was a new side to Albert; it had taken months for us to arrive at this discussion, and I realized that I was not the only person to keep my cards close to my chest. It sometimes took just a passing comment to reveal where another person stood, but it also took courage in those days to share these thoughts with another person, even someone one worked alongside. When I had started at Daimler-Benz big Bruno had been free with his opinions but as the years passed by even he had become, I hoped, silent.

In August Albert was given leave and my unit went back to Berlin. We travelled wherever our fighter group went. I preferred Berlin because it meant that I could visit my home and the chess club, and sometimes stay with big Bruno and Marie. If I remember rightly it was about this time I became aware that Johann Epp was virtually living with them, and rarely attended the chess club. Johann told me that the State had demanded that he add a second name to his given name, so he was now known in official documents as Johann *Israel* Epp.[12] Big Bruno saw this as yet another way of humiliating Jews and he was becoming more and more worried about Johann's safety. Later, that very year, he would be proved right.

I had told him about Hans and Erik and how they had managed to leave the country, and he whispered to me (and it was unlike him to whisper anything), that he was already looking into the possibility for Johann. He had already been to see Pastor Heinrich

---

[12] On 17 August 1938 it was decreed that from 1 January 1939 all Jewish men were to add Israel to their names, and Jewish women had to have the second name of Sarah.

Grüber at the protestant church,[13] and it might be arranged. Johann was so overwhelmed that German Christians were prepared to help him that at times he was almost in tears. I told big Bruno about the passport officer at the British Embassy and Dr Ho at the Chinese Embassy, but he preferred to work through his Church, using the contacts that his own Pastor Niemöller had quietly fed him.

At the end of August we were back in Munich. I felt like a puppet on a string being picked up and put down somewhere different every month. In the middle of September I knew that something important was happening: I thought it might be another visit by the *Führer* because all the planes were being lined up as if on show. It turned out to be a visit by the British Prime Minister, Mr Chamberlain,[14] and we were told it was to enable the *Führer* to cement international relationships. I have to say I was impressed that the British had come to Germany to meet the *Führer*. Franz, on the other hand, had a different viewpoint, and one that turned out to be very close to the truth. He claimed that the *Führer* was warning the British Prime Minister not to interfere with Germany's determination to free Germans on the Czechoslovakian border. He added that the *Führer* would claim back the Danzig area,[15] which separated Germany from some of its Prussian roots.

'He will not risk a major war,' Friedrich said.

'If he has to make war to return our lands, he will,' Franz replied. None of us knew how right Franz was.

I was more preoccupied at the time with learning about the Junkers Jumo engine inside the Stuka we were repairing. Both Albert and Franz were experts on this engine, but I was learning fast. I also felt more detached from what was happening in the world about me, than I had been when I had been a member of the Hitler Youth. I wanted to be detached; I just wanted to do my job well and make myself indispensable. Having felt a kind of rejection by being

---

[13] Pastor Heinrich Grüber, the Dean of the Protestant Church in Berlin, organized escape routes for Jews through Holland. It became known as the 'Grüber Office' by the Jews.

[14] He was taken from Munich to the Berchtesgaden to meet Hitler at the Berghof.

[15] The so-called Polish Corridor.

termed a *mischling* I was beginning to feel the need to prove myself.

My awareness of being a *mischling* came to the fore again a few weeks later, when Franz announced that he had read that Aryan doctors could treat only Aryan patients.[16]

'Why?' Albert asked.

'Would you want to go to a vet?' Franz retorted. 'The Jews are more animal than human.'

As I tightened up some holding bolts I wondered whether I would be regarded as part animal; this was all beginning to make me feel both scared and angry. I was beginning to change; events surrounding me were affecting my personality in a very real way. I could feel myself becoming more introverted, at times less confident, more reflective and, dare I say it, more sensitive about other people. My fondness for Johann Epp had made me look at Jewish people in a very different light. When Franz called them animals I knew he was wrong. When I had called them animals years before I had known they were not, but now I was worried that people like Franz actually believed it to be true. My father was not an animal, nor a part animal, but it had taken the shock of my own *mischling* status to make me sympathetic towards people like Johann Epp. Big Bruno had been right from the very beginning, but my immature, selfish nature would not listen to him until it happened to me. I suppose when I look back it was all part of growing up, but they were not easy times for anyone young to develop naturally.

My inner confusion and tension increased when I heard that, because the Swiss did not want any more Jews over their border, all Jewish passports had to be marked with a large 'J', as in the case of the ration books.[17] It was not long after this that I also read that all passports belonging to German Jews had been cancelled.[18] I did not have a passport, nor did my parents, but it still added to my growing paranoia. Franz was also jumping with joy because his forecast was proved right when our troops occupied the Sudetenland.[19] We were not directly aware of this; we knew

[16] On 30 September 1938 this decree was promulgated.
[17] 5 October 1938.
[18] 15 October 1938.
[19] 1 October 1938.

something was going on because our planes were coming and going, our flight never needed rearming, so we reckoned it was peaceful. The papers saw it as our right to reclaim this area, and being politically naïve I had no problems with this view. I knew nothing at the time of the international tension it caused, nor where all this would eventually take us as a nation. My main desire was that any plane I worked on was in first class condition, and my main source of relaxation was still chess.

Just after the second week of all this activity we were back in Berlin and I was able to spend a few weekends at home. I arrived there one Saturday morning at the same time as my father, and I could see at once that something was upsetting him. At first he would not say what, but after some breakfast he talked to my mother and me about what he had seen. During the previous week he had been detailed to do some long hauls, and on the Monday and Tuesday he had taken thousands of Polish Jews to a place called Zbasyzn.[20]

'You can have no concept of what I saw,' he said. 'Thousands were packed into carriages and some into cattle trucks by armed SS guards. When we arrived at Zbasyzn they were herded off the train like cattle, and when I returned the next day they were still outside the station because the Poles wouldn't let them in, and it was freezing.'

'What's going to happen to them?' my mother asked.

'God knows, there was no food for them, no shelter, but there's worse to tell.'

'What?' I asked.

'The SS guards were brutal; if people didn't move immediately they hit them with their rifle butts. I saw one guard hit a child, a child I tell you, and when the mother complained he literally smashed his fist straight into her face; there was blood everywhere.'

'That can't be true,' my mother said.

'It's true all right, and when my fireman shouted at him, he turned towards us, and I saw Josef; I'm not lying, it was Josef.'

We were all silent for a moment, and then my mother asked, 'Did he see you?' My father was not sure and we fell back into

[20] On 18 October 1938 12,000 Polish Jews were expelled at once and only allowed to take one suitcase. Some 8,000 were denied entry by Poland.

silence. My mother and I were stunned by the apparent brutality, but the news that Josef was involved made me feel quite sick. When I was a boy, I had had a vision of my big brother being a smart soldier fighting the enemies of the *Reich*, but here he was brutalizing women and children. My mother had intended to go to Memmingen with Aunt Ingrid for a week, but she decided to postpone the visit until the beginning of November; she and I could see that my father was in a deep state of shock. I could understand why. He had seen brutality and sheer cruelty, and then to add to his horror he had seen his estranged son as one of the perpetrators. He was also upset because he would have liked to step down from the train cabin and remonstrate with Josef, but he was now all too aware of his own *mischling* status and the distinct possibility that he might soon be named as a Jew. He was still trying to come to terms with this shock. All his life he had been German, he had fought in the German army, he was awarded a medal for bravery, and now officialdom was telling him he was a Jew, a man of no worth, only an animal. He felt the guilt of being one of those who had once agreed that Jews were profiteers and anti-German, and like me he was confused. I detected in him a real element of anger, and only my mother's insistence made him keep a low profile and not speak out. He had lost his friend Otto who, like Ruddie, had disappeared, and had probably been sent to Dachau. 'All the best Germans are in Dachau,' big Bruno had warned me once, and now I was beginning to believe him. My mother was keenly aware of the danger that the family was in, and she would sit calmly with my father, trying to convince him that the best means of survival was discretion.

Some time in early November, just after my mother had gone to Memmingen and my father was back at work, events suddenly seemed to erupt like a volcano. I had two weeks' leave and I was staying either at home or at Aunt Ingrid's flat, and playing chess with big Bruno. I was trying to treat this as a minor holiday, but because I did not have sufficient funds to go away I thought that by moving from one residence to another I would feel refreshed before returning to duties. I learned that big Bruno had managed to get Johann Epp out of Germany and into Holland. 'Grüber's Office' had done the trick and as far as Bruno knew Johann was now staying with relatives in Amsterdam. He had heard no news but was expecting a letter any day telling him that his old friend was safe. Many years later I found out that Johann had made it safely to Amsterdam but that after the invasion he had been rounded up with other Jews and sent to Auschwitz, where he died in November 1944. In 1938 we had no idea of the horrors to come, and considered Holland to be as safe as the other side of the world.

Times suddenly changed: it all started with a newspaper report that a Polish Jew had killed a German diplomat in Paris.[21] The paper proclaimed that collective punitive measures would be announced very soon. Memories of another assassination were invoked, the incident involving a German Jew called David Franfurter,[22] whose case was constantly being re-reported, and passions were running high. I knew there would be trouble and thought that perhaps some leading Jewish rabbis and other leaders might be arrested. How wrong I was; I should have known better, with all the anti-Semitic violence simmering just below the surface. When I heard that all Jewish newspapers and magazines had to close down, and that Jewish children could no longer attend Aryan state schools, I thought that those were the measures referred to.[23]

It was on a Wednesday or Thursday night[24] that I decided I would stay at Aunt Ingrid's flat while she was in Memmingen with my mother. I arrived late in the centre of Berlin and was amazed at the crowds walking around the expensive shopping area chanting *'raus mit den Juden'* ('away with the Jews'). Then I came across the fashionable Kurfürstendamm completely in ruins, shop windows smashed and all the goods scattered over the street. Every now and then some furtive person would snatch some of the goods and then

[21] On 7 November 1938 Herschel Grynszpan shot the German Attaché Ernst vom Rath, who died from wounds two days later. Herschel Grynszpan was angry at the way the Nazis had treated his parents. A week later the SS ordered the destruction of Jewish property, shop fronts and synagogues. Nearly one hundred Jews were killed and an estimated 20,000 were arrested.

[22] Three years earlier David Frankfurter had killed Wilhelm Gustloff, the head of a Nazi organization in Switzerland.

[23] Both these measures were taken on 8 November 1938.

[24] *Kristallnacht.* 9–10 November 1938.

disappear. I walked quickly by onto Unter den Linden and to Alexanderplatz, where a huge retail store called Israel, four floors high, was being totally ransacked. It was dangerous to walk past because goods were being thrown out of the windows. I spotted a news-stand with the headline 'the deed of murder falls on all Jewry';[25] now I realized what was meant by 'collective punitive measures'.

I asked a policeman what would happen to the rioters and he simply asked me why I was not joining in. 'It is the duty of every good German to drive these animals out,' he said, and I moved on. He shouted after me that soon all the synagogues would be burned down. I decided that it was too dangerous to stay in the city centre that night, and boarded an almost empty tram back to my home. We had only been travelling a few minutes when I saw a huge building on fire, which the person sitting behind me said was one of the famous synagogues. Enough was enough, and I wanted to go home, I wanted to pretend it was not happening.

But the riots had followed me. We did not live in a large retail area but the one shop I knew was Frau Goldblatt's and there was a crowd standing outside shouting at her and calling her a Jewish whore. Frau Goldblatt must have been in her seventies and I was amazed when she threw open her top window and called out that she was as good a German as they were, and her sons had died for Germany in the war. Then somebody shouted out a phrase I had once used: 'They just died from fright.' I felt so ashamed that I had once used that joke, and then I saw Big Dick, not in uniform, leading the hostilities. The crowd was mainly Hitler Youth and some thugs that I recognized as Brownshirts in civilian clothing. Before Frau Goldblatt could close her window she was being pelted with stones and even bricks. Like a real coward I shrank back in the shadows and watched as her shop windows cascaded to the ground. From my vantage point I could see that Big Dick had broken the door in and disappeared inside, only to appear a few minutes later dragging Frau Goldblatt by her grey hair. She was in a flimsy nightgown, and to my horror Big Dick pulled it off her leaving her standing amongst all the men and boys stark naked. He thrust a

[25] From Goebbel's paper *Angriff*.

small brush into her hands and told her to clean the gutter. She refused at first but Big Dick smacked her across the face, drawing blood from her mouth, so she got on to her knees and started to scrub the gutter. I wanted to go across and help her, but I was scared stiff, and knew that I could not take on such a crowd. I would dearly have loved to have one of the machine-guns from the Bf109 so that I could cut them down where they stood, I was so angry. Suddenly Frau Goldblatt collapsed and Big Dick kicked her; when she did not move the crowd seemed to lose interest and the shout went up that the synagogue was next. Within minutes the crowd had gone, leaving Frau Goldblatt in the gutter.

I crossed the road with considerable caution; there was no one around, so I got on my knees; I could sense at once that Frau Goldblatt was still alive. Taking another look around I picked her up; she seemed all skin and bones, no weight at all. I took her back into her shop and up the stairs to her apartment. There were no lights on in the house but the street lamp enabled me to see what was where. I covered her with a blanket from her bed and with a damp towel I wiped the blood from her mouth. I saw a bottle of cognac on the sideboard, and I tried to give her a small glass to drink. At first nothing happened and then she sipped it a little, spluttered and thankfully seemed to come to life. When she looked at me she was terrified but when I smiled and wiped her forehead with the towel, she began to relax a little.

'Why? Why? Why?'

'I don't know.' What else could I say? She asked for another nightgown, which I found, and then I put the kettle on the stove to make a drink. There was a good deal of shouting outside but when I looked through the smashed windows the street was empty. I made her some coffee and put a large cabinet across the smashed window. Then I decided to go home. She thanked me profusely but I did not deserve her thanks, I had only come to her rescue when it was safe.

I left her shop with caution after scanning the street to see if all was clear before making for my own home. Once outside I decided to walk around the area for a while; I headed towards the train station. The area now seemed quieter and there were very few people around, but I saw Big Dick walking up the steps to the old stone bridge across the railway lines. I felt a very deep hatred for him and for what he had done to Frau Goldblatt, and without considering what I was doing I ran up the steps behind him, and called him a swine.

He turned round, surprised to see me there, and sneered, calling me a 'Jew-lover'. My fist went straight for his face but he ducked, and in doing so slipped at the top of the steps and crashed to the bottom, about thirty steps down. Even before I got down to him I could see, by the position of his head that his neck was broken; a closer look told me that, although his eyes were open, he was dead. At the time I did not feel a moment's remorse and simply looked around to see if anybody had witnessed the deed. There was nobody in sight but I checked and double-checked before taking a back road home as fast as I was able. That night I worried that I might have been seen and could be facing a murder charge; I even worried that some people might blame the Jews for his death and carry out further reprisals. In the early hours of the morning I awoke with a start: I had been dreaming that Big Dick's body was sitting at the end of my bed. Then I felt a deep sense of remorse about the magnitude of what I had done to a man who had once been my friend. The next few days passed very quickly, but even today I can still see Big Dick's dead face looking up at me from the bottom of that flight of steps.

My father was away and my mother and Aunt Ingrid were in Memmingen, so I took myself off to see big Bruno and Marie. Big Bruno was at work, so I stayed with Marie until he returned. I told both of them all that had happened. Big Bruno looked at me very intensely, and Marie looked at the clock on the mantelpiece.

'Did you intend to kill him?' big Bruno asked.

'No, I just wanted to beat him up for having humiliated Frau Goldblatt.'

'Whether it was murder or not is irrelevant,' big Bruno mused. 'Any normal person would have lashed out at a thug like him for what he'd done; it was an accident, and I suspect the police will see it as an accident. He simply fell down the stairs. I doubt whether they will investigate much.' I understood Bruno's point but felt sick with guilt.

Big Bruno had heard that hundreds of synagogues had been burned down, most Jewish shops had been destroyed and any Jewish man caught out on the streets or at home had been arrested and sent to Dachau or Sachsenhausen.[26] We also read the next morning that no Jew could be a retailer or exporter, or manage any business, and that from that day[27] Jews could no longer attend cinemas, theatres, dances or even music halls.

'I'm glad Johann is in Holland,' Marie said. 'They are making this a country where Jews are either dead or in prison.'

'There's one synagogue they didn't get,' big Bruno said, 'that large one on the Oranienburger Strasse. I'm told the local police looked after it because it's a major landmark.'

'The police in the city centre almost insisted I joined in,' I observed.

'Not all the police are bad, not the old guard,'[28] big Bruno said.

We sat around the table all night discussing what was happening. Both big Bruno and Marie believed that the events of what was called *Kristallnacht* had changed the old Germany for ever. Young as I was I was inclined to agree with them. I spent nearly all the rest of my leave with them, only returning home the day before I was due to report back to my unit.

There was no sign of Frau Goldblatt at her shop, which was closed and boarded up. I was pleased to see that my mother was home, and to learn that there had been no policemen at the door – not that I confided to her the reason why I was concerned. My father had been and gone, and my mother was feeling terrible about *Kristallnacht*.

'It was dreadful in Memmingen,' she said, 'and when that lovely pastor you played chess with spoke out about the persecution of the children of Abraham, half the congregation walked out, then

---

[26] Any male Jew aged between sixteen and sixty was liable to be arrested.

[27] 12 November 1938.

[28] 1938 November 10 the Synagogue in the Oranienburger Strasse was saved by the head of the local police precinct, a police lieutenant called Wilhelm Krützfeld. He stopped it on the grounds that the ancient Synagogue was a famous landmark. He was reprimanded for this and later RAF bombs destroyed the building.

some thugs dragged him from the pulpit and beat him so badly he nearly died.'[29]

'I'm sorry, he was a kind man,' I said somewhat lamely.

'By the way, Frau Goldblatt has left, but she asked me to give you this small parcel. I gather you helped her.'

The parcel was small but heavy, and when I opened it I found it contained an old-fashioned brass fob watch. Attached to the chain was a note thanking me, and adding that the watch did not work, but to treasure the contents. My mother and I were intrigued about this, so I opened the back of the watch and, where the spring would normally sit, were five large diamonds. We were astonished; we had no idea how much they would be worth or what to do with them, but my mother suggested that I kept the old watch and continued using it as a hiding place for the diamonds.

'Nobody,' she said, 'will try to steal that old watch from you.'

I tried not to look guilty when my mother mentioned that Big Dick had died accidentally by falling down the railway steps; apparently he had been drunk. Big Bruno had helped me cope with my inner turmoil, but I was still suffering from terrible nightmares. When I returned to my unit I spent some time talking to Albert about what happened at a Catholic confession. I did not want to arouse his suspicions, so I asked about all aspects of the Roman Catholic Church. The traumas of that fateful night continued. During the day or every time I woke up I would let my mind dwell on Frau Goldblatt naked and scrubbing the gutter. If I did this for a few moments, the pain of having caused Big Dick's death abated. I did not go to confession then as big Bruno had advised, but I kept it in my mind and later in life I did as he had suggested.

For me 1938 was the year when the Nazis revealed their true colours, and it was the year that irrevocably changed me. I felt nothing but distaste for what was happening, and I have always felt contrite that for many years I continued to be a faithful servant of the regime through my work in the *Luftwaffe*. As the year drew to a close I recall being horrified when I heard from Franz that the evangelical churches that once had Hebrew names over their doors,

[29] Pastor J. von Jan of Menningen was beaten up by some Brownshirts and then imprisoned.

such as Bethel or Jerusalem, had taken them down and more often than not replaced the script with a swastika.[30] Franz also read out that the Jewish community was being fined one billion marks for the destruction of property on *Kristallnacht*.[31] Even dear old Friedrich said that was 'a bit rich', but shut up to avoid Franz giving us a political lecture. Albert whispered to me, 'Nothing good will happen when you burn God's house,' but we kept it to ourselves. Later that evening Albert passed me his Bible, in which he had ringed one of the Psalms; it simply seemed to express the situation perfectly: 'They set thy sanctuary on fire; to the ground they desecrated the dwelling place of thy name. They said to themselves, "we will utterly subdue them"; they burned all the meeting places of God in the land.'[32] After reading this text I started to take the Bible more seriously.

I read one evening that the Nazis had executed a girl,[33] a student, because she had been involved in political activities against the regime. I could hardly believe that they would execute a woman, a mere student. This is what marked 1938 for me; it was the realization that I was living through a wicked period, a period with no love, no compassion, not even a modicum of decency. It was a year that left me with images of the naked Frau Goldblatt scrubbing the gutter, the lifeless face of Big Dick and the burnt out synagogues. It was the year that made me a killer, the year when I knew I was a coward, the year I found myself committed to my work, but in doing so supporting a regime I now detested.

[30] Following a directive on 20 November 1938.
[31] 12 December 1938.
[32] Psalm 74 verses 7–8.
[33] Lilo Hermann, the first woman to be executed by the Nazis for opposing them at university.

Chapter 7

1939

I had no idea what the future might hold for me in 1939, but young as I was I felt all did not bode well. I had always thought that Daimler-Benz worked me hard, but from January onward my unit was enlarged[1] and we seemed to work every hour that God made. The only break we had in January was when we were obliged to attend the opening of the new *Reich* Chancery,[2] but apart from that it was work and more work. I was based mainly in Berlin but every now and then we would be picked up and flown to some remote place where teams of other experts turned an amateur landing ground into a *Luftwaffe* airfield. Most of the fields I worked from were deep in the countryside, north of Berlin and with rich villages nearby. It was exceptionally cold as it was in the north. We sometimes worked on engines when the temperature was minus 10 degrees Celsius and the reason it did not bode well was that there was a growing consensus that the number of aircraft we were beginning to see could only mean that war was imminent.

Huge numbers of He111s and Do17s passed through our hands; they were, of course, twin-engined bombers which could serve no purpose in a peaceful world.[3] We serviced the Ju86k and the

[1] By 1939 the *Luftwaffe* had one and a half million men in its ranks.
[2] Opened on 9 January 1939. Hitler spoke to 8,000 construction workers who completed the whole building within twelve months.
[3] In 1939 the Germans had 1,270 twin-engined bombers and were producing 700 planes a month.

infamous Stuka, the Ju87. Thanks to Albert and Friedrich, I learned a great deal about the Jumo engines that powered these planes. It was not an impressive engine; it had a power punch of only 600 hp, and although it had a top speed of 200 mph, its best cruising speed was about 175 mph, and a limited range of less than 1,000 miles. Not only was the Stuka slow, but it had only two machine-guns and was not armoured. Years later I came to realize that it was a deeply feared plane because of the psychological impact its dramatic dive had on those below, but later enemy fighter planes found it easy to shoot down.

We all belonged to a flying group known as a *gruppe*, to look after about thirty aircraft. A subdivision was a *staffel*, the leader of which was a *staffelkaptän*. Our *staffelkaptän* was Heinrich Müller, but we saw little of him; he was an administration officer who left us mechanics to our engines. As we were a mobile unit we were rarely with the *gruppe* as a body, as we were always being taken from one spot to the next at the drop of a hat. I can vaguely recall that the *Führer* reorganized the *Luftwaffe* at the beginning of the year[4] into three air fleets as we called them. It was of little significance to my small group because we simply went where we were told. Franz, of course, had a deep interest in these manoeuvres, but none of us wanted to listen to his views; we were too busy ensuring that none of our planes killed a pilot. The one time I did listen to him was when he read out part of the *Führer*'s speech in which he said, 'if war erupts it will mean the *vernichtung* ('extermination') of European Jews.'[5] I was playing chess at the back of the hangar during a break, and I can recall thinking to myself that the *Führer* was in fact anticipating war, but wondering how he could possibly exterminate all European Jews. I can still recall the cold shudder the language of *vernichtung* sent down my spine, and can still see the game I was playing against Albert, which was a variation of the Queen's Gambit Accepted.

I have to confess I was the odd man out, with the possible

---

[4] On 1 February 1939 Hitler established three air fleets with generals Kesselring, Felmy and Sperrle in charge.

[5] Part of Hitler's *Reichstag* speech on 30 January 1939.

exception of Albert. Friedrich only cared for engines, but everyone else I met at work seemed positively excited about the increasing strength of Germany. Time and again officers would tell us we were building the largest and strongest air force in the world, and no one would be able to stand against the might of the *Luftwaffe*. Despite my *mischling* status, which had coloured all my views, and despite the horrors of *Kristallnacht*, which had reinforced my changed attitudes, I still took immense pride in my work, and I was proud to be part of the team that was producing the finest aeroplanes the world had ever seen. In 1939 I was twenty years of age, hardly an experienced man, so when I look back I do not find it too surprising that my attitude to my work did not clash at that time with my emerging political views. The press, the radio and all our officers seemed to think we were moving towards a 'glorious destiny' and as I worked on an engine I felt part of that journey, but every now and then I would suddenly stop and question myself. I was aware that some of the amateur airfields we took over had to be extended, which was done by what I now realize was slave labour. I can recall Albert coming back into the hangar late one afternoon and saying that he had seen the living dead.

'The living what?' Friedrich asked.

'Those workers extending the runway, they are as good as dead. I saw one of them collapse, they're so thin and undernourished. I tried to go to his assistance and the SS guard as good as chased me all the way back here. They started work at seven this morning, first light,' Albert continued, 'and as far as I can see they're the same prisoners. We've worked ten hours, we've had breaks, hot food, coffee, and been able to stroll off to the lavatory; those poor sods are being worked to death. They've been here from dawn to dusk and they have worked non-stop as far as I can tell.'

We worked on in silence.

During February we saw a film of the launching of the new battleship, the *Bismarck*,[6] by the *Führer* in Hamburg. It was the most incredible sight, and once again I had that strange mixture of feelings, between a natural pride in that beautiful ship and the

[6] Launched on 14 February 1939.

uneasiness that such a vessel had been built to wage war. During one weekend break I met big Bruno for a game of chess and found he was of the same opinion.

'I tell you, little Bruno,' he said, 'that *Bismarck* has been launched as a warning to France and England that Germany is powerful. If the *Führer* marches into the Polish Corridor in order to bring Prussia back into the German fold – and that's the rumour – the Poles have no navy worth speaking of; so that ship's been prepared to warn our old enemies to keep their distance, especially England, which has a large navy.'

That same weekend I managed to catch up with my father. He was still the same person I knew from my younger days to look at, but he was more subdued. The shock of what I can only describe as his 'Jewishness' had changed him completely. He had once, like me, believed that all Jews were rich profiteers who had brought ruination to Germany, although he had at least acknowledged that ordinary Jews like Frau Goldblatt were not the problem. Now that he realized he was of German-Jewish origin he had been forced to reappraise the whole Jewish issue. Again, like me, he felt himself to be as German as anyone else, and resented the fact that some minor civil servant had declared him virtually an alien. My mother, who was keenly aware of the situation, seemed to be even more tender towards him than she had ever been. He was still driving trains, and was becoming aware, like me, of a military build-up. His train was often commandeered by the military, and several times normal services had been disrupted by sudden troop movements from one part of the country to another. He noted that there was a build-up of troops near the Czech border, and we wondered what was happening.

That weekend I went with my father into central Berlin where we saw the first Volkswagen[7] on display. According to the advertisement the *Führer* expected that every German family would own one within a few years. It was an exciting thought that one day we might actually own a car, but even then it seemed no

[7] At the opening of the International Automobile Exhibition in Berlin Hitler announced the arrival of the 'cheap people's car' – to be within reach of lower income groups.

more than a dream. We had tea with Aunt Ingrid, and I recall quite clearly that although we talked about family matters and events, we did not mention Ruth and Hans, or speak once about the problem of being half-Jewish; it was a taboo subject about which we all kept quiet.

From early March that year my *gruppe* was transferred back to Berlin, where we became very busy, with more and more planes arriving each day. Albert and I both knew that something major was taking place, and because of my father's observations about troop movements, and leading newspaper articles, we were not surprised when our troops marched into Czechoslovakia.[8] Suddenly the newspapers were full of the establishment of Bohemia and Moravia; and Czechoslovakia as we once knew it, no longer existed. Franz was in high spirits and for a whole week was talking about the re-emergence of Germany's greatness. 'It was not an invasion,' he claimed, 'but an act of unity that brought German-speaking people together.' Friedrich seemed to agree, and both Albert and I decided that perhaps it was right; it had been an artificial border. But I still nursed a few quiet doubts. Our planes took part in the annexation, but they were not really necessary, according to their pilots, except as a sign of German might.

We had only just become accustomed to this new venture when it was announced that Memelland,[9] which adjoins East Prussia, had also been annexed. It goes without saying how Franz viewed all this, and I have to confess that it had always struck me as nonsense that East Prussia, part of Germany, should be artificially separated from the rest of the country by the Versailles Treaty. We all knew that the *Führer* would eventually claim what was called the Danzig or Polish Corridor and reunite the country. It was generally anticipated that Poland would understand the necessity for such a move, and accede to the correction of what seemed such a strange anomaly. Looking back, it would appear that we were all being

[8] On 16 March 1939, in Prague Hitler issued a proclamation establishing the Protectorate of Bohemia and Moravia as being *lebensraum* of the German people.

[9] On 23 March 1939 Hitler arrived by the battleship *Deutschland* and delivered a speech to the people of Memel.

drilled into a pattern of nationalistic thinking. On the other hand I have often wondered how the British managed to hang on to Gibraltar, on the southern tip of Spain, and how the British would feel if Cornwall had been ceded to France following a dubious defeat. In 1939 this recouping of lost German lands seemed quite natural, and it was generally observed that the rest of the world seemed to agree with our actions because, apart from a few mild protests, nothing was done to try to stop them.

One of the pilots, who frequently played chess with us, said that none of the recent actions had any element of *casus belli*, which I learned was the Latin for a 'cause for war'. He believed that the *Führer* was simply putting right the iniquities of the peace treaty, and the major nations quietly understood why these actions were being taken. We were slightly in awe of officers, and I therefore believed him. He was also a non-political person, who was always very polite and pleasant, and treated us mechanics with respect. His chess was passable and I think he was surprised to find a mechanic who could beat him. Not all the pilots were of the same calibre; many would bark out instructions to us and accuse us of not servicing their planes correctly if engines overheated or did not perform one hundred per cent of the time. It was probably the same the world over, but the more pleasant the pilot the more we looked after his machine. He flew one of the Bf109s and his machine had big Bruno's signature on it, which always gave me pleasure when I spotted it.

As we were based mainly in Berlin I still managed to see big Bruno and attend the chess club, but the numbers were dropping. In the old days there had been nearly thirty members, but now there were fewer than twenty. Quite often I took Albert along with me. He enjoyed big Bruno's company, but we were guarded in our conversations, avoiding political issues and only discussing chess moves. It was becoming common knowledge that it was dangerous to talk freely to anyone; even family members could not always be trusted.

Albert and I went to the cinema one night after a game of chess to watch the launching of the battleship *Tirpitz*;[10] once again it was

[10] At Wilhelmshaven on 1 April 1939.

a magnificent piece of naval engineering and design and looked extremely powerful. We also heard the *Führer* complain that Britain was encircling Germany with its enemies even though Germany had no intention of attacking anyone.

The very next day we heard that Mussolini had invaded Albania,[11] which meant we were subjected once again to Franz's views on the power of fascists. 'Strong countries need leaders, democracies are weak,' he said, and this was to remain the central theme of his observations for the rest of the year.

'At least Germany's not involved in this one,' Albert whispered to me.

Nevertheless, the same day our mobile unit had instructions to move back north to the airfield we had established near Sachsenhausen, and I noted that there were new barracks and army units posted right across the area.[12] As we flew in I could see the growth of different military groups spread over a vast area. By the time we had settled in and our planes had arrived, we became aware that nearly all the *Wehrmacht* forces had disappeared. Apparently, they were needed for a large parade in Berlin[13] and we had the place to ourselves; even our officers had disappeared. Mercifully Franz was on a week's leave. Friedrich was feeling lazy, so Albert and I played non-stop chess for four days, carrying out only the lightest of duties. One afternoon we went on a long walk; the birds'-nesting season always seemed to make me want to walk in the countryside. We came upon Sachsenhausen concentration camp and looked at it from a distance; it looked terrible.

'Your brother may be down there,' Albert observed.

'He's probably wangled himself a place on the parade.'

'Do you want to go and see?' Albert persisted.

'I don't think so; let's wander back.'

I felt a little guilty about not wanting to see Josef, and Albert

[11] Mussolini ordered the invasion on 8 April 1939.

[12] Hitler had projected *Fall Weiss* (Operation White) and was already beginning to concentrate *Wehrmacht* forces near Polish borders threatening the annexation of Danzig.

[13] On 20 April 1939, Hitler's fiftieth birthday, a massive four-hour military parade was held.

kept a discreet silence on the matter. He and I had started to become close friends and we shared more and more. I had not told him about my *mischling* status, but he knew I was not very happy with my brother. He put it down to what he described as my milder views on politics. As we rounded a corner we came upon a group of prisoners being escorted back to the camp; mercifully Josef was not one of the guards. The prisoners looked as if they had risen from hell itself. They wore striped prison garments and they were all totally emaciated. The thing that struck us most was the way they walked with their heads down, only daring to take a sideways glance at the two *Luftwaffe* mechanics before swiftly looking away, as if they were terrified of us. The three SS guards waved at us cheerfully and we waved back, but once they had passed both Albert and I sat on a fence and caught our breath.

'Did you see they way they looked at us?' I said.

'They were scared.'

'Of mechanics?'

'It's not us.' Albert paused. 'It's our uniforms; they're scared of uniforms, can you blame them?'

I was glad I had not tried to find Josef, and remembered what my father had seen of him on the Polish border; I would never be able to tell my parents what I had seen. Albert put together an old Anti-Semit[14] and I lit my pipe, which I had recently adopted instead of cigarettes; we sat on a fence in silence to smoke companionably.

During May and June life at the airfield seemed to fluctuate between extreme business and laziness. The *gruppe* was busy enough, but occasionally every plane for which we were responsible was elsewhere going through some kind of exercise. I was glad of Albert's friendship, which was especially valuable to me as I did not see big Bruno as regularly as I was used to. We still corresponded but he was very busy and I was away from Berlin more often than not during the summer of 1939. Albert and I did manage to set up a chess competition at the airbase, and several pilots, and one senior officer, joined in. It lasted all summer long and I was pleased to win, but only after a tough struggle with

[14] The brand name of a rolling tobacco introduced by the Nazi propagandists in the early days of their struggle; it could still be bought very cheaply.

Albert, who had come to understand the nature of my tactics and strategy. Whether we were heading for war or not was a constant source of conversation. When we read, in May, that Italy and Germany had signed a 'Pact of Steel'[15] it did not augur well, but a few days later we also heard that Germany had signed a non-aggression pact with Denmark,[16] and this sounded more hopeful.

Despite all this tension it was a pleasant summer, hot and balmy, with plenty of work to do. Albert and I also found time to play many games of chess and take some pleasant meandering walks in the countryside. At the beginning of the summer nearly all our pilots disappeared for a week; they had gone to some special address given by the *Führer*.[17] While they were away we were introduced to the mechanics of a recently developed plane, a new four-engined Focke-Wulf Condor.[18] It had four BMW-Bramo nine-cylinder radial engines. It was quite interesting and, apart from the problem of accessing parts, it would not be too difficult to service.

The build-up of troops continued during the summer, as did a massive build-up of Stukas. We were attached to the First *Fliegerdivison*[19] based to the north-east of Berlin, and were told by a fairly senior officer that we would be providing support for the Fourth Army Group. Even this tiny piece of information made all of us realize that something was happening; and by mid-August the pilots were keeping themselves very much to themselves. Normally they would chat and answer our questions, but I had the distinct impression that they knew a good deal more than we were allowed to know. A small detachment of SS guards stayed near our barracks for a week, but they were not there long, because the *Luftwaffe* always guarded their own airfields. An SS guard saw Albert and me playing a game of chess one evening and asked for a game. I played him and won easily, but he managed to reach a draw with Albert.

---

[15] On 22 May 1939 the foreign ministers, Ciano and Ribbentrop, signed the so-called 'Pact of Steel'.

[16] On 31 May 1939.

[17] On 6 June 1939, Hitler gave an address to all those pilots who flew in the Condor Legion during the Spanish Civil War.

[18] On 6 July 1939 Hitler was flown around Berlin in this new plane.

[19] Later known as *Flieger-korps*.

He seemed surprisingly pleasant and I eventually plucked up sufficient courage to ask him if he knew my brother. He did not, but he was heading for Sachsenhausen and said he would look out for him.

'Who are the prisoners there?' Albert asked with as much innocence as he could manage.

'They come from one of the many camps in the area,' he replied. 'They're just given the overall name of Sachsenhausen.'

'What are they for?' Albert persisted.

'It started as an overflow centre for *Gestapo* interrogation.'

'Overflow?' I interjected.

'Yes, normally they were interrogated in Columbia House[20] but it was too small for all the prisoners.'

'Are they all political criminals?' Albert asked.

'Mainly, many of them are Communists and Jews, and some are those who tried to oppose the *Führer*.' He seemed quite relaxed with us, even sharing some of his tobacco. The latter part of August was the end of normal life as I had come to know it from the previous seven months. We were told that because the Poles had been provocative by challenging the integrity of our borders, the army was going to invade. Not just the Danzig area, as many of us had predicted, but the whole of Poland was the intended target, and the *Luftwaffe* was going to lead the way. In the early hours of 1 September, which I recall was a Friday, we were all up in order to see plane after plane passing overhead, and our own planes flying up to join this huge gathering.[21] It was a bright morning and the sun was starting to rise in a cloudless sky. By breakfast the Stukas and some fighters had returned and needed rearming and refuelling. Although we were mechanics we all helped in these procedures because none of the returning planes needed any mechanical attention. There was a real sense of excitement in the air, and one pilot told us that he, and his wing, had completely obliterated an entire Polish airfield; because all the planes had been placed in neat

[20] The old Berlin centre for the *Gestapo*.
[21] On 1 September 1939 at 4.45 a.m. Hitler unleashed *Fall Weiss* ('Operation White'). German troops crossed the border at this time; fifty-three divisions in all.

rows their destruction had been easier. The next day, Saturday, one Stuka pilot claimed there were no aircraft targets left, and now they were bombing troop formations.[22] Information was posted on our notice board and we watched and listened with fascination to the news about how rapidly the troops were making progress.

There was no leave that month; any time off was spent in the barracks, and we often went without sleep. Our aircraft were up and down every hour, and soon we were working on overheated engines, broken fuel lines and similar problems. Impatient pilots were a nuisance, and Friedrich had to point out that an engine had to cool down before work could be started. On the Sunday evening we heard over the radio that Britain and France had declared war on us. That caused some confusion and consternation. The confusion was due to the fact that we were unable to understand why these two countries would care about a border dispute between us and an eastern neighbour, and the consternation arose amongst those who had experienced the trench war of twenty years before. This meant that some fighter planes were now held back in reserve, but not many because it was believed that our control of the skies would inhibit any bombing raids. Albert and I talked a great deal about what the future might hold, but I was very keen to speak to my father and big Bruno; however, I was not to have that luxury for another month.

All my initial excitement and enthusiasm faded away at the end of the first week, when I read a notice that had been dropped on the floor. I think it must have been dropped by a senior officer, because it was not meant for the likes of Albert and me. It was a directive from the *Führer*, stating that he did not believe the British and French were strong enough to attack from the west, but, more to the point, that the army was not to interfere when special SS units exterminated Polish Jews and any intelligentsia.[23]

'Exterminate?' Albert said. I did not reply, I simply reread the notice, a cold feeling developing around the back of my neck. Suddenly Franz was with us asking what we were so interested in;

[22] By 2 September nearly all Polish aircraft had been destroyed.
[23] Issued on 7 September 1939.

we had no choice but to show him the notice.

'That's what the SS men were here for the other day; one of them played chess with you, Bruno.'

'What do they mean by exterminate?' I asked.

'What we all mean by it, what's been promised by the *Führer*; they're going to wipe out, kill, all European Jewry, and that could include you.'

I froze for a moment; had he somehow heard about my being a *mischling*?

'What do you mean?' I asked.

'Chess players belong to the intelligentsia, don't they?' He grinned at me and walked off. His little joke had misfired.

We decided that they were going to be put into concentration camps, and this was confirmed later when we heard that they intended to create ghettos[24] in Poland, to keep Jews in the same place. This seemed bad enough but it did not mean mass murder.

We lived for the news of the day, whether it was by wireless or newspaper. The war certainly seemed to be going our way. We heard that the army was just outside Warsaw[25] and that one of our U-boats had sunk a major British aircraft carrier.[26] There was a glass of free beer for everyone that evening. We also gathered, much to everyone's surprise, that the Russians[27] were on our side and were advancing into Poland. We were surprised because until now we had all become accustomed to the belief that Communism was the next great evil to Jewry. I continued to have mixed feelings: the German side of me rejoiced in the news of almost daily victories, but the *mischling* side was in a perpetual state of nervousness every time I heard the word *Juden* mentioned, which was all too often. Both Albert and I, as young as we were, felt some doubts about being at war with nations like Great Britain and France. Franz was becoming too jubilant for words, and only Friedrich could shut

[24] On 21 September 1939 Heydrich issued a directive for the establishment of ghettos in Poland.

[25] On 6 September 1939 the 3rd and 4th armies advanced on Warsaw.

[26] On 17 September 1939 the aircraft carrier HMS *Courageous* was sunk by U-boat U29.

[27] On 19 September 1939, at Brest-Litovsk, Soviet and German troops met.

him up by telling him to get on with his duties. Franz was predicting that France would soon fall, that Great Britain would sue for peace and that the Russians might well be the next target. We refused to believe him on the former count, as we knew from the 1914–18 war that France had a powerful army and Britain a powerful navy. We did think he had a point, however, when he argued that the *Luftwaffe* was all-powerful and our navy's U-boats were brilliant. This was again confirmed when we read about a British battleship being sunk within its safe harbour by the U-boat hero Günther Prien,[28] and that the *Luftwaffe* had attacked and damaged British warships along their very coastline.[29] It seemed, in 1939, that Germany was invincible and the *Führer* was becoming more and more popular. I recalled how I also had once hero-worshipped him, but since the Jewish question had come home to roost, I was now much more uncertain; big Bruno had taught me to question everything I heard – but not out loud.

At the end of the year I was able to spend a few days at home. It was good timing because my father was at home after a long period of work away. We discussed all that had happened, not least the *Führer*'s victory parade in Warsaw,[30] and his doubts about the declaration of war by France and Britain.

'They will fight,' my father said, 'and that could mean an ugly return to the attrition of the trenches.' He also had a similar view to Franz; he reckoned that the agreement with the Soviet Union was only temporary, because the Party, as he still called it, 'is fundamentally opposed to Communism'. I told him that the *Luftwaffe* was going to be an all-powerful factor, and one of our units had serviced planes that were dropping special mines off the British coast[31] that could well destroy all British shipping.

'They still managed to sink one of our best battleships,' he said, 'not that we heard much about how they did that.'

---

[28] On 14 October 1939 U47 sank HMS *Royal Oak* inside Scapa Flow.

[29] On 16 October 1939 German aircraft attacked the Firth of Forth, damaging cruisers *Edinburgh* and *Southampton*.

[30] Hitler flew to Warsaw on 5 October for a victory parade.

[31] On 11 November 1939 German aircraft were seen for the first time dropping mines off the English coast.

'That's news to me,' I replied.

'Beginning of the month,' he said. 'They sank the *Graf Spee*.'[32]

I had certainly missed that in the papers, but I gathered later that although Günther Prien had been given full coverage for sinking the *Royal Oak*, the sinking of the *Graf Spee* was given a mere paragraph. I was to learn as I grew older that this type of selective writing was a worldwide feature.

We never discussed our *mischling* problem, but my father had driven some of his trains right through Germany and into Poland, and had been horrified that attached to his train were cattle trucks full of Jews being sent to a ghetto in a place called Piotrów. Apparently all Austrian and Czech Jews were being sent to Polish ghettos,[33] and in Poland itself, Jews were forced to wear an armband or a yellow star.[34]

'It's no wonder someone tried to kill the *Führer*. They say it was foreign agents,[35] but I wonder.' My father almost whispered this, even though we were sitting in our own kitchen. I think we were both wondering whether the *mischling* status would soon become an issue once again. Big Bruno, whom I caught up with for a whole Sunday, was broody about events. When we read that Pope Pius XII had made an appeal for peace, big Bruno said, 'He might as well pee into the wind; this *Führer*'s set on war.'

Before I returned to my unit late on 31 December, which was a Sunday, I heard the *Führer*'s New Year message, in which he stated that 'the Jewish capitalistic world will not survive the twentieth century'. The capitalistic world did not worry me, the word 'Jew' and its companion term 'half-Jew', *mischling*, meant it was not with a light heart that I settled down to face the beginning of the New Year.

[32] On 17 December 1939.

[33] Started on 12 October 1939.

[34] As from 23 November 1939.

[35] On 11 Nov 1939 Hitler visited Munich to attend the victims killed in the explosion. Some believe this was arranged by Hitler in order to incite public hatred against the enemy.

Chapter 8

1940

It was a bitterly cold winter, freezing beyond belief, and in the barracks we spent as much time as possible beside a wood burning stove. Working in the hangars was particularly unpleasant and starting up the engines in the early morning often took longer than expected. I had only been back for a few days when I received an official-looking letter stamped KZL – Sachsenhausen: KZL stood for *kazetlager*, which was the German for what we now know to be a concentration camp. My heart thumped as I opened it, but when I saw a brief handwritten note from my brother Josef the relief was overwhelming. I felt nervous because I knew this was one of the dreaded camps, but in a more rational mood I realized that they would not write to one of their victims. I was quite surprised, indeed shocked, to see that Josef had bothered to write. He suggested visiting me sometime in February when he was due some extensive leave. I left it for a couple of days, but eventually replied, writing that I was on the base for a time but that we could, being a mobile unit, be shifted at any moment with little or no notice. I was not happy about the proposed visit, because I knew how deeply he had hurt my parents.

I have read the various histories of the war, and much of what I have read has been revealing, but the initial impact was a shock. As ground crew we were not privy to the plans of the OKW (High Command) and the *Führer* certainly did not consult *Luftwaffe* mechanics; we simply did our duties, as ordered by our officers.

However, we did learn a good deal from the newspapers, and around any airfield rumours were always rife. Unlike an ordinary army barracks we had plenty of senior officers around, as well as important figures passing through, and a mechanic, with his head inside an engine, was still capable of picking up bits and pieces of conversation. In January we were preoccupied by the Soviet invasion of Finland and there was a great deal of humour around about the ways the Finns were defending themselves against the greater force.[1] Franz reckoned, correctly as it later transpired, that Stalin had killed off his best generals in his various purges and that the Soviet soldiers were ill trained.

One of the most important pieces of gossip which Friedrich overheard was that one of our planes had been obliged by mechanical failure, or poor navigation, to land in Belgium, with senior officers on board who were carrying plans for the invasion of the west. Friedrich said it was because of this that the invasion of the west had to be postponed. That there was going to be an invasion of France was news to me; I knew they had declared war, but I thought that with the invasion of Poland it would simply be a matter of defending our borders. Later I read in the various history books that this gossip was true, but that the invasion had been postponed because of the bitterly cold winter.[2] The possibility of a war in the west became yet more dominant in our minds when we read that Belgium had refused the French and British the right to cross their borders.[3] Then, at the end of the month, we all had to attend a speech by the *Führer* at the Sportspalast, in which he stated that the first phase of the war was over with the end of Poland and that the second phase would be a 'war with bombs'.[4] We all knew then that we were really at war, and that the conquest of Poland, or annexation as we then called

[1] The 44th Russian Assault Division had been annihilated by the Finns under General Siilasuvo, on 8 January 1940.
[2] On 13 January 1940 Hitler postponed the Western Front because of weather and also issued a directive that senior officers must not carry important documents over foreign territory.
[3] On 15 January 1940.
[4] A speech by Hitler celebrating his seventh anniversary as Chancellor.

it, was not the end of the matter. I remember that speech because it was given on a Tuesday and we were given Wednesday and Thursday off, which meant I could go straight home for a few days. Sadly my father was away at work, and had been for several days. My mother was delighted to see me and made Albert, who came with me, very welcome.

'The mother of one of your old friends called the other day,' she said.

'Who was that?' I asked, thinking that Erik's mother had returned from Poland.

'Frau Bier, Adolf's mum. She told me he had been injured in the fighting in Poland and was hoping some of his old friends would call in to cheer him up.'

I had once admired Adolf, he had been my Hitler Youth leader, but my views had changed sharply and I really did not want to take up his somewhat dubious acquaintance again. My mother, however, was persistent, pointing out that poor Frau Bier was desperate because her son was so lonely, stuck at home with his wounds. Albert and I went round to his house that evening with some beer and cheese, and Frau Bier hugged us for coming. We found Adolf in what we used to call the front room, in a large bed. He was in such a mess I stood in the doorway stunned, and held Albert back. He was lying on top of the bed, and it was immediately clear that he had lost one leg from the thigh, and the other from the knee, one of his hands was missing, and his face was so scarred it looked as if he had been cooked on an open grill.

'My God, Adolf, what happened?' I blurted out.

'I got blown up and was then crushed by one of our trucks,' he replied angrily. He seemed hostile and showed no interest in either Albert or me but stared at a fixed point on the opposite wall.

'I'm really sorry, do you have any pain?' I sounded rather feeble but I have always found it difficult to find the right words in situations like this. The fear of saying the wrong thing tends to make whatever I say inappropriate or pathetic.

'Of course, my legs hurt, though they're somewhere near Warsaw, my missing hand itches and my private parts were blown off, a fact that cuts me to the quick.' My eyes inadvertently looked below his waist, but he appeared to be swathed in a large nappy.

'Are the army looking after you?' Albert asked.

'They kept me alive and then delivered me here for my parents to feed and wipe my arse. If you're the friend you used to be you'd shoot me.'

'I couldn't do that,' I said.

'Then find me a revolver.'

'God, Adolf.' I sat down by him. 'You can't do this, I'm sure you will find some joy when you are feeling better.' I said this more to comfort myself, but I have to admit that I wondered how I would feel; I had my chess and my reading, but the sense of uselessness and dependency on others made Adolf's future look horrifically bleak, to say the very least.

Both Albert and I sat there in total silence, there was nothing we could say in the face of such total despair. In fact, it was nearly five minutes before I broke the silence, offering Adolf a beer; he refused.

'I drink as little as possible because every pee is agony.' Another silence followed and I was beginning to feel embarrassed at not being able to find the right words.

'Do you believe in God?' Adolf suddenly asked.

'Yes,' I replied.

He looked at me for the first time and held his eyes to mine as if trying to see if I were telling the truth.

'Do you?' he asked Albert.

'Yes.' I could see that Albert was feeling the same strain as me, and I was sorry I had put him into the situation. I had brought him with me for purely selfish reasons – to keep me company, not to expose him to such pain.

'If you believe in God,' Adolf continued, 'then pray that he takes me quickly, and forgives me.'

'Forgives you?' I asked.

'I killed a lot of people, and they were not enemy soldiers; women and children who were Jews, we just killed them when we came upon them.'

'That's part of your pain now?' Albert asked. I did not reply, but sat pondering what a world we were creating.

Adolf did not reply; in fact that was the end of the conversation. I suggested he might like to see a priest, but he just shook his head. As we stood up to go I put the beer and cheese on his table. I said farewell but he just nodded. Then just as we got to the door, he called me back. 'Bruno,' he almost whispered, 'it's all wrong, we've got it all wrong.' As he said this he moved his face towards the wall but not before I saw that his eyes were full of tears. I heard months later that someone had taken pity on him and left him a Polish handgun, some trophy, and he had shot himself.

'Why a priest?' Albert asked me as we walked back to my house.

'I somehow think a priest would handle sin better than a Lutheran minister; they don't seem so judgmental. Just a thought,' I added.

'The authorities keep the injuries out of the papers,' Albert said. 'In fact they tend to suggest that only a few heroes have been killed while a few others have minor injuries.'

'I really felt sorry for him,' I eventually replied, but in reality I felt more sorry for his mother.

We also managed to catch up with big Bruno and Marie. Needless to say, big Bruno had some strong opinions, but once again he was cautious, as Albert was there, even though he was beginning to discern that Albert and I held similar views. He had tried to listen to programmes from Britain on the wireless, but Marie had begged him to be careful. The authorities had forbidden this, and a mutual chess friend had been in trouble for doing so, having been reported by a neighbour. People who listened to foreign broadcasts were called *feindhören* and could be held on a capital charge for being *volksschädling*, a word which meant antisocial vermin. As we left them on their doorstep, I wondered how long big Bruno would exist in a country where free expression was a potential death trap.

I had been back at work for hardly a day when I had another trip out, but this time with Friedrich. Albert and Franz were sent off with a small convoy to pick up spares for the Stuka engines, and Friedrich and I were detailed to visit the Deutsche Ausrustungswerke (DAW – 'German Armaments Works')[5] near

[5] Under SS direction.

Munich, to pick up some special machine-guns for the Heinkels. It was a long and interesting trip, which gave me an opportunity to get to know Friedrich better. He was technically my boss, but although we were young he always treated Albert and me as colleagues. I discovered that he liked Franz well enough but was tired of being subjected to his political tirades. Friedrich was patriotic about the war, but reading between the lines he was obviously not what we used to call a Party man. His main fear was that a war with France and Britain would not be over as quickly as the Polish campaign.

'They will fight long and hard, they will dig in for another war of attrition,' he said.

'Like the last war,' I offered.

'It could be worse,' he replied. 'This time the weapons are more destructive; tank power has increased, and we have much better aircraft and plenty of them, and heaven knows how they've improved the gas.'

I had not even considered gas, and when Friedrich suggested that they might drop gas canisters everywhere, I have to confess it scared me.

'This *blitzkrieg*,' I said, 'could make the war quick.'

'Maybe, but the British are just across the sea, and they will fight like the very devil, they're fundamentally the same race as us.'

'Same race?' I questioned. Then I discovered Friedrich's great love of history. For the next hour I listened as he explained that the people of England came mainly from Germany, the Saxons from Saxony, that the Prussians and British together had defeated Napoleon, that during the eighteenth century the Hanoverians had ruled Britain, and that Victoria's husband had been German, and that even their current royal family was Germanic. I have to confess that these historical insights were entirely novel – and thought-provoking. The rest of the crew were obviously bored by Friedrich but I found him fascinating.

When we arrived in Munich we found that the works were carefully guarded by the SS whom we found overbearing and arrogant, and they treated us like lesser mortals. 'Glad we aren't Jews,' Friedrich grumbled. I held my breath as we stowed the crates in the lorry and felt grateful to be off again within three hours. On the way back we all decided that although we were dedicated to our work, as were the pilots and officers, there was not the same degree of fanaticism we saw in the SS every time we encountered them. It was not surprising therefore, that on our return Friedrich raised his eyebrows when a duty guard said an SS soldier called Josef had been looking for me. I was glad we had missed each other; he had not even troubled to leave a note.

What few of us could understand was the way Germany seemed to be hand in glove with the Communists of the Soviet Union. I had been told that the concentration camps were full of Communists, and we had had it drilled into us, based on the *Führer*'s book *Mein Kampf*, that the Communists in Russia were all part of a Jewish plot, and that we needed their space in order to expand our living conditions, what we used to call *lebensraum*. Yet my father told me that when he was not carting prisoners to the east he was hauling back from the Soviet Union tons of wheat and wagons of oil.[6] We also heard from one of the pilots that Norway was causing the *Führer* concern because it was not as neutral as it claimed; in fact, it was dangerously unreliable. It had allowed armed British merchant vessels into its waters to capture some prisoners. As a result the *Führer* had warned the British that such vessels would be treated as warships.[7] Despite all this I still found it difficult to imagine that we were actually at war with Britain and France; it all seemed so unreal.

Albert and I visited an exhibition in the Zueghaus (Berlin's old arsenal) about the campaign in Poland.[8] There were many amazing pictures, some of our own Stukas diving on the enemy. The war, from the German side, was obviously carried through with great efficiency. There were no pictures of any dead or wounded Germans, only Poles.

[6] On 11 February 1940 Germany and the Soviet Union made an industrial treaty.
[7] This incident probably refers to the time that the destroyer *Cossack* raided the *Altmark* in Norwegian waters to rescue 299 prisoners; the *Altmark* was the supply/support ship for the *Graf Spee*.
[8] Hitler opened this exhibition on 10 March 1940.

When we returned to the airfield Franz was full of the news that the Italians would be fighting alongside us.[9] 'That will make a change,' quipped Friedrich. 'I fought against them in the last war.'

More stunning than this information was the news that came five minutes later; we heard from a fighter pilot that hundreds of RAF planes had raided one of our bases at Hörnum on the small island of Sylt.[10] Several mechanics had been killed in one of the hangars but not a great deal of real damage had been done.

'Mechanics?' Franz asked him.

'Only mechanics, so no real problem.' At least the pilot had the decency to grin as he said this.

We did not have much time to cogitate on this news because within an hour we were ordered to mobilize as a unit and be prepared to fly to a new base. Four hours later, we were sorting out our new barracks on the outskirts of Hamburg and plane after plane was arriving; we knew that something was about to happen.

Next day, after an unpleasantly early start, we actually heard that we were going to invade Norway. Franz was almost jumping up and down with excitement and Friedrich was puzzled. 'I should imagine it's to do with the British naval activity in their waters,' he mumbled as we watched hundreds of soldiers boarding the transport planes.[11]

I could now see why we were in Hamburg; it was closer to Norway and only a hop, step and jump away from Denmark.

'What about Denmark?' I said. 'They've always been good neighbours.'

'They won't fight,' Friedrich replied. 'They're far too small and they know it.'

As it transpired, the very next day, he was proved absolutely right. As the spring blossomed we remained in Hamburg and

[9] Hitler and Mussolini met at Brennero on the Brenner Pass on 18 March 1940.
[10] In fact it was a fifty-plane raid on 19 March 1940.
[11] On 9 April 1940 German troops invaded Denmark and Norway. Denmark accepted the German ultimatum on 10 April. The *Luftwaffe* supplied 400 fighters, 70 reconnaissance aircraft and 500 air transport.

became greedy for every news item, and piece of gossip coming back from the pilots. I would have appreciated the chance to visit Hamburg itself, but all leave was cancelled and we were busy day after remorseless day. One interesting feature of my time there was watching paratroopers loading up. I could not but help admire their courage; they were obviously the best of our fighting troops and they looked tough. I did not like the idea of jumping out of an aircraft, hoping that the parachute would actually open.

I gathered that the *Luftwaffe* controlled the skies, and had it not been for our aircraft the invasion of Norway would not have been such a success. It was not such good news for our navy because I heard that several of our ships had been sunk.[12] On learning this news I reflected on what big Bruno and my father had said about the British having a powerful naval force. Nevertheless, our troops seemed unbeatable and we read that at one stage thousands of Norwegian troops had surrendered on one day.[13] I have to admit that despite my misgivings, I was taking a lot of pride in German military might: Albert was a little more reserved than I was, not least because one member of his family was Norwegian.

We were unbelievably busy, with planes arriving for repair day after day – not so much from battle scars, although there were a few flak-scarred fuselages, but from engines that had been pushed to the very limits for too long. At the beginning of May there was a quietening down of activity but just as I was hoping for a pass to go into Hamburg another phase of activity started, with an early morning start. I remember clearly that it was a Friday morning because I was hoping for a long weekend, but all hell broke loose as plane after plane took off to start the offensive in the west. It really had started; the war against France and Britain which had seemed like make-believe or just skirmishing until now – I learned later that the British called this phase the Phoney War – was moving on with real ferocity. We were told that our planes would dive-bomb enemy positions, the tanks would follow

[12] The German cruisers *Blücher*, *Karlsruhe* and *Königsberg* were sunk, and seven destroyers.
[13] On 1 May 1940 4,000 Norwegians surrendered in the Lillehammer sector.

through with the infantry and it would be short and sharp. We watched as paratroopers piled into transports, intending to land at Rotterdam, Dordrecht and Moerdijk in Holland. We heard that Rotterdam was subjected to a very heavy bombardment. I have to admit we never discussed the awful consequences of bombing during that period; they were our planes, and we kept them flying and loaded, as we were at war. It would not be long before I started to contemplate the terrible nature of this aspect of warfare. But it was not the time for contemplation as we were caught up in the turmoil. Later we were suddenly told, to Franz's delight and Friedrich's horror, that our mobile unit was to go with a large group of soldiers to take over a Dutch airfield in the Hague. Now we understood the reasoning behind the establishment of mobile units. One of the soldiers told us that the airfield was already in our hands thanks to airborne troops, and they were hoping to catch the Dutch royal family. I felt quite nervous on that flight because we were stuck in the back of a transport plane with no windows, and we knew that British and French fighters had been seen in the vicinity. We were accompanied by some Bf109s, which I hoped had big Bruno's engines in them.

When we arrived we discovered we had taken over one of the civil airports. There were several burnt-out planes by the side of the first runway and some bomb damage around the edges, but little more. Some soldiers were organizing the clean-up using prisoners, while some of our unit set to with mobile anti-aircraft guns. We assisted for a few hours, but soon we were back at our normal task of ensuring that our planes were ready and safe for another flight. We heard, that day, that some of the airborne troops we had watched take off had taken the Belgian fortress Eben Emael, which was supposed to be impregnable. Franz reckoned that airborne forces, aircraft, tanks and poisonous gas would be the hallmarks of future wars. We saw all sorts of planes coming and going but not once did we see any sign of the enemy.

The dive-bomber force of *Flieger Korps* VIII, with its fighters, refuelled with us several times. We heard from the pilots that they were putting the *blitzkrieg* theory to the ultimate test – smashing the way open for the tanks to rush forward – and apparently it was working well. The war in Holland did not last long, and just before Antwerp was taken,[14] the Dutch army capitulated.[15] By the end of the month we heard not only that the King of Belgium had surrendered,[16] but that the British army had been trapped in Dunkirk, although quite a few, we were told, had somehow scurried back to England. It felt as though events were moving too fast to keep up with. As Friedrich put it, 'The German army has got further in a month than they did in four years in the previous war.' Franz put it down to the leadership of the *Führer*, and Albert, who was becoming more and more fractious with Franz, claimed it was because of the *Luftwaffe*.

We had made our billets in the back of one of the hangars and the pilots had used an old reception lounge. The prisoners, mainly Dutch soldiers, were kept in the hangar next to us. They were used as manual labourers whenever there were onerous duties to perform. I walked over to their hangar one afternoon when we had been given stand-down time, and saw that they were sitting around just watching the planes coming and going. I spotted two of them playing chess and offered to play the winner. I shall never forget that moment; they both looked up at me, and without speaking picked up the pieces and walked away. I was reasonably popular at school, found it easy to make friends in the Hitler Youth, then at Daimler-Benz, and also in the *Luftwaffe*, but these two men looked at me with a mixture of utter disdain, if not hatred. I now know that my *mischling* status was the first and most serious knockback I had experienced, the second was the sight of Adolf Bier's suffering, and the third was the look of pure hatred in the eyes of those men. I was twenty-one years of age and felt very sensitive about being so disliked. I never went into the Hague after this experience, but chose to stay within the confines of the airfield; I simply did not want to have another meeting with Dutch people. I was, compared to others on the base, quite sensitive, and on reflection think that this was caused by my own awareness of being a *mischling*.

[14] On 18 May 1940.
[15] On 15 May 1940 at 11 a.m.
[16] On 20 May 1940.

During my time there I became very friendly with Karl, the pilot of one of our fighter planes. It was our mutual love of chess that brought us together and we spent what spare time we had together over the chess board. His skill and approach to chess were very similar to mine, so they were interesting games. He also told me about how the war was going. There was next to no resistance in the air and the army was moving across France with great speed. Paris soon fell, one of our bomber groups had bombed it,[17] but it was swiftly declared an open city[18] in order to avoid the kind of damage we had inflicted on Rotterdam. Then Dijon fell[19] and eventually France surrendered.[20] Karl showed me a newspaper with photographs of the *Führer* in Paris[21] and the news that two of our battleships had at last gained a victory against the British navy by sinking an aircraft carrier.[22]

June moved like a swift and conclusive game of chess. Never had the *Führer* been so popular; he was seen as a military genius who had repaired all the damage done to Germany in the first war. Karl thought he had been sent to the German people by God himself, which drew criticism from Albert. However, Karl was such a genuinely pleasant person that his views never got in the way of our growing friendship or the three-way competitive chess we played outside the hangar. It was a really hot summer and when we were not busy with the planes it was actually quite pleasant basking in the sun, playing chess. Karl's love of the game brought pilots and mechanics together, because both groups would wander over to the chess table and offer the occasional challenge.

The gossip on the base was that England was the next target.[23] Nobody knew for sure what the plans were but I was told that

---

[17] On 3 June 1940.
[18] On 16 June 1940.
[19] On 16 June 1940.
[20] On 22 June 1940.
[21] On 23 June 1940.
[22] On 8 June 1940 HMS *Glorious* sunk by the *Gneisenau* and the *Scharnhorst*.
[23] On 16 July 1940 Hitler issued *Seelöwe* – Operation Sealion to land 20 divisions on the south coast of England.

invasion barges were being stored on the coast. On Saturday 6 July the *Führer* had a massive victory parade in Berlin. There was considerable rejoicing on our base but it was not shared by the surrounding population. I heard from Franz and Karl that the residents of the Hague looked as if they were all at a funeral. I had some sympathy for them, but apart from whispered conversations with Albert, it would have been seen as almost traitorous to be anything but happy. On reflection I was happy because I did rejoice in the might of Germany, it was only my *mischling* status that caused me to stop and ponder the future from time to time, which made me somewhat sensitive.

I think we were all astonished when we read that the British had sunk a major portion of the French fleet[24] but we worked out that they done it in case our navy took them over.

'I can hardly believe that they would kill their own allies,' Karl mused.

'It tells us one thing,' Albert replied. 'They are really serious about this war; if they are prepared to sink the French, and kill their sailors, they're not about to capitulate or sue for peace; they're deadly serious.'

Karl and I thought about this and agreed: the British had done a dreadful thing to the French but their action made it evident that they were not going to 'roll over' like France. There was a general feeling that the French soldiers had not put up a spirited fight, and those units that had done so had managed to escape to Britain with the British army.

During that month many of our pilots, and ground crew, had returned to Germany for a break, but our small mobile unit stayed in Holland. Then just before the end of July we were attached to a *flergerkorps* in *Luftflotten* 2, a tactical fighter command, and were taken by lorry to Lille in France. It was clear to us that another phase in the war was about to begin. During the journey I managed to sit at the rear of the lorry and saw for myself the damage of war. There were some places where nothing had happened and others where it looked as if hell had visited the

[24] Vice-Admiral Somerville attacked and seriously damaged French warships at Oran and Mers-el-Kebir.

earth. There was one area near the French coast where British tanks, artillery and lorries were burned out besides the road, for what seemed like miles and, more to the point, there were many hastily dug graves.

I was relieved when we found our airfield near Lille, to find that Karl and his group were already there. Chess had helped Karl, Albert and me to form a close friendship, a thing to be treasured in such difficult times. In fact, we had barely unpacked before Karl appeared and gave us a couple of bottles of French wine, which we shared with Friedrich and Franz that evening, once we had sorted out our billet. This was again alongside our aircraft in an old and draughty hangar that had seen better days. It was a hot summer and so we did not mind our circumstances too much.

The next day the pilots were assembled inside our hangar, and we were allowed to listen to the plans for the next few months. We were told that the *Luftwaffe* had been given a major role in bringing Britain to its knees. It was proposed to take control of the skies over the French coast in order to allow the invasion to take place. Air control would mean that the British navy could not interfere with our ground troops crossing the channel, and in order to achieve that control our pilots were to destroy the RAF headquarters and all their aircraft and airfields. Apparently the British had an excellent radar system that allowed them to detect our aircraft in the air, and these stations were to be destroyed by Stuka dive bombers. Once this was achieved the airfields and planes were to be annihilated. It was to be another *blitzkrieg*, and according to the officer it should all be accomplished within the month. After the fall of the Low Countries, Norway and then France, none of us doubted him.

'I'm surprised,' Franz said, 'that the British have this radar system. I thought we were more technologically advanced.'

'It's all they've got,' one of the bomb-loading crew said.

'They've got good planes as well,' Karl added. 'They have Hurricanes and Spitfires, but not too many; they say most of them were destroyed in the invasion of France.'

Later that evening, Karl confided in Albert and me that the pilots had been warned not to parachute out or land in England, because they would be subjected either to instant death or torture.

'I doubt that,' Albert said. 'They're like us, fairly civilized.'

'What about the French fleet?' Karl shot back.

Throughout the war everyone believed this rumour that to land, or crash in England would lead to being tortured or shot. It caused me to wonder what sort of people the British really were; strangely it provoked a desire in me to try to understand some of the English language. Karl spoke English, as did Friedrich to a lesser extent, and so Albert and I made a point of learning the language together; after all, according to what we had heard we would be living over there very soon.

Albert and I thought we might try to attend a local Catholic church in the town, but that was ruled out as on the Sunday we had planned this venture, we had to help arm the Stukas as the raids on the radar stations were to start that very day.[25] On their return we were told that they had met no resistance and that all the pylons had been destroyed. That evening we could smell victory in the air, but later we were to learn their radar was still operational: the British were craftier than we had thought.

On the Tuesday of that week I saw more aircraft in the sky than I thought existed.[26] None of us could believe that it would be possible for the British to resist such an attack. I actually thought the British war would be over by that evening, because with such a devastating assault[27] they would surely capitulate. If one out of three planes hit their targets the potential British control of the skies would be lost. Back at base we waited with bated breath and a keen sense of anticipation. I wished Karl good luck as he headed for his Bf109 and anxiously awaited his plane's return; I was responsible for his engine, and as he had become such very good friend, I was concerned for his safety.

That evening Karl told us that although they had taken the English by surprise it had not been as straightforward as they had

[25] On 11 August 1940 German aircraft attacked radar stations at Portalnd, Weymouth and Dover.

[26] On 13 August 1940. *Aldertag* ('Day of the Eagle') was the code name for the *Luftwaffe* attack on the RAF.

[27] The *Luftwaffe* sent 1,485 aircraft; they lost forty-five and the RAF thirteen.

anticipated. The Stukas had proved to be an easy target for the British fighters, as they had a maximum speed of less than 200 mph, whereas the British fighters could reach 375 mph; in addition the Stuka had a ceiling of 11,000 feet whereas the British could fly up to 33,000 feet and dive out of the sky from nowhere. However, the German fighters had the advantage of gaining height over the Channel, while the British planes only had a few moments to scramble and gain any height. Karl was confident that we would win within a few weeks because the British had fewer planes than we did. On the Thursday of that week another massive flight flew over us as our fighters joined them.[28] I really could not begin to envisage the damage they would create and was sure the British would soon sue for peace.

That afternoon a Stuka just managed to land on our airfield: it should have landed elsewhere, but the urgency of his situation demanded that it came in at once. I joined the emergency team and rushed over to the plane. It was in a dreadful state, with bullet holes everywhere and most of its fin was missing. The pilot could not open his cockpit and it was evident from the blood on the screen that he was badly wounded. I was just about to jump on the wing to help him, when a sudden uplifting blow threw me high into the air. I can remember to this day being airborne and twisting my body in order to land on my feet. I failed and came down on the grass with a thump that knocked all the wind out of me. I could feel heat all around me but could hear nothing. I was conscious of being dragged along by my arms but it took a supreme effort to try to get up. It was Albert who had pulled me clear and I could see at once that the plane had exploded. I was very lucky to be alive. It was several hours before my hearing returned, by which time we were all busy again on our fighters.

This time the repairs took longer, and some of the planes were so badly shot up that the best we could do was put them to cannibalize for spare parts. This was a different scenario from those of Poland and France; we were for first time working on planes that had been damaged in aerial combat. We could also see

[28] On 15 August 1940 over 1,000 planes took off against the RAF: the Germans lost seventy-five and the RAF thirty-four.

from the pilots that it was no joy-ride. Some were still as jaunty as ever, but most of them looked more solemn than we had ever seen them before. I suppose that is not surprising given that many would have seen their friends shot down. In fact quite a few were missing even from our small airfield. It was not long after this that they withdrew the Stukas from the battle over England,[29] and we heard that the RAF had actually bombed some ammunition plants in France and Germany. After five days I could feel that this new phase of the war was not progressing as everyone had anticipated. Karl was much quieter than usual and I detected a loss of enthusiasm when he was preparing to fly.

'Those British planes,' he said, 'Spitfires and Hurricanes, live up to their name. They're as fast as we are, the Spitfire can turn more quickly, and their pilots don't seem to care whether they live or die; and there's more of them than we were led to believe.'

The general opinion amongst many of the pilots was that they had been given the wrong information about the British. Their pilots were skilful, and as many as we shot down, others seemed to appear. Furthermore the British seemed to know fairly accurately when, and where, our planes would be. We were really shocked when we heard that the RAF had even had time to bomb Berlin,[30] despite the fact that the head of the *Luftwaffe*, Herman Goering, had claimed that this would be impossible. This was all a very different story from Poland and France, and it started to dawn us during that month that although Germany was militarily stronger we now faced an enemy that would not just give up.

One day near the end of August, I was working on a Bf109, replacing the entire exhaust system, when I heard a commotion outside. Everyone was looking up at the sky, where one of our fighters was in trouble, being pursued by what Franz said was a Spitfire. The Bf109 was on fire, and seemed to be diving straight towards us when the pilot fell from his plane and opened his parachute. The Spitfire circled him and Franz said that the crew would shoot him as he floated helplessly in the air. I also thought they would, but the plane dropped away from the pilot and

[29] On 17 August 1940.
[30] On 25 August 1940 and again on 10 September.

zoomed down towards us, its guns blazing at two of our planes on the side runway. It was deadly accurate blowing both of them up as we watched, powerless. We only had one anti-aircraft gun and the crew were still running towards it as the Spitfire came around the second time. This time I could see the pilot's face, and I think he must have run out of ammunition because he just swooped along our field and up to the descending pilot where he waggled his wings and disappeared. I shall never forget the sound of his engine; it sounded really powerful and with a very deep hum. It was not long before I discovered that the lucky German pilot was actually Karl.

'I thought he was going to shoot you when you were parachuting down,' I said to him that evening.

'So did I,' Karl replied. 'But when he came up the second time, and I was preparing to hit the ground, he actually waved at me and waggled his wings, which is a sort of greeting.'

'The English can't all be bad,' I said.

Albert and I did eventually make it to a church in Lille, but it did not feel right. Although we had been trying to learn some English, we had no French, and so we sat in the pews as if watching a foreign performance. It was not quite as bad as Holland, but I did notice that, even if we smiled or nodded at someone, they managed to avoid our gaze. No one looked at us, not even in the church; it was as if we did not exist. I found it quite difficult to cope with being so despised.

No one said anything specific about what was happening but Karl told us that he thought the invasion was probably off because the RAF was still managing to get fighters into the air. The pilots had been told that the British only had a few planes left, but on the very day he and the other pilots had been given this information, they were met by hundreds of Hurricanes and Spitfires. Apparently we were now trying to bomb the British into submission, and our fighters had become the bombers' 'shepherds'. This was quite dangerous because the Bf109s could only just make it to London before their fuel capacity meant that they had to start returning, hoping that a British fighter would not detain them. There were a large number of missing pilots and new ones were turning up each week; some looked very young and, I have to admit, frightened. Our bombers made easy targets and by October of that year we stopped sending them over in the daytime, and did it under cover of darkness.[31] As Friedrich said, 'We are not losing this war, but we are not winning it.' It was a world war now, because Italy, which had invaded Greece,[32] had joined with Germany and Japan to form a worldwide alliance.[33]

I reflected upon the fact that the *Führer* had been right when he said the next phase would be a 'bombing war'. It was however, a two-way process; we were told that we had eliminated a city called Coventry,[34] which caused me think of Erik who was still in England, but we also heard that the British had bombed Essen[35] and the Kiel naval base.[36] I had been on duty for nearly a year without a break so I was delighted to be told that I had been granted two weeks' leave just before Christmas. I managed to wangle a flight back in one of our planes, thanks to Karl. My parents were thrilled to see me and wanted to hear about what I had been doing and where I had been. My father had seen the bombing raid over Berlin from his train, but his main news was about his trips to Poland. He had taken train-loads of Jews to Litzmannstadt (the Lodz Ghetto) before it was closed.[37]

'So many people, Bruno,' he said. 'It was like moving an entire city population into a village. I have been transporting them to Warsaw[38] for most of the year. The SS squeeze them into cattle trucks. There's nothing we can do. I have never seen anything as terrible as this. I mentioned it to another driver friend of mine who has been taking troops to and from France, but he refuses to believe me.'

It seemed that we were moving all Jews from the west into the

---

[31] This decision was taken on 5 October 1940.

[32] On 28 October 1940.

[33] On 27 September 1940 the Rome Berlin Tokyo Axis was formed.

[34] On 14 November 1940.

[35] On 3 November 1940.

[36] On 16 October 1940.

[37] On 7 May 1940 the Lodz Ghetto was sealed with 165,000 people squashed into an area of 1.6 square miles.

[38] Sealed with 500,000 people on 16 November 1940.

east, which I supposed was what the *Führer* had meant by *lebensraum*. I never mentioned our shared *mischling* status to my father, but talked to my mother about it after he had returned to work. She was concerned that when all the Jews had gone they might well turn on the *mischlings*. She, like me, had had a letter from Josef but she had not replied. I know this hurt her deeply, but she felt that it was people like Josef who were destroying the lives of people, such as Frau Goldblatt, besides putting his own father in danger. She asked me about the diamonds Frau Goldblatt had given me because she knew that one day they might become useful. I showed her that they were still in the brass watch, which I always carried with me. That night she asked me for the diamonds so she could sew them behind my *Luftwaffe* badge to make them more secure. I felt that this was somewhat paranoid, but I never argued with my mother. I was interested to hear that she attended my father's church more than her own, because she thought it important that married people worshipped together, and she was pleased that my father had started going to church more regularly than he once had.

I also caught up with big Bruno and Marie: he was as cynical as ever; I would have been sad had he changed.

'I tell you,' he said, 'the British are not fools, and they'll soon have more aircraft in the sky than we will. If their backs were against the wall they would cut their own grandmother's throat. They've smashed up the Italian army and taken more prisoners than they know what to do with.'[39]

'They sank the French fleet,' I added.

'For them, that would only be like killing your mother in law.'

Marie brought us in some bread and cheese. Apparently I had eaten well in France compared to Berliners; people were being encouraged to have hot-pots or stews to conserve food, because so much money was being spent on armaments.

'I met some prisoners who were English officers in the last war,' Bruno said, sipping his beer. 'They were really charming, but later they slit the throat of one of their own because they

[39] On 9 December 1940, British troops in Egypt broke through the Italian lines at Sidi Barrani and on 23 December took 35,949 prisoners.

suspected him of giving away secrets. They might be English gentlemen of our joke, but they can be cold blooded when necessary.'

'We will beat them eventually?' I said.

'That is what Napoleon said.' Bruno shot back.

'We may find it difficult to cross the channel,' I said, 'but so will they.'

'They haven't got an empire for nothing; look at all their colonies. I bet you a thousand marks that the Americans will eventually side with them. Bruno, we are heading for trouble.'

Given that this conversation occurred at the end of 1940 I now realize how discerning big Bruno was in his own astute way. No one else in Germany, including me, harboured any doubts that the successes of 1939 and 1940 would continue. I now know what a clever man he was; he thought for himself and never allowed propaganda or newspapers to dictate what or how he thought. If I had not had his support at Daimler-Benz the day I discovered I was a *mischling*, I dare not think how I would have reacted. I keep big Bruno and Marie in my prayers to this day.

Back at the Lille airbase 1940 ended on a sad note, because I heard that the day before I had returned Karl had been forced to parachute out over enemy territory, shot down by a Hurricane over the River Thames. Albert and I went back to the Catholic church in Lille and said prayers for him, and lit a candle.

Chapter 9

1941

The airfield was not the same without Karl, and Albert and I missed his company. Friedrich rightly pointed out that half the original pilots had been killed, seriously wounded or captured, but it is not until a close friend is lost that the ghastliness of the situation truly dawns. Much later in the year I received a letter postmarked Munich; it had been sent by Karl's father, Heinrich von Richter. Karl had landed safely in England, and was now in a prisoner of war camp, but all was well; he had asked his father to let me know. 'Doesn't sound as if he was tortured,' Albert said. Perhaps our prayers had been answered; but we were sure that when we did eventually invade Britain Karl would once more be free.

Most of the war seemed to be happening elsewhere while we were in Lille. Our fighter planes flew up each day to guard the coastline and at night many were busy escorting the bombers on their raids. According to the papers and rumours, the Italians were not doing well: the Greeks were now attacking them,[1] and they were being beaten by the British in North Africa.[2] But all was peaceful for us in Lille – busy, but peaceful. When Albert and I had free time we would walk through Lille and were pleased that the French shopkeepers and café owners did not show the same hostility as we had experienced from the Dutch prisoners. Franz

[1] On 4 January 1941 the Greeks launched an attack on Valona from Berat.
[2] On 5 January 1941 Bardia fell to the British.

said it was because the French had seen it all in the previous war. We went to church several times, and although there were quite a few Germans in the congregation, the French people we saw there did their best to avoid eye contact; thank goodness for the café owners.

On 12 January I had a shock. Albert and I had been to church in Lille and were walking up the path to our billet when an SS soldier came away from our room. It took me a few minutes to recognize him as he walked towards us. 'Albert,' I said, 'meet my brother, Josef.'

Albert shook hands with Josef and said he would leave us to talk; I really did not want him to go because I felt closer to him than to my own brother. Josef seemed to be taller, and he smiled readily as we met.

'How did you find me here?' I asked.

'Mum told me.'

'You've seen Mum?'

'Yes, but she wouldn't let me in the house. She told me where you were, saying she wouldn't hold brothers apart.'

'I'm sure,' I said a little uncertainly, 'that if you apologized to Dad, Mum would welcome you with open arms.'

'I'm not apologizing to any Jew.'

'He's not a Jew, he's a *mischling* like you and me, and he's your father.'

'He's a Jew. An intelligence officer double-checked for me in case I could become an officer; he's a Jew, and if it weren't for Mum being truly German, we'd both be in serious trouble.'

'He's still our father.'

'Yes, unfortunately, but if we don't marry a Jewess, we'll be all right. The new laws will breed Jewishness out of German blood.'

We were sitting down at one of the mechanics' tables because it was beginning to rain outside, and it was quite chilly. As I looked into Josef's eyes I could see that nothing I could say would change his mind. He was a total fanatic. I recalled the day when he had argued with my father over going to Frau Goldblatt's shop, and I pondered on the fact that two brothers, from the same stable, with the same upbringing, could differ very much. We were both *mischling*, which had caused me to question not only the race laws, but also the official attitude towards the Jews. Josef, on the other hand, retained his obsession about Jews and his unquestionable loyalty to the Nazi Party. I had the distinct impression that if he were ordered to shoot himself he would obey instantly. He was bitter about Ruth marrying Hans, the Jew, and he told me he would never speak to her again. I could not help but point out that since she now lived in America that would be difficult anyway.

'We will rule America in our lifetime,' he replied. 'Japan in the east and us in the west, we cannot lose.'

I could not argue with him: I could not see how we could be beaten, but I really did not believe we would ever control America. Josef was truly the child of propaganda. He was not at all interested in my work, and although I tried to show him the engine I was working on, I once again felt like a little boy trying to get his big brother interested in his toy soldiers.

'I may not be an officer because of our father,' he said, 'but I have wangled a posting to a proper fighting division, the SS Adolf Hitler Division.' He was almost bursting with pride as he told me this, and I half expected him to stand up and salute at the *Führer*'s name. I asked him if he wanted to stay the night, but he was off to Paris before joining his new division. We talked for another hour about the war, but when I asked him about the concentration camp he just said they made life unbearable for the enemies of the state and killed the Jews. I did not believe him at the time, and thought he was just trying to impress me.

'So you'd kill your own father?' I asked.

'If ordered,' he replied without hesitation.

I shook hands with him when he left, and then he stood back and gave me a '*Heil Hitler*' salute; I gave the traditional military salute in return, though even that seemed ridiculous with my own brother.

On the Monday morning after Josef's visit, twenty of us in our unit, including the four mechanics, were ordered to join another airfield – in Sicily, of all places. Before midday we were on a transport plane and airborne. We landed in Graz for refuelling, and by late evening we were in an airfield just outside Palermo. Having left a cold winter's day in western France we felt completely taken aback by the heatwave that hit us when we stepped on to the runway.

The next day we all assembled, after having unpacked, and met many others who had been dropped in just as swiftly as us. A senior officer explained the importance of the Sicilian airfield, and how it would continue to grow over the coming year. We were attached to the *fliegerkorps* X, under the command of *General der Flieger Geisler.*[3] Some of the planes were specially designed to carry torpedoes, but our particular job once again was to work with the accompanying fighters. The build-up in Sicily was happening to ensure that the Sicilian Straits were closed to enemy shipping, and to destroy the British bases of Gibraltar and Malta. There were about 200 aircraft around the island,[4] which kept us fully deployed from day one. Unlike Lille, where we had felt the cold, we worked wearing just our boots and shorts. In all my life I had never experienced such heat, and it was supposed to be winter.

During February nearly every plane was on patrol looking out for British naval vessels, because many of our own troops were beginning to cross to North Africa.[5] Vessels were not easy targets, but they sustained serious damage when hit by bombs and torpedoes. We were told that some slow-flying JU87s had seriously damaged a major British vessel, the *Illustrious.*[6] The British were being hard pressed, defending their own country as well as trying to fight in the Mediterranean; on the other hand we were obliged to support the Italians because they were beginning to crumble in the face of British opposition.

Joining our team in Sicily was an unusual member of the crew; he was not German but a volunteer from South Africa who hated the British, a Boer. He was an expert in bomb-aiming devices and he was lodged next door to us in our billet. His name was Jan. His German was understandable but flawed, and his dialect had a

[3] *Oberst* Harlinghaussen, an anti-shipping expert, was his Chief of Staff.
[4] A year later there were 425 aircraft based in Sicily, of which 190 were long-range bombers, and 115 Bf109s.
[5] On 3 February 1941 Hitler decided to send the *Afrika Korps* to Libya.
[6] On 10 January 1941.

strange twang. What was interesting was his ability to speak English, even though he hated the British. This suited Albert and me because we were still trying to learn the language, and with Karl in a POW camp and Friedrich fed up with trying to help us, Jan was quite useful and seemed keen to teach us.

We were told to keep our distance from the Sicilians, especially the women. When we did go into town it struck me that they were either stunningly beautiful or really haggard. All the men appeared old, and watched us with a look of deep suspicion in their eyes. Albert and I went to the local church again, but it was even more of a mystery than the one in Lille. The main part of the service was in Latin, and gabbled at speed, while the local congregation, mainly women, looked through us as if we did not exist. Albert was deeply religious, and I have to confess I was becoming more so. Following my conversations with big Bruno I was more and more inclined to take 'God-talk', as Franz called it, more seriously. I remember sitting on a hill full of olive trees one afternoon with Albert. We had been playing chess but were now just resting in the glorious Mediterranean sunshine, when Albert suddenly asked me about my belief in God. I told him that my parents, especially my mother, were devout, and that I had always had a residual belief in God. I explained that the Pastor in my mother's home town had made me think more about religion, and that, because of my huge respect for big Bruno, I had begun to consider the question of faith. I confessed that I had found my father's Catholicism more spiritual than my mother's Lutheranism, but I still found the resurrection of Christ difficult to take on board.

'The thing to consider there,' Albert said, 'is whether the evangelists who wrote about the resurrection were bad or mad, and why Christianity has survived for nearly two thousand years, with thousands of people willing to die for their faith.'

'Will it survive this war?' I asked. 'Some of the Churches in the evangelical tradition have taken to putting swastikas up above their pulpits.'

'As an institution it may well wobble because not all the clergy are faithful, but when this war is done and dusted the Christian faith will still be there. Look at the Lille church last time we were there: about forty locals and nearly twenty Germans.'

That afternoon felt almost like being on holiday; basking in the sun and talking about religion. There were no sounds of war, just some birds in the background, and we had a bottle of wine and some ham to feast on.

We spent three glorious months in Sicily; we were busy but not worked to death, and we enjoyed our meanders into the Sicilian hills. We were hoping that we would be spending the duration, as we had come to call it, in the Mediterranean, when Franz gave us the news that our unit was once more on the move. We had heard that Rommel was doing well and the British had been forced out of Benghazi,[7] but victory was still a long way away. We were told very little before boarding one of the bombers, and a few hours later found ourselves setting up house in southern Austria on the outskirts of Graz.

We lost our English teacher Jan, because Friedrich told us two senior officers had arrived by plane and taken him away. It was all very friendly, and cigars and handshakes indicated that he was not in trouble. Friedrich thought that because of Jan's English they were either going to use him as a spy or drop him in a British POW camp to gather information.

When we arrived the airfield was already busy, and there was plenty of action out on the airfield and in the hangars. This was the largest airfield our small group had worked on, and we soon discovered that Germany had invaded Greece and Yugoslavia.[8] This base was for Stukas and the Bf109s in which we tended to specialize. There had been a major bombing raid on Belgrade and the planes were just returning to base.[9]

April was a period of frenetic activity and once again we followed the progress of the war with avid interest: Sicily now seemed like another world. We read that the German 2nd Army, under Von Weiches, was advancing rapidly and the XLI Motorized Corps was moving in from Romania. It was no surprise

[7] On 3 April 1941.
[8] On 6 April 1941.
[9] The *Luftwaffe* operation, codenamed Castigo, carried out a terror raid on Belgrade on 6 April 1941.

to hear that the Yugoslav army had been destroyed.[10]

That said, it was not all good news; we gathered from a fresh group of pilots who had just arrived from Berlin that the RAF had carried out a devastating raid on the city.[11] It might have been easy to beat Yugoslavia but the British planes were becoming quite a thorn in our side. When I said that I found it strange that a little offshore island like Britain could be fighting all over the place, Friedrich pointed out that 'it was because England was an island that she could survive,' and he said, reminding me of previous conversations, 'They're like us, they will fight to the end.' Some time during our first month in Graz I heard that the *Führer* was in the city, but it was all very hush-hush and I did not hear any more about it, apart from the fact that he had been there.[12] Normally we would all have been on parade, but this time we were busy, with more and more planes coming and going.

When Albert and I did have a free long weekend we visited Graz and went to the cinema, where we watched a newsreel of the *Führer* visiting the great battleships, the *Bismarck* and the *Tirpitz* at Gottenhafen.[13] I always got a great thrill from seeing these huge monsters: there was a sleekness to them which was pleasing to the eye, and their sheer size gave a real sense of devastating power. But Albert pointed out that 'One of our planes could sink such a vessel with one lucky hit.' On the way out of the cinema we saw a fairly large group of boys and girls being rounded up by the police as they came out of a hall. They were being put into trucks, and driven away without protest.

'What have they been up to?' I asked a policeman who was watching from our side of the street.

He looked at my uniform and I could see him wondering whether he would bother to answer. 'They're *Swingjugend*,' he said.

[10] On 17 April 1941.
[11] On 10 April 1941, when Hitler attacked Goering for allowing this to happen.
[12] On 26–27 April 1941 Hitler visited Graz and Klagenfurt to meet his old history teacher, Dr Leopold Poetsch.
[13] On 5 May 1941; Gottenhafen was formerly the Polish port of Gdynia.

'*Swingjugend*?' I queried.

'Deviants,' he replied. 'They've been jitterbugging to American music.'

'Is that a crime?' Albert asked.

I shushed Albert and did not argue because I knew he was right. I remembered that in my Hitler Youth days we had been warned against such music, but I also knew that some of the most fanatical Hitler Youth leaders liked it, including Adolf Bier. I had taken it for granted that American music was degenerate, but having experienced Albert's perceptive thinking and big Bruno's influence, I could not help but wonder why, with a war being fought, grown men would bother to arrest fifty-odd boys and girls for dancing to any form of music.

We were very busy at the airfield with engines that were worn out. They were not returning battle-scarred as they did from the sorties over England, but they were flying long distances in order to bomb and strafe the countryside ahead for our troops.

During May we heard that the Bismarck had sunk a major British battleship[14] and then a few days later that the British had sunk the Bismarck. We found it incredible that such a large, modern vessel could be sunk, but when we heard that aeroplanes had been involved in the battle, I remembered Albert's point about battleships and aircraft. In the same month came the strange news that the *Führer*'s deputy had lost his mind, and with one of our more recently developed Messerschmitts had flown to England.[15] None of us could begin to fathom why he should do this, and since the news took so long to percolate out, we guessed that the Reich's leaders had no explanation. We also heard that Crete had fallen[16] which made us feel that the war was about to finish, apart from the British opposition. I was becoming more and more suspicious of the *Führer* and his Party, but I have to confess that I felt a great pride in the German military machine of which I was part.

Apart from the one weekend in Graz, Albert and I had to work

---

[14] *The Hood*, on 24 May 1941.

[15] Hess on 10 May 1941

[16] On 1 June 1941.

day in and day out, which meant we were due leave. It was therefore something of a shock when we were told, again with only a few minutes' notice, that we were off once more. This time they would not tell us where we were going until we were on board the Dornier. 'It's like a circus,' Friedrich said. 'Put down, pitch up, do a show, pull down, pack up and move on.'

'At least we're seeing the world.' Franz was always optimistic, and he was happy about the move, even though he had found a girlfriend in Graz.

'Perhaps it's another phase of the war, back to Lille,' Albert suggested. On this occasion he was wrong; a small compass that Friedrich kept in his pocket, showed that the plane was heading east. We were followed by a swarm of our fighters, and we pulled Friedrich's leg about the safety of the Dornier, because he and Franz had serviced and prepared this particular plane.

Even after we had landed it was at least two hours before we realized that we were on the outskirts of Warsaw, in a district which, if my memory serves me correctly, was called Ursus. We had seen busy airfields before, but this one was a hive of frenetic activity.

'Something big is going on now,' Friedrich observed.

'I know what it is,' said Franz.

We all looked at him expectantly, but he carried on stowing his gear into a large tent which had been set aside for us.

'All right, know-all,' Friedrich said, 'tell us.'

'Russia. The *Führer* always said that the Soviets are our natural enemies.'

'That would be a war on two fronts,' Albert said.

'The British are not at war, they're just playing,' Franz replied.

The conversation ended abruptly when a senior officer appeared and told us all to get a move on, and leave the thinking to the leaders.

The tent was uncomfortable, not so much because of the weather, which was quite warm, but because there was no protection from the noise; Friedrich snored enough for a whole battalion. We had our fighters to service and check, as well as a large number of Stukas to work our way through. One of the pilots, having sworn us to silence, told us one Saturday that the next day all hell would break loose. He was right; we were kept up all night arming nearly every plane on the field. It was all hands to the pumps, because of the number of planes that needed ammunition. Just after 4 a.m. all the planes started taking off one after another, until the airfield was virtually empty. More planes were coming from the west. We just stood looking up in amazement, finding it hard to believe that there could be so many planes in the air at once.

'So we start another war on a Sunday,'[17] Albert said aloud.

'What's wrong with a Sunday,' Franz replied. 'The Soviets won't be at church.'

'It's a Holy day.' Albert replied sharply.

'You believe in all that rubbish?' Franz asked.

'I do.' Albert was obviously intent on standing his ground.

'You actually believe in God?' Franz was now looking at Albert and not the planes.

'I do.'

'Well, I don't care whether you do or don't,' Franz said, 'but if God exists he's going to be on our side with that amount of aircraft.'

'I wouldn't mock God, Franz.' Albert sounded angry.

'I'll mock God because he's as silly as garden fairies.'

'I guarantee you one thing,' Albert shot back. 'That if you were on the point of death, you would be praying not to garden fairies, but to God and hoping like mad he was listening.'

'All right, all right you two,' Friedrich interrupted. 'Cut out all that shit and let's get something to eat before our planes return.'

I was pleased Friedrich had intervened, because knowing Albert well, and being aware of his growing dislike of Franz, I was beginning to wonder where this conversation was going. We were four men who had worked together for a long time, and it was important that we managed to get along together as a team. This was Friedrich's strength; he held us together and ensured that we helped one another, despite any differences of opinion.

When the pilots did start returning we gathered that the Soviets had been taken completely by surprise; most of their

---

[17] On 22 June 1941 Operation Barbarossa was launched at 4.15 a.m.

aircraft had been destroyed while still on the ground, and our army was pushing forward with unbelievable speed. Of course we were pleased with the news, but I could recall hearing, several months before, a similarly optimistic view from some of the very same pilots, that all the RAF planes and radar systems in England had been destroyed. They had been wrong then and they could be wrong again.

Near the end of June I had a letter from my mother. It had taken some time getting to me and for some reason my instincts told me that it was not good news. I took the letter away to the perimeter fencing and opened it when no one else was around. Josef had been killed in April at some place called Ioannina in the Greek campaign.[18] My mother told me the news in one sentence, and the rest of the letter was asking after my health; I suspected that even in death my mother had not forgiven Josef. I found this hard, but I would come to understand it more later. I felt sad for Josef, but the way he had treated my father was beyond belief. As I walked back to the hangar I saw Albert looking at me over the cowling of a Bf109, and I knew then that I would have felt sadder and more distressed had it been Albert who had been killed and not my own brother. I suspect that in war it is quite often the case that a person draws closer to his comrades than his own family, because of their shared experiences.

The bombers were exceptionally busy; one day they seemed to be in the sky all day.[19] In the middle of July several flights from our area took part in the bombing of Moscow[20] and it really did seem that we were invincible. Big Bruno wrote and informed me that the RAF had seriously bombed Bremen, Cologne and Wilhelmshaven.[21] It was quite clear, although big Bruno did not say so, that there was still a war on the Western Front and that the British were still very much in contention.

One morning, when we were having problems because of a lack of spare parts, Albert and I were ordered to go with a convoy

[18] 1941 April 21; the SS Adolf Hitler Division took Ioannina.
[19] Probably 28 June, when Minsk was bombed.
[20] On 12 July 1941.
[21] During the Wilhelmshaven raid on 8 July 1941 the RAF used its first B17s.

to another airfield which had Bf109 exhaust systems we badly needed. It was exciting because we had not left the airfield for over a month, and it was the first time we had had an opportunity to see Warsaw for ourselves. The two soldiers who went with us had done the trip many times, and on the way they took us past the Jewish Ghetto. They were laughing at the fact that half a million Jews lived behind the walls in a few flats. I felt sick. The wall was still being built in places, and the driver stopped to 'show us the view'. We were always hungry and missed good food, but I could see instantly that the people lolling around on the pavements were starving; they looked as emaciated as the prisoners I had once seen in northern Germany. There were guards at the entrance to the road, and we all watched as a small boy, probably no older than seven or eight, was stopped by one of our soldiers. For a moment I thought the soldier was going to pat him on the head, but then he took his rifle and slammed the wooden butt down on the boy's head; he collapsed at once. A woman rushed over towards his prostrate body and started to drag him away, but not before the other soldier had kicked her in the ribs and sent her sprawling. Despite her pain she still managed to drag the boy away and as she did so both soldiers laughed and lit their cigarettes.

'That's criminal,' Albert said. 'They'll be on a charge for that.'

'Don't be stupid,' one of our *Luftwaffe* guards said. 'They're just Jewish rats.'

'Jew or no Jew, soldiers don't kill kids,' Albert said. 'We should find a senior officer.'

'You do that and we'll be seen as Jew-lovers and find ourselves the wrong side of the wire. Let's get a move on.' The guard was obviously worried that Albert was about to jump out of the truck and make a scene.

'So senior officers know about this type of behaviour?' I asked.

'Haven't you heard of *Endlösung*?'[22] he asked me.

'What?'

'The liquidation of Europe's Jews.'

'Liquidation?' I asked.

[22] An order given by Goering.

'They're put into these ghettos and they will have to eat one another or starve.'

'I don't believe it,' I said.

'I don't care what you believe; take it up with the *Führer*.'

For the rest of the journey the two guards sat in silence and Albert and I, lost in thought, did not break that silence. As we drove back through Warsaw I told myself that those guards were thugs, and there was no way that the senior command would countenance such behaviour. And when we were alone, fitting the exhaust system to the Bf109, we agreed that the senior command was in ignorance of such brutish behaviour.

'But,' Albert continued, 'I think we're cocooned from the reality of the ground war. We're flown from airfield to airfield and we're always well behind the lines of the fighting. The pilots, on the whole, are educated men, but some of these soldiers are just criminal thugs.'

We did not mention the incident to Franz, but spoke to Friedrich who, I was happy to find, was just as shocked as we were when we told him about the young boy and his mother. Like us, he believed we had witnessed a one-off incident by two psychopaths, but he said that it was too late to report it. I did not have to go into Warsaw again and I did not volunteer to leave the base. If we were cocooned from the brutality of the outside world I wanted it to stay that way.

By late October we thought the war would be finished by Christmas. Our troops were only sixty-five miles outside Moscow[23] which we had also bombed,[24] and few could see how the Russians could possibly survive such an assault. But despite this the gossip at the airfield was not all good. As I have said, the airfields, with personnel coming and going, were rife with gossip that was quite often correct. We heard that Hamburg had been seriously bombed,[25] but on the other hand that our troops were now in the Crimea.[26] Perhaps the most disturbing rumour was

[23] On 20 October 1941.
[24] On 31 October 1941.
[25] On 26 October 1941.
[26] On 25 September 1941 the German onslaught on the Crimea began.

167

that over 30,000 people had been massacred somewhere near Kiev.[27] When we asked why, we were brushed off with the answer that they were just vermin: Jews and Communists. Albert and I agreed once again that it was just a rumour, because we could not imagine how such a massacre could be organized: the sheer amount of ammunition and manpower needed in the middle of an all-out war seemed, quite frankly, ridiculous. During November we heard that Tikhvin had fallen,[28] as well as Yalta and Rostov.

Near the end of the month we were packing our bags again. This time we guessed that it was happening because many of our planes, especially our fighters, were reaching the limit of their fuel capacity. The army had advanced so far and so quickly that Warsaw and the Polish airfields were too far behind the lines. After flying to the front line and attacking ground targets, some fighters barely had sufficient fuel to return, and there had been several unnecessary accidents.

We landed at a small and unpleasant airfield somewhere deep in the Ukraine. We looked at a map and saw that we were in the middle of nowhere, somewhere south of Kiev at a large town called Poltava. Our planes were already there and once again we were billeted in large tents. The place was busy with more troops than we had ever seen before: a mixture of *Wehrmacht* and *Waffen-SS*. It was also a holding camp for prisoners, and we were camped unpleasantly close to the enclosure which contained them. It was mid-November and there was snow on the ground; we froze and Friedrich worked out that we were sleeping in temperatures twelve degrees below zero. We did not have the right clothes, and our blankets were totally inadequate. We slept in our working gear, with our uniforms over this, plus greatcoats over the top, but we still felt the intense cold. Next morning I realized that the Russian prisoners had spent the entire night out in the open. While we were working on the planes during the day we saw that the prison pen was still filling up, and the prisoners

[27] On 28 September 1941 at Babi Yar 34,000 Jews were massacred.
[28] On 8 November 1941 Northern Sector XXXIX Armoured Corps captured Tikhvin.

were fed by some of the guards throwing bread over the fence. It was hardly sufficient for so many, and so they fought like dogs for the scraps.

'They're just like animals.' Franz said.

'So would you be,' replied Friedrich, 'if you'd been out all night with no food.' Had Albert said this there would have been a debate, but Franz made a point of not tangling with Friedrich.

It was a strange atmosphere, working with such suffering staring us in the face. We were all quiet that day. In the early evening we saw some SS troops bring in about thirty men wearing Soviet uniforms: they looked a good deal smarter than the ones in the cage. They were ordered to stand beside the concrete wall of a large storage hut and were guarded by several men. We watched a truck draw up and guessed that they were going to be taken to another camp, because the one at Poltava was obviously too full. We were very wrong; the truck reversed towards the men, and as it did so the rear canvas was raised revealing a machine-gun which pointed straight at the prisoners. I was standing with Franz close to the scene, and so could see that most of the Russians did not look like soldiers; they were middle-aged and wearing spectacles. I could see the fear on their faces, and just as I was about to say something to Franz the machine-gun opened up, spraying them with high-calibre bullets. I was transfixed, watching blood and bone spray all over the concrete wall, and the man I had been studying started to run towards us. He did not get far because machine-gun bullets ripped up his chest towards his face, which seemed to explode in a fountain of blood and brains. The machine-gun was deafening, and continued to spray its lethal lead into those bodies that showed no sign of life. I felt my stomach heave, and I vomited on the ground before me. This caused one of the SS soldiers to laugh, and to my astonishment Franz took me by the elbow and led me away – an act of consideration I had not expected.

'Who were they?' Franz asked an SS guard standing by.

'Political commissars,'[29] he said. 'We've orders to shoot them at once.'

---

[29] On 3 March 1941 Hitler's Directive No.13 ordered the SS to eliminate all Bolshevik chiefs and commissars without a court martial.

As Franz and I walked back to our area I heard him mutter under his breath, 'Bastards.'

'Who?' I asked, thinking he meant the commissars.

'The SS,' he replied. 'They showed no compassion.'

Later I told Albert, who had seen everything from a distance, about Franz's reaction.

'Perhaps we've got him wrong.' Albert suggested.

Next morning the bodies were buried by some of the Russian prisoners, under the watchful eye of two SS men. Life was becoming miserable for our little team as we worked all day in the freezing cold, the rations were insufficient, we hardly slept at night because of the low temperature, and all day we were obliged to watch the Russian prisoners bringing out their comrades who had died in the night from hunger or who had simply frozen to death. The impact on Franz was noticeable; for once he was silent. I am sure he was as surprised as I was by the sheer barbarity of what was happening all around us.

Just as I was thinking matters could not possibly get any worse we were confronted by an horrific sight, as were some *Wehrmacht* soldiers standing by, when the SS brought in a small huddle of Jews, men, women and children, put them up against the same blood-spattered concrete wall and shot them with their MP34s.[30]

The four of us had been working on a Stuka, and we just stood looking at the scene not knowing what to think, let alone say. One of the *Wehrmacht* soldiers was the first to speak, telling us he had complained to a senior officer about the SS doing this, and had been told to mind his own business, as the SS were under orders from the highest authority.

'The *Führer*?' I asked.

'That's the person to whom we all swore allegiance,' he said.

I looked over at the Russian prisoners and many of them were standing with their backs to the scene; a few were looking directly at us, and if I thought the Dutch prisoners in the Hague looked at us with distaste, these Russians were looking at us with pure hatred.

---

[30] *Maschinenpistole* 34 made by Waffenfabrik Steyr, machine-guns mainly used by the *Waffen-SS* and still used after the war.

To try to obliterate the events of the afternoon Albert and I played chess that evening, but we played in uncharacteristic silence, both of us immersed in our own thoughts. As we were trying to get some sleep that night Friedrich, who had been out all evening, returned and said all hell had broken lose. Apparently one of our fighter pilots, who was a respected ace and a member of one of the old Prussian families, had witnessed the same events as us, and had complained to the most senior SS officer he could find. He had argued that he objected to having to watch public executions, and more to the point he was angry because such behaviour was upsetting the mechanics, who needed to concentrate fully on the planes to ensure that they were in full working order. There had been threat and counter-threat, and the airwaves had been busy with demands and counter-demands, even as far as Berlin. Friedrich did not know what the conclusion of this debate would be, but suggested that either we would all be moved away from the airstrip or the SS would find another killing spot.

'How can we be moved from the airstrip?' Franz asked.

'That's right,' Friedrich replied, 'so I reckon they'll move their executions elsewhere.'

Food was running short, the temperature was dropping daily, and in the morning there was snow so deep that we knew no planes would be taking off. By mid-morning the Russian prisoners were being organized to clear the snow from the one hardcore runway we had. We were allowed to set up our billet in the concrete sheds where the killings had taken place. There were no bodies outside, but the walls were shattered with bullet holes, and even the drifting snow did not cover the smeared blood on the concrete.

At least it was warmer inside the concrete shed, especially once we had managed to build a fire. Friedrich, who was a brilliant scrounger, came back with two chickens; it was the best supper we had eaten since arriving in Poltava. The smell of the roasting chickens brought several visitors into the shed, but we kept ourselves huddled together in a corner.

The events of the past couple of days had given rise to much discussion, but after our meal we followed Friedrich's example and dropped the subject. I was astonished by Franz's reaction to all this and realized that there was more to him than I had hitherto believed. Friedrich never entered into debates about politics, but Franz and Albert tended to be outspoken. I kept myself to myself because of my fear of being found out as a *mischling*.

We had only just finished our supper when our shed was surrounded by SS troops. A plane was standing on the runway and several fighters were flying around above us. All the senior officers were standing by the plane and we thought that some general must be inside. When the plane door opened, however, all the officers immediately discarded their cigarettes and we knew instantly that the *Führer* had arrived.[31] He stepped down from the plane, completely ignoring the salutes of the senior officers, walked towards the main building while everyone else fell in behind him.

'Didn't expect to see him here,' Albert said.

'Well he hasn't come for your advice,' Friedrich said.

One of the SS soldiers, still standing stiffly to attention, then told us that it was only because of the adverse weather conditions that the plane had landed. He remained at the airfield all that day, not that we saw him, but later the following day we saw a figure, stooping against the wind, hurrying back to the aircraft, as the weather had cleared. He was heavily guarded, almost totally surrounded by SS men. No doubt this was to protect him from being ambushed by bands of partisans operating in the area despite the invasion.

That December was bleak; it was so cold we could not afford to touch metal without gloves on, and we had to melt ice in order to boil a kettle for hot water every day. Engines were difficult to start, and on one occasion we spent half an hour separating some tools which had been left under a wing and had therefore frozen together. Most of the Russian prisoners had died from the cold, but the few that were left were used to keep the snow off the runway, which was an impossible task for people in their condition.

[31] On 3–4 December 1941 Hitler was obliged to put down at Poltava because of weather conditions. He was not happy with the situation and this was to be his last visit to any of the front lines.

Small fires were lit under the two *panzer* tanks in order to be able to start them immediately in the event of an attack.

We heard on the news that Goebbels was asking the German population for winter clothing for the troops. I was surprised, because spare parts for engines were still being delivered, but Franz said it was because everyone had anticipated that the Russian war would be over by the winter. It still struck me as downright stupid that they had sent us into a winter war without appropriate clothing, and were now expecting old women to knit woollen socks.

During that cold December we heard that the *Führer* had declared war on America.[32] We did not hear about Pearl Harbor until later, and I do not think there was a man on that airfield, officer, pilot or even mechanic, who could begin to understand why this had happened – not that it was ever discussed, except amongst the closest of friends. Albert thought the *Führer* had become a megalomaniac; once I would have hit him for this, but now I agreed. It had been a strange month, what with the unexpected arrival of the *Führer* to our base in the middle of nowhere and the declaration of war on America. Now, the pilots told us, the Russians were beginning to fight back.[33]

As my twenty-third birthday approached, I realized that the experiences of 1941 had changed me completely: I was no longer an idealistic youth. My *mischling* status, the treatment of Frau Goldblatt, the reaction to me of the Dutch prisoners, the deliberate starvation of the Russian prisoners, the killing of the commissars without trial and the senseless murder of Jewish women and children, had all caused me to feel differently about everything. Big Bruno and Albert had challenged my way of thinking, and although I still kept my opinions to myself, I now hated the *Führer* and all he stood for. I was a coward, however, because unlike big Bruno and Albert I never expressed an opinion. I now hated the very regime for which I laboured, but I still worked hard at my job because Germany, despite the race laws, was my homeland: I was still German.

[32] On 11 December 1941 Hitler and Mussolini declared war on the USA following the attack on Pearl Harbor on 7 December.
[33] On 8 December 1941 Russian counter-offensive began.

Chapter 10

1942

The New Year began with us being assembled to listen to a broadcast by the *Führer*; he spoke in a frenzied, almost hysterical voice, 'The Jew, will not exterminate the people of Europe; he will be victim of his own machinations instead.'[1] As we stood around in the freezing cold, I could see in my mind's eye, the terrified Jewish family lined up against the wall, and the little girl, dressed in a green skirt, clutching a doll. How could people like that be a threat to the people of Europe? It beggared belief. It was noticeable that no one cheered the speech; we were a mixture of *Luftwaffe*, *Wehrmacht* and *Waffen-SS* troops, and apart from a few of the latter who gave the obligatory '*Heil Hitler*' salute, there was a general silence. It could, of course, just have been that we were frozen rigid, both physically and through our concerns that the Russians were fighting back and heading in our direction. In fact, it was only a few days after this broadcast that Berlin radio admitted that the Russians had penetrated along our lines at several points.

On my twenty-third birthday I was sharing some cheese and biscuits my mother had sent me with Albert and Franz, Friedrich having been called away, when a fresh contingent of SS troops moved into our shed, and made themselves a temporary billet. At first they simply nodded in our direction, and I hoped that they

---

[1] First broadcast on 1 January 1942.

would stay by the main door, but our fire soon brought them to our end of the building. Earlier Friedrich had estimated that the temperature was now about thirty degrees below freezing, and we could hardly expect them not to move towards the warmth. Even Franz, for all his pro-Nazi fervour, however, treated them with some reserve. They were an *Einsatzgruppen*[2] and to our horror we discovered that their job was to exterminate Bolsheviks and Jews. They looked like ordinary soldiers, and when they produced some brandy I confess that we accepted their company and let them share our fire. None of us had had any leave during 1941, and apart from some wine in Sicily and a few beers in Graz, this was the first strong drink we had tasted in a while.

'Where are you heading?' Franz asked.

'Just east as far as we know,' a tall, lean man answered as he poured brandy into our mess cups. 'We have been called in from Auschwitz to bolster the front; the Fuhrer has issued an order that has forbidden any retreat, so as many SS troops as can be mustered are being brought in.'[3]

'And,' another one added, 'we're pleased to be able to fight on the front line; all we've done for the last two weeks is herd Jewish rats into the gas chambers.'[4]

'Gassing?' Albert asked.

No one answered his query. They were more interested in telling us that the best SS troops were heading east because there was a real danger that the Russians were breaking through in the Ukraine. As we were in the centre of the Ukraine, I hoped our troops would hold. They also told us that Field Marshal von Reichenau, who had commanded the 6th Army, which had taken Kiev and Kharkov (the nearest cities to us), had died from a stroke.

---

[2]Mobile killing units or execution squads of Security Police and SS. They moved in to Russia in June 1941.

[3] On 27 January Hitler ordered no retreat, claiming that racial superiority would win in the end, and adding ominously that he would be *eiskalt* (ice-cold) if German people were not prepared to give absolutely everything for the sake of self-preservation.

[4] The gassing of people in Auschwitz-Birkenau started at end of 1941 and beginning of 1942.

In fact, they said that the *Wehrmacht* was in danger of being split by Russian forces.[5] By this stage we were well into the brandy, and the visitors appeared to be saying that they were superior to the *Wehrmacht*, and that was why they were coming to the rescue.

After nearly three hours of solid drinking they mentioned Auschwitz again. We had no idea where or what it was, until they told us it was a concentration camp in Poland. They seemed to enjoy telling us how Jews and other perceived enemies of the Fatherland were being systematically exterminated using gas. Many years later, after the war, I heard many Germans claim that they had no idea what was happening in the death camps. Yet I was only a mechanic but I heard about it within months of it happening. It is true that at an airbase, as I have mentioned many times, we heard much more than ordinary citizens and soldiers, but no one who had fought on the Eastern Front could plead ignorance of the atrocities. If one did not witness the brutality directly, or see some of the consequences, it was certainly widely known.

There was no air activity at the base, owing to the plummeting temperatures and freezing conditions, and apart from checking and rechecking the planes we had plenty of spare time. Albert and I wrapped ourselves up like bears and played chess by the fire. One of the pilots wandered in and asked for a game. He was in his late twenties and had a very pleasant manner; his name was *Hauptmann* Braun, but we were soon calling him Ricky because first names were adopted after several games. Pilots and mechanics rarely mixed but an appreciation for chess brought us together at most airfields if we had time to spare. We were four weeks without a plane taking off, and we were rapidly running out of food. On one occasion Ricky produced some cheese and cold meat and Franz discovered that one of the SS had left a bottle of brandy behind in a cupboard; that was probably the most pleasant afternoon we spent during that wretched winter. Ricky was highly educated, but he rarely mentioned his political views. He seemed to be of the opinion that there was a war on and he was a serving pilot, and that was as far as his opinions went.

[5] In fact on 29 January the German army was split at Kaluga.

He could speak English, and Albert and I were soon practising our limited skills on him. Whenever we played chess we used English expressions, and I think Ricky was bemused to find two mechanics wanting to learn a language out of mere curiosity.

There was a great deal of activity with the *Wehrmacht* troops stationed nearby; they were coming and going, using horses mainly because many of the trucks and track machines were impossible to start in the freezing conditions. Ricky said he had heard the Russians were breaking through the lines north of us, and that while the winter held they would hold up better than our forces. Our aircraft were still grounded and we had run out of supplies which, as we were now too far from Germany for our supply lines to reach us by land, made the future look bleak.

'You would have thought that the generals would have taken the winter into account,' Albert said.

'Indeed,' Ricky replied. 'But they were confident Moscow would fall before Christmas, and we are not accustomed to weather like this.'

At the beginning of March there were signs of a thaw and at last the aircraft were taking to the skies once more. This meant we were active again, but the *Wehrmacht* were still experiencing serious problems with their vehicles because the thaw had turned everything into a quagmire. We were all terribly hungry and suffering from a lack of essential components for some of our engines; we had at least four fighters grounded because we lacked spare parts. We thought of stripping one of them to use for spares, but as they all had defective, or shot-up cooling systems, there really was no point. We heard on the radio that Berlin had admitted there was a food shortage, especially for the 16th Army, which was on the front line. This was not welcome news, especially when we heard that the Russians had retaken Yucknov[6] and that the RAF had not only attacked Kiel but had done some serious damage.[7] Ricky said the main problem was that the *Luftwaffe* was too preoccupied with the Russian war to give sufficient attention to the west of Europe. Big Bruno had once said

[6] On 5 March 1942.
[7] 12 March 1941.

177

that a war fought on two fronts was a war lost.

One wet, cold Sunday morning we were approached by a senior officer who told us that a Bf109 had made a forced landing twenty miles east of us, towards Kharkov, and said we were to go with a contingent of soldiers, to strip this aircraft for parts, so that we could hopefully get some of our grounded fighters back into the air. Friedrich selected Franz and me to do this, and so, for the first time in the war, I found myself armed and travelling with about twenty *Wehrmacht* soldiers towards the front lines. It was the first time I had actually been off that airfield, and I was surprised by the size of Poltava and the number of soldiers there. As we headed out towards Kharkov I have to confess that I felt some trepidation about what we would find, and was quite happy to sit by the engine-lifting gear stacked at the back of the lorry. The soldiers thought we would be safe but said that the occasional small band of partisans or group of troops, who used to penetrate the lines as reconnaissance, could cause us problems if they crossed our path.

The countryside was not beautiful; it was very flat, and where there was no snow the ground was thick mud. For the first few miles we could not see any sign of the war, but in one spot we saw a group of tanks and trucks that had been burned out. There were half-frozen bodies everywhere; one in particular caught my attention because he appeared to be standing, still frozen to the side of a Russian tank. The soldiers told me that they buried our men, but they never bothered to do so with the Russians. Suddenly we turned off the main road and headed towards a more hilly area. I only hoped that someone was reading a map, and that we were heading in the right direction. I also wondered how long we would be out because it was already noon and we had not yet reached the Bf109 site.

When we did find it I could see that only the engine would be worth saving; how the pilot had managed to get out of this aircraft was unfathomable. Franz pointed out to the officer that we would need nearly all the men to assist with the lifting gear. They were just as keen as we were to get the job done as fast as possible, so he ordered five men to stand as look-outs while the rest worked with Franz and me. Franz removed the guns and bits and pieces that could be taken out quickly, while I checked the engine. This was not a five-minute job and I had to explain to the *Wehrmacht* officer the nature of the problem.

'We don't want to be out here at night,' he said. 'It still gets cold and I have the distinct impression that we're being watched.'

We had about five hours of daylight left, and we would need every minute. Somewhere in the background, to the east of us, we could hear artillery explosions, and at one point another Bf109 swooped down towards us; I could see that he was about to attack us but some frantic waving of arms persuaded him we were friends, and he moved off waggling his wings.

Franz and I managed to resolve most of the problems and had removed all the engine holding bolts by four in the afternoon. I was about to ask one of the soldiers helping us to pass me the grip chains when there was the crackle of gunfire and I became conscious of bullets passing close by my head, sounding like fast-flying bees. I turned to look in the direction of some nearby trees, and saw that the soldier to whom I had just spoken was flat on his back with a gaping wound across his face. Franz grabbed me by the leg and pulled me down, screaming, 'Get down you bloody fool, you'll get yourself shot.' I fell across the body of the soldier, who although dead was still twitching. Even under fire I still felt sickened by the sight of a fallen comrade who was twitching even after death: I had no idea that a dead body could still move.

I was aware that the enemy were in a wood about 300 metres from us, but could not see exactly where. Our soldiers were true professionals. They had already fallen flat to the ground and were immediately seeking cover behind the plane. Several were returning fire where they could see the flash of a gun. Franz passed me my rifle, which I had left by the plane's smashed undercarriage. Our officer was trying to make contact with our base on a small radio but it was apparent that it was not working. He told us all to fan out as widely as possible and to try to close in on the small wood, which projected out from more trees behind. I wondered how many of the enemy were hiding amongst the foliage. Franz was taking the stick-grenades from the shoulder strap of a soldier who had been killed with the first shots. I waited for him, and then we and three or four others worked our way round to the left-hand side of the wood. I had to admire the soldiers who, instead of following my instinct to get clear, were now pushing towards the enemy. The firing from the wood was spasmodic but seemed all too accurate; especially when spurts of dirt flew up in front of my face. The light was not very good by this time, and I feared I would be lost in the dark, so I made a point of keeping my eye on Franz.

One of the soldiers had managed to get very close to the wood and was trying to signal something to the others that I could not quite understand. Suddenly, to his right, I saw someone moving towards him. I looked very carefully along my rifle through the sights and squeezed the trigger. In my early training I had been a good shot at the rifle range, and I hit this target with ease. I saw him stand with his arms outstretched and fall forward into the field. As he fell there was a massive explosion, which I think was caused by a hand grenade he had been about to throw. After this the firing increased and Franz touched my leg, telling me to keep down. Two of our soldiers had entered the wood at the flanks, and the officer yelled at us to identify our targets before shooting our own men amongst the trees. There was some more gunfire, then everything fell silent. We were ordered forward and found that the partisans had disappeared into the larger woods behind; they had been firing at us from a sort of woody salient. It was now almost dark, and we were told to penetrate the woods by 100 metres or so to make sure it was clear. That was when I had the fright of my life. I had walked forward with considerable caution, and was just returning when I saw Franz pointing his rifle directly at me from thirty metres. I was about to ask him what the hell he was doing when he fired and I swear I felt the draught of his bullet as it passed my cheek, killing a partisan, who had appeared directly behind me. Franz had saved my life by watching my back; the partisan was about to shoot me but Franz got in first. In fact, Franz had probably saved my life three times that afternoon. He could say what he liked in future; I knew I would always be indebted to him for my life.

As we regrouped by the edge of the wood I saw the figure I had killed and was stunned to see it was a young woman. 'Don't feel bad about that,' the *Wehrmacht* officer said. 'They're just as dangerous as the men, and she was about to put that bomb into Werner's mouth. You did well to shoot her when you did.'

I nodded but did not say anything; I could not feel elated about killing anyone, let alone a woman, but in a situation like that one fights back. Years later I had nightmares about some of the things I had seen, but the young female partisan, dead and twisted at my feet, became more prominent in my mind when, years later, I started to question why we were in the Ukraine in the first place.

'In fact,' the officer continued, 'for a pair of *Luftwaffe* garage boys you were quite impressive.'

I was about to reply when we were obliged to hit the mud once more; a Russian fighter, a Yak, had suddenly zoomed down towards us and strafed the ground. I pressed my face closely into the mud, hoping the ground would swallow me up. Three times the Yak returned. It was absolutely terrifying being under attack from a fighter plane; the increasing noise of the engine and the blazing guns gave me the sensation that it was diving straight at me. On the third sortie he hit one of our trucks, then the Bf109, as well as three of the soldiers. He then seemed to run out of ammunition because he was up and away in seconds. We were stuck in the middle of nowhere; one lorry and the Bf109 were in flames. In that strange, alien field, by the light of the fires and the disappearing sun we hastily dug four graves for our comrades. We left the two dead partisans where they had fallen. By the time we had finished we were all exhausted, and it was pitch dark; apart from flickering shadows caused by the burning truck and plane we could see nothing.

'Gather round,' the officer said. 'We're going to move away from the edge of the wood; it's too dangerous to stay here. But we shall not try to make it back tonight; we're going to find somewhere to bivvy down until first light.'

We could not all get in the truck, so it moved slowly along to enable those who were walking to keep up. After nearly two hours we found a deserted, burnt-out farmhouse and parked the truck beside a fallen barn. The officer divided us into two groups; one would sleep in the truck while the second kept guard, and every three hours we would change over. I was glad to sleep for the first three hours, and despite my taut nerves I slept like the proverbial log. When it was my turn to be on guard duty I was positioned to the east of the farm building. I have to confess I was terrified. Every sound, every shadow made me jumpy. At one stage I thought I saw someone sneaking towards me but it was nothing, just fear. Even though it was bitterly cold I felt as if I were sweating, and I kept the safety catch on my rifle off throughout my two watches.

Nothing happened during the night and at first light we started to head towards the main Kharkov to Poltava road. Our luck had changed; the only planes we saw were ours and within an hour of finding the main road we met a convoy heading in our direction, and the walkers were given a lift. I was walking at the time, and when I jumped into the back of the truck I discovered it was full of wounded men. Some of the wounds were simply appalling. The floor of the truck was slippery with blood, and although the men were quiet, I could see from their faces that every bump the truck hit caused many of them excruciating pain. One man asked me for a cigarette; I offered him my pipe but he refused. Another man pointed to his pocket, where I found a packet, so I lit one for the first man and placed it in his mouth.

I was extremely glad to be back in the safety of the airfield, away from all the suffering. I told Albert that we were really fortunate to be so cocooned, having seen something of what the soldiers had to live with; they must become accustomed to living in constant fear, always alert, with the prospect of being badly wounded hanging over them all the time.

'While you were away yesterday,' Albert said, 'they flew in eight planes of wounded soldiers. There's obviously a fierce battle taking place east of Kharkov.'

That night I thanked Franz for saving my life, but he brushed it aside and said he knew I would have done the same.

By the end of April the four of us were all pretty fed up at having had no leave. We had been on the go for nearly a year and a half, with only the occasional weekend off. The post from home only came through every now and then, and was weeks out of date by the time it reached us. Our food had improved, but it was still not enough to make us feel comfortable; and we found that the easiest way to wind Friedrich up was to talk about different meals that we would like to eat.

Ricky was right about the influence of weather on war; as spring gave way to a warmish summer our troops started to go on the offensive once again. The troops in our area[8] were attacking Izyum, which was a salient east of Kharkov, thus halting the Soviet offensive which had started to draw uncomfortably close to our area. Then we heard that we had won a major battle at Kharkov,[9] which made it as though the war was going our way once again. The news from Germany was not so good; we heard that the RAF had bombed Cologne[10] reducing it to rubble by using over a thousand bombers.

'I didn't think the English had that number of planes,' Franz said.

'I bet they are producing them faster than we are,' Friedrich said.

I have to confess that I believed that Franz was right; like him, I thought the British were just a thorn in our side, but this massive raid made it clear that they had the materials, and were keen to destroy us.

At the end of May the airfield was suddenly flooded with *Leibstandarte*, a special SS unit used to guard the *Führer*. That night, Ricky confirmed that the *Führer* was coming next morning: he was to take his plane up to check that there were no Russian planes lurking in the area.[11] We never saw the *Führer* because he was totally surrounded by the *Leibstandarte*, and we were busy in the hangars trying to keep the Bf109s in the air despite a lack of spares. We were, however, very aware of the high degree of security in the area. We heard on the radio that the *Führer* was returning to Berlin for the state funeral of Heydrich,[12] who had been killed by agents flown in from England. It seemed amazing that the British could carry out such a mission without getting caught until after the deed. The amount of security surrounding

[8] Army Group South.
[9] On 28 May 1942. Kharkov was the second largest city in the Ukraine.
[10] On 30 May 1942. The first 1,000 bomber raid was against Cologne.
[11] On 1 June 1942 Hitler visited Army Group South HQ at Poltava.
[12] On 9 June 1942.

the *Führer* started to make sense. We were also quite surprised that he had returned to Poltava, which I had learned from my sortie out of the airfield was not far from the front line.

During that summer the tide of war really seemed to be turning in our favour once again. On the other side of Kharkov a battle was fought in which a whole Russian army was crushed, and by the end of the month there was a major victory for the German 6th Army, led by General von Paulus, at Kharkov and Donetz, where we established bridgeheads over the Don.[13] There was no question that we were once again in the ascendancy, but there was a price to pay. Several times we put our work aside to help carry the wounded on to planes heading for Germany. I shall never forget some of the horrific injuries we saw. How some of the men remained alive after having been so hideously injured, was beyond belief, and said a great deal for human endurance and the will to live. One man had no legs, one arm was missing and half his jaw had been blown away, and still he lived. He had been pumped full of drugs and as I saw his transport plane take to the air I asked myself what the medics could do for him, and if they succeeded, what his life would be like afterwards. Another man had his stomach in a bag. A medic said that he was being taken back for the sake of the other wounded soldiers who were watching, but they thought he would be dead by the time the plane landed. I could see in their faces the horrors they had endured. I was also constantly amazed at the number of new troops arriving daily; they were either younger than the men we had been used to seeing or much older, but they continued to come and we wondered when this human resource would dry up.

We were told that our troops were fighting their way to the oilfields, and that the next city to fall would be Stalingrad. We also heard that the Russians were resisting with true grit and great determination. I detected a growing respect for the Russian soldiers amongst some of the ground troops to whom we occasionally spoke.

We saw less of Ricky during the summer because his plane was airborne nearly every minute of the day and he needed sleep after

[13] On 26 June 1942.

his missions. We were unbelievably busy, with serious problems with spare parts. At one stage I had three DB601 engines in the hangar that needed parts and could not therefore be put back in their planes until we had the promised delivery. It was only when we were flying at fifty per cent of our capacity that the senior officers really started to shout and parts started to arrive. That in itself was pleasing, but for three weeks during August we were working eighteen-hour days without any breaks.

We could tell by the wounded coming and going through the airfield that the fighting at the front was fierce. Our troops continued to be successful: Tikhovetok fell in the Kuban area and we seized Armaviv on the River Kuban.[14] Then a few days later Surovikino,[15] just west of Stalingrad, fell to Army Group B, whilst Army Group A captured the oilfields at Maykop and Krasnodar in the Caucasus. It seemed that our military prowess was once again in the ascendancy, especially when we heard that a British raid on the French coast at Dieppe had been repulsed with ease.[16] Ricky was able to tell us that Stalingrad was on the verge of collapse, and the *Luftwaffe* was bombing that city to a pile of rubble. I was pleased to hear we were doing well, but Albert was concerned about the rise in civilian casualties, though he only ever dared mention this to me.

At the start of the winter, just as Ricky had predicted, the Russians seemed to gather strength and hold the line inside Stalingrad. We soon gained the impression that our troops' summer successes had come to a halt, and they were not alone; the Russian resistance could also be seen in the air. The number of Soviet planes was increasing and some of their aircraft were not only faster than ours but could turn more quickly in combat. They had a new ground-attack plane which made a sudden and devastating appearance and was causing our troops serious problems.[17] Indiscriminate bombing of Stalingrad had to be avoided as our troops were involved in hand to hand fighting with

[14] On 6 August 1942.
[15] On 8 August 1942.
[16] On 19 August 1942.
[17] The Il-2 Shturmovik. A total of 36,163 were built.

the Soviets in the centre of the city.

During that winter we began to realize that we were not the only country able to create effective technology. Our planes were falling behind both in development and in production. The good old DB601 engines were no longer up to fighting standards. We were obliged to modify the Bf109s by changing the somewhat vulnerable cooling system, and by removing all the external fittings in order to improve the aerodynamics, as well as adding heavier armament. We also saw the arrival of the FW.190, which was more capable of challenging the increasing dexterity of the Soviet aircraft. I foresaw that the FW.190 would soon replace our beloved Bf109s, although none of us were fully trained to work on this particular aircraft.

Not only did the temperatures start to fall rapidly during November, making life in our concrete shed once again extremely uncomfortable, but the general news was far from good. We heard that the Russians had started a major counter-offensive[18] and that the British were starting to gain the ascendancy in North Africa. It struck us as incredible that they were not only defending themselves but were attacking Germany and successfully advancing in North Africa. The worst news of all was that the Red Army had met at Kalach, thus encircling the whole of the 6th Army which was still fighting in Stalingrad. We had been well and truly outwitted by the Russian generals.

It seemed that 1942 was going to end, as it had begun, with icy cold weather and defeat staring us in the face once more. Then, like a bolt out of the blue, a relief team of mechanics arrived and we discovered that after nearly two years we had been given leave. Within three hours of the new team arriving we had packed and were sitting in our transport plane waiting to fly to Berlin. I never saw Ricky again and learned years later that he had been shot down somewhere on the Eastern Front in January 1943.

I was overwhelmed with happiness to be going home to Berlin. Leaving when we did probably saved our lives, because the situation on the Eastern Front deteriorated rapidly, and soon the only way home was walking. But we did not escape completely

[18] On 19 November 1942 at 8.50 a.m.

We had been airborne for about five minutes when our plane came under attack by a Soviet fighter. We could see nothing, but were tossed about and turned upside down as our Dornier tried to avoid the hail of machine-gun bullets. When a trail of bullets ripped through the fuselage I caught one in the shoulder. At first I thought I had just knocked my weak shoulder against the door hinge, but Franz held me down, pressing his scarf against my shoulder, from which seemed to pour an endless stream of blood. Strangely I experienced no pain but I felt faint. The Dornier survived the skirmish and Franz and Albert took turns in trying to stem the bleeding from my wound: I was worried, but like all young people did not think for one moment I would die. When we arrived in Berlin I said my farewells to my friends from a stretcher as I was carried to a truck, which took me to hospital. As soon as they had disappeared from sight the wound in my shoulder really hurt, probably because my friends had been applying direct pressure to the wound, which had helped stem the pain. I spent that Christmas in a military hospital, and thought it best not to let my parents know where I was, as they would have been too distressed by my plight. My meeting with them would have to wait until January, when I hoped to be discharged. Albert, Franz and Friedrich all visited me at different times, and I realized that despite the evils of war we had formed the closest of friendships; we were like a close-knit family.

Chapter 11

1943

I was fortunate not to suffer a great deal of pain from my wound, for although the bullet had damaged the muscles, the bones were intact. When I eventually left the hospital they told me to keep my arm in a sling for at least three weeks, exercising it gently each day. It was impossible for me to lift anything because my left arm felt as if it had lost all its power. I felt fortunate, despite my injury, because I was surrounded in that hospital by men so badly wounded, and in so much pain, that it put my one bullet wound into perspective. The man in the next bed was in agony all the time, and only slept when he was pumped full of morphine. The hospital was packed, and in my ward there was barely room for a nurse or doctor to walk between the beds.

I left the hospital on 11 January to make my way home, only to discover that there was no one there. I had not written to my mother because I did not want to worry her. I found the back door key under the stone, where we kept it for just such an eventuality. The house was as familiar as ever, but I could see, and feel, that it had been empty for some time. I sat at the table with a growing sense of panic, wondering what on earth had happened. It was impossible for my mother to be away on holiday, those days were gone. The first clue was the clock on the sideboard which had stopped; when wound up it would go for four days at a time. The second was that there was no food in the house, and the final straw came when I saw all the post on the doormat, some of which was two weeks old. I was full of foreboding; I found the whole situation alarming. Eventually I asked our next-door neighbour, Frau Braun. She was very surprised that I did not know that my parents had left a month before; no one had seen them since. She looked at me extremely oddly, almost scrutinizing me, but I put this down to the fact that I must have changed since she last saw me.

Then I remembered Aunt Ingrid, who lived in the Sophienstrasse, and made my way to the centre of Berlin to call on her. I caught a train and, as it travelled along, I was astonished at the vast swathes of the city that had been seriously bombed or abandoned. I had known that Berlin had been bombed, but had no idea as bad as I found it. I noticed that the city looked drab and tired, as did many of my fellow travellers, and I guessed that the war was also beginning to take its toll on the civilians. At the front I had always imagined that life at home was continuing as usual, and certainly my mother's letters had given me that impression.

I arrived at Aunt Ingrid's flat at 4 p.m., by which time it was already becoming dark. I knocked on the door but there was no answer. I knocked again and still there was no answer. By this time I was both baffled, and a little scared, about what was happening. I walked the streets for another hour and tried again, but still no response. Standing outside I could see a light on in one of Aunt Ingrid's windows, so I went up and tried again, and bellowed through the letterbox that I was there. Immediately the door was opened and my mother fell into my arms.

'I've been knocking for hours,' I said as I hugged her. 'Why didn't you answer?'

My father appeared looking so different I could hardly believe my eyes. He had lost at least half of his body-weight and his face was sallow and drawn. His jowls had turned to layers of skin. I shook his hand and then hugged him.

That evening they told me all that had happened to them. Josef, in his anxiety to prove he was not Jewish, had had some official double-check my father's background, and it had transpired that both his parents were Jewish. The fact that they were Christian Jews was irrelevant; my father was therefore a Jew and as a consequence of this he had been thrown off the railways a year ago. He had had no idea that he was of Jewish extraction, but once the officials knew, he was fired from his job the very same day.

'Are you ashamed of me?' my father suddenly asked.

'Why should I be ashamed of you? You're my father and I shall always love you.'

I cannot recall the whole of the conversation we had that evening, but it was mainly gloomy if not downright depressing. Once my father had been branded a Jew some of the neighbours had been extremely unpleasant, especially Frau Braun, of all people. This angered me, because my mother had always looked after her when she had been ill, and my father had always dug over her small vegetable patch for her so that she could plant vegetables. When my mother heard that the *Gestapo* were rounding up all the Jews in Germany and transporting them east, they simply fled and hid in Aunt Ingrid's flat. She no longer worked as a manager in the shop; she now assisted in one of the many makeshift hospitals, which were becoming fully stretched. As they feared a call from the *Gestapo* they made a point of never answering the door, which was why I had been left outside until they heard my call through the letterbox. My father hid under the bed when anyone knocked on the door.

'I am a decorated soldier from the last war,' my father said. 'I have served Germany all my life, and now I am reduced to hiding under the bed.'

I described what I had seen in the east and told my father that it was best to keep hiding, because *lebensraum* was complete nonsense; most of us suspected the Jews were being exterminated. I felt that this was a bitterly cruel thing to say, but I did not want my father to be caught and transported to Poland. I need not have told him because as a train driver he already had some idea what was happening to the Jews. My mother was working as a bus cleaner, and by using their savings, plus some help from Aunt Ingrid, they were just about surviving. As I had already discovered, food was very scarce, even in Berlin, and ordinary families were finding it difficult to cope.

When I asked my mother why they had chosen to live with

Aunt Ingrid, she said it was because she had so few neighbours nearby and there was less chance of discovery. It was unusual for the buildings in Sophienstrasse to be used as ordinary flats because it was such a commercial area. My father was virtually a prisoner in the flat; he rarely went out of the building for fear of being rounded up.

I told my parents all that had happened to me, and shared some of the views which I now held as a consequence of meeting big Bruno and Albert. My mother was anxious for me, saying that I should always keep my ideas to myself. She snatched up a Bible and told me to read Psalm 31 verse 13: 'I hear the whispering of the crowd; fear is on every side, as they scheme together against me as they plot to take my life.'

'Bruno,' she said, 'your work has put you in danger, but as your father is suddenly a Jew, you are a *mischling*, which means you are in even more danger on the streets of this city.'

I was tired and so slept on a mattress on the floor in the dining room. By the time I woke up next morning Aunt Ingrid was asleep in her room, and my mother was out. My father was sitting at the table, looking at me whilst I slept. He helped me to clean my wound and we ate some ghastly brown bread and drank ersatz coffee together. He was now a deeply distressed man, but I noticed that after all that had happened he harboured no sense of bitterness.

'The only regret I have,' he said, 'is the way I used to judge Jews. Not just because I now know my parents were Jews, but because I, like all the others, am as human as anyone else, and just as German as any Nazi.'

'What I don't understand,' I replied, 'is how, in the middle of a serious war, the *Reich* can spend so much time and energy persecuting Jews who would willingly fight for their country.'

My father agreed with me, pointing out that there had been times, when he was on the railways, when trains meant for troop transport were being used to ferry Jews to the East.

I decided to go for a walk, but my father thought he had better stay indoors. I could see from the shops that the merchandise was limited and very expensive, and there was not much food. I saw some bomb damage close to the centre of the city as I walked along towards the Tiergarten Park where I found a seat and smoked my pipe in relative peace. There was a smattering of snow on the ground, but after the Ukraine it did not feel cold. I had not been there long when a *Wehrmacht* officer joined me to smoke his pipe. Like me he had one arm in a sling and it was not long before we were chatting about how we had been wounded. He had been flown out of Stalingrad a few weeks before, and considered himself lucky. His wound had looked more serious than it was, and as no planes had been able to land near Stalingrad since he was evacuated he was relieved to be alive. He told me that the fighting in the city had been hand to hand and ruthless: no prisoners were taken and no mercy was shown. Apart from the fighting the main problem was a lack of food. They were lucky to get a slice of bread and a bowl of thin soup. Dogs and horseflesh were considered a treat and he suspected that rats were being grilled when the opportunity arose.[1] He told me in a conspiratorial way that he thought the 6th Army would not be able to survive unless they were rescued by Manstein's army, or the *Luftwaffe* were able to bring more troops in. The trouble was that the *Luftwaffe* no longer had control of the skies. He also told me that he had heard that the siege of Leningrad was not going well.[2] All in all the future looked depressing, even though the Berlin radio stated that we were winning the war. Many civilians believed the wireless until they were told in confidence, by a family member who had been to the Eastern Front, just how grim it all was. As we sat there I noticed that the park was full of people in uniforms, many of them, like me and my companion, obviously recovering from various injuries.

I popped back to the flat to tell my father that I was going to see big Bruno and Marie. I was there that evening, and stayed for the night. Big Bruno had also lost weight, but seemed more angry than sad about the war.

'We're not fighting on two fronts but on several,' he said. 'We are being bombed from the west, we're fighting for our lives in

---

[1] By January 1943 the German rations in Stalingrad were 1¾ oz of bread and 1¾ pints of vegetable soup.

[2] On 11 January 1943 the siege of Leningrad was broken.

the Soviet Union and now in Africa the British have the upper hand, as they do in the rest of the Mediterranean.[3] Even the Berlin broadcasts admit there are problems in Stalingrad, and from what I hear we are going to be defeated there as well.'

I told him about my father's plight, and he warned me that he was right to stay hidden. The *Gestapo* had rounded up every Jew that big Bruno knew, and they were now seeking out those Jewish men married to German women: I found this especially frightening because that was my father's situation.[4]

'We're living in dangerous times,' big Bruno said. 'The rest of the world are at war with us, and we're at war with ourselves. If you talk about anything other than victory you talk in a whisper.'

'We are being heavily bombed,' I said.

'That I do not understand,' big Bruno replied. 'Goering claimed they would never reach Berlin, and all our planes are in the east, so why are we under no pressure to build more; we're still building the same amount of planes as we were three years ago. We're led by hyper-egotistical and evil men.' He explained that the mass of the population still believed that the *Führer* would lead Germany to victory, and the bombing was making them hate the enemy as much as the *Führer* did; it unified them. For years we had been told that the Third *Reich* would dominate the world for years to come, and most people still believed this to be true.

I was back at Aunt Ingrid's flat in time to celebrate my twenty-fourth birthday. Aunt Ingrid had managed to get some sausage meat, and I found some beer for my father and me, and some fortified wine for my mother and Aunt Ingrid. I cannot say it was a happy occasion, and although Aunt Ingrid pulled my leg about not having a girlfriend, most of the evening we discussed the war and my father's safety.

The next morning we heard that the Americans had bombed Wilhelmshaven and set much of the city on fire. I think that was the first time that the Americans had bombed Germany, although I gathered from my father that they had heavily bombed Lille,

[3] At 5 a.m. on 23 January 1943 the British Army entered Tripoli.
[4] The deportation of German Jews started as early as October 1942.

where I had been in France. In the same depressing broadcast we were told that all men aged between sixteen and sixty-five years of age and women from seventeen to forty-five years were to register for defence work.[5] My mother and Aunt Ingrid decided to ignore this, since they were in full-time work; my father was the problem, because my mother would not even use his ration card because it had *Juden* stamped across its cover.

On the last Saturday of the month I made my way to big Bruno's house for a game of chess that evening, intending to stay over until the Monday morning. I was walking down the Sophienstrasse when I heard planes in the sky and the 'clack-clack' of anti-aircraft guns. The sirens started to sound, and people ran for cover; trams and buses stopped as people fled to the nearest cellar or shelter. I could see, high in the sky, a large fleet of bombers, and even as I watched bombs cascaded down on the south of the city. It struck me that there were no *Luftwaffe* fighters in the air, and the enemy had the audacity to bomb the capital city in broad daylight.[6] I did not rush for a shelter but watched out of sheer curiosity the British planes descending with impunity; the anti-aircraft gunnery seemed to be totally ineffective.

Eventually I did find a shelter, when the planes wheeled in my direction. I could feel the ground shudder, even though the bombs were dropping a fair distance away. A woman was crying in the corner of the shelter, and a man shouted at me, asking why the *Luftwaffe* was not doing something about the problem. I pointed out that I was a mechanic not a General, but nevertheless decided to risk the outside rather than suffer his personal abuse. It was a quick raid and I saw the planes turning away as I surfaced. Even from ground level I could see smoke rising from several directions, and I decided to check that the Sophienstrasse had not been hit, so I retraced my steps. All was well; it seemed

[5] On 13 January 1943 Hitler approved special measures for mobilizing all men and women, and on 21 January *Gauleiter* Suckel ordered all men and women of certain ages to report and register for defence work.
[6] On 30 January 1943 the RAF bombed Berlin in daylight and there was also a saturation attack on Hamburg.

that this area of Berlin had remained unscathed. Nevertheless, it was a frightening experience and reminded me that, thanks to enemy aircraft, civilians were also under attack. Apart from my skirmish with the partisans in the Ukraine I had always felt safe, even when just behind the lines. On Sunday, at big Bruno's, we heard that the Russians were heading towards Kharkov, which made me wonder whether we would be returning to Poltava when my leave finished after all. We also heard that Hamburg had been seriously hit; even the Berlin radio admitted that the city appeared to be on fire.

At the beginning of February the weather seemed a little brighter, and it almost felt as if a touch of spring were in the air. I was beginning to miss Albert's company, but the hospital had signed me off until the beginning of March. Normally, I would have been grateful to have time with my parents, but I was actually beginning to miss my work mates, and home life was stressful. Big Bruno and I played chess quite often, but I felt guilty if I stayed away from my parents too long, so I was careful with my time.

One Wednesday morning we were all listening to the radio when the news broke that Stalingrad had been lost, and General von Paulus had surrendered.[7] As a result of this defeat all theatres and cinemas were closed for three days as an act of mourning.[8] Big Bruno said it was the turn of the tide against us, and that in a few years the Russians would be in Berlin. I was not sure whether to believe him or not, but his predictions had been on the ball in the past, and I felt he could be right once again.

February was a strange month for me; I was not used to having nothing to do, and although my wound had healed, my arm was still very weak. I tried but failed to make contact with Albert, and I guessed, having heard that Kharkov was virtually in Russian hands,[9] that my team would not be going back to the Ukraine. One Wednesday evening big Bruno and I were listening to the

[7] On 31 January 1943 General von Paulus surrendered with some 250,000 troops.
[8] On 4–6 February 1943.
[9] On 16 February 1943 the Russians were inside Kharkov.

Führer on the radio; he sounded strained but defiant as he said, 'We shall break and smash the might of the Jewish world coalition, and mankind struggling for its freedom and we will win the final victory in the struggle.'[10]

'I don't know where he gets this Jewish coalition from,' big Bruno said. 'As far as I know the Soviets are not the greatest lovers of Jewish people, and very few of them live in England, or so I'm told.'

'The English aren't anti-Semitic, are they?' I asked.

'Only some in their upper classes. I heard once that when some Fascists marched through London both Jews and English people threw bricks at them.'[11]

As I travelled home that night I heard bombs falling in the distance; the bombing was occurring almost daily.[12] However, the raids were put into perspective once I arrived at Aunt Ingrid's flat, as I found my mother in a terrible state: that afternoon the *Gestapo* had broken the door in and taken my father away.[13] I wanted to try to find out what had happened, but my mother gripped me by the arms and made me swear that I would do no such thing. All the rebellion in me turned to pure hatred. My father had fought for Germany, I was fighting for Germany and was currently giving the country the best years of my life, and yet they had taken him away. It is difficult now to express the sheer hatred I felt then.

I have never known a woman with as much love and loyalty as my mother. Next morning she was up and out of the house at first light to try to find out where they were holding my father. Apparently they had taken him to an old Jewish community centre in the Rossenstrasse, which was a little side street not far from Alexanderplatz, and quite near Aunt Ingrid's flat. She told me that there were a lot of German women standing outside

[10] Broadcast on 24 February 1943.

[11] Probably a reference to Oswald Moseley and the East End riots before the war.

[12] On 28 February 1943 the RAF began round the clock bombing offensive.

[13] On 27 February 1943 the Berlin *Gestapo* rounded up 4,700 Jews married to non-Jews.

demanding the return of their husbands, but they had been told that the Jews were going to be transferred to Auschwitz. I froze; I recalled all that I had heard of that camp and my heart sank. I also knew that a group of German housewives would not be able to convince the *Gestapo* to change their minds, or to overrun the SS guards at the entrance. Even the Soviets feared the fanatical ferocity of SS troops.

My mother went back that afternoon and I followed at a discreet distance. She was absolutely right, in the Rossenstrasse hundreds of women were standing outside the old Jewish centre, which was being guarded by SS troops. I had promised my mother that I would keep my distance, but when she saw me, she and another woman, Frau Friedenthal if I remember correctly, told me to go. I never disobeyed my mother, not even as a 24-four-year old. I went round the corner but returned a few minutes later to find another vantage point from which to observe what was happening. One of the women, or it might have been one of the many children present, threw a brick through the window. Within seconds the SS troops had surrounded the crowd. For a moment the women fell silent, but then I heard Frau Friedenthal scream at the officer on the steps. I found the whole scene totally incredible, as did others when I related this story later in life, but it happened, and I have since read an account by someone else who knew Frau Friedenthal. She was like me, clearly German, tall, fair haired and with blue eyes. She mounted the steps to the SS officer and bellowed in his face: 'You bloody swine, you're shooting at German women and children here instead of protecting us from the Russians, aren't you ashamed of yourself? Call yourself a soldier?' I could see even from where I stood that the SS officer was clearly embarrassed and called his men away, leaving the women to continue their protest.

My mother went back and forth to the Rossenstrasse for days; she would come home, snatch something to eat, sleep a few hours and then return once more. The women had worked out a rota so there was a large group of them there day and night, shouting and protesting. I knew it would get them nowhere, as did big Bruno when I spoke to him about it later.

I find it difficult to express the incredible joy I felt when, on the first Saturday in March, I went home in the evening and found my father sitting at the table. To my utter astonishment I learnt that the authorities had relented, and most of the Jewish men had been released to their wives.[14] After all that had happened – the atrocities in the east, the bombing in the west, the transportation and extermination of Jews – a few determined German housewives had faced down the hard-nosed *Gestapo*, and made a stand against the cold steel of the SS, and won!

We did not have the food or the energy to celebrate my father's release, as I would have wished, but it was the first happy evening we had shared for a long time. My mother was braver than anyone else I have ever met, either in war or peace. I had seen senior *Wehrmacht* and *Luftwaffe* officers quail before the SS, but not her. She stood her ground and won. This was a sacrificial love that changed my whole perspective of the devotion my parents shared; it personified for me strength, loyalty and love second to none. From that day I hated the Nazis, and I have never entirely trusted any state authority ever since. After the war people have said to me, 'It is easy now to say you hate the Nazis,' but when I tell them of my *mischling* status, followed by the arrest of my father and the Rossenstrasse incident, I think they begin to understand.

The next day I had to call in at the local *Luftwaffe* headquarters, only to find that my leave was over. After the tensions at home and in the city in general it was almost a relief. However, it was immediately clear that I would not return to my usual unit, because my left arm was hardly capable of lifting a spanner. At first I thought they were going to extend my leave, but I was wrong; I was being sent back to Lille, of all places. Apparently the bombing in the west was causing serious

---

[14] On 6 March 1943 Goebbels agreed to avoid a public demonstration. He called the released Jews 'the privileged few'. The incident became known as the Rossenstrasse Riots.

problems,[15] and now that von Manstein's armoured division had recaptured Kharkov,[16] it had been decided that the bombing raids were to be resisted with greater zest. I was given a pass, and having said goodbye to my parents and Aunt Ingrid, I posted a letter to big Bruno and Marie, and made my way out of Berlin to Paris and then on to Lille.

The town had been well and truly devastated by the bombing raids[17] and the destruction I saw caused me to realize how tough the British were if they were prepared to bomb their old ally and friend, just to get at us; but then it was not very long ago that they had sunk the French fleet. I reported to the officer in charge and found that I had become an office boy. I was to answer the phone, do the filing and run errands. I was billeted in town, in the home of a middle-aged woman who obviously resented my presence; for once I understood her feelings and showed her the greatest respect. I looked through the hangars but saw no sign of Albert, Franz and Friedrich anywhere. It was a useful tour because one of the mechanics was struggling with the cooling system on a BD601 engine and I was able to point out what he had to do. After that I was always welcome in the hangars. The rest of 1943 was easy for me in terms of work. Being the office boy was not demanding and I had more free time than I had ever had, and more freedom than anyone else on the airfield. Wherever I went everyone assumed I was on an errand, so, equipped with a brown envelope in my hand, I could come and go when and where I pleased. I might have a weak arm and a hole in my shoulder, but I had certainly landed on my feet.

The airfield at Lille now had several components. There was a small *transportgeschwader* ('transport wing') and a small

[15] On 5 March 1943 during a raid over Essen 150 4,000 lb bombs were dropped in forty minutes. On 17 March Berlin radio announced that 20,000 people were homeless in Munich and a further 100,000 in Essen, Duisburg, Bottrop and Stuttgart. On 27 March the RAF carried out the heaviest bombing raid on Berlin.

[16] On 10 March 1943.

[17] On 9 October 1942 a heavy bombing raid was carried out to destroy industrial plants.

küstenfliegergruppe ('coastal defence group') and some fighters, which were mainly used at night. With the increase in bombing raids it had become a battle of technical ingenuity. Some of our fighters were now equipped with *Lichtenstein* (airborne radar) and the *Luftwaffe* began to use a system code-named Wilde Sau, in which single-engined fighters worked in liaison with searchlight teams. The British and Americans dropped metal strips to confuse our radar, and sometimes they flew in a different direction to make us think there would be a raid in the south, when the main attack was in fact taking place in the north.[18] We had to devise an overland plotting system, so the Observer Corps suddenly grew in importance. Every now and then we were visited by *Oberst* Herrmann, who was responsible for the night defences. The Lille airfield was now basically an early-warning station, especially as most of the raids were occurring north of us, many passing over Denmark.

The chief man, as far as I was concerned, was *Oberst* Georg Freisher. In a twist of fate he almost became a friend of mine, despite the fact that I was at the opposite end of the pecking order in rank. Needless to say it was chess that brought us together. I had entered his office in order to collect some files from him, to take to another building and he was on the phone. Whilst waiting I saw on his desk a beautiful chess set with a game in progress, and after looking at the game could see that if white sacrificed his rook against the black castled-king, then checkmate followed.

'You play chess Sonn?'

'Yes sir, all the time.'

'What would you do with that position?'

I told him and showed him the results, and I could see that he was impressed. The game on the table was a correspondence game with a fellow officer in Paris, and my move pleased the *Oberst* no end. Two days later I was called to his office late in the afternoon to play chess; I definitely had the upper hand. Our games increased as the months went by; in fact there were times when we played chess when we should both have been working.

---

[18] Sometimes called a 'spoof' route.

I had found a senior officer who was as obsessed with the game as me. I was also treated to a cognac every time I played, and although I always respected his rank, we became good friends.

Early in April I was ordered to go with a *Luftwaffe* soldier to collect a British pilot, whose Hurricane had been shot down near a small village which I believe was Estaires. I was given an MP38 sub-machine-gun. As I already had my service Walther-P38 with me, this indicated it might be dangerous. I was somewhat surprised to find that a French *gendarme* was guarding the prisoner. I would have thought that he would have helped him to escape, but I knew that not all the French loved the British. The Englishman was about my age and he, like me, had fair hair and blue eyes. He was obviously annoyed that the Frenchman had informed us of his presence. He was the first Englishman I had ever met which made me curious about him. He shook his head at the Frenchman, and although my English was weak I heard him call him a bloody traitor. The Frenchman raised his fist to punch him, but I deflected the blow with my machine-gun. I saw no point allowing him to hit a man whose only weapon was already in the Frenchman's hand.

The pilot did not even look at me, but gazed around as if there was a bad smell in the air. He was not so much arrogant as aloof, and I sensed that he was not frightened, more disdainful and annoyed with himself for being caught. The *Luftwaffe* soldier searched him for more weapons and took his gun from the Frenchman. We put him in the car and I sat in the back to keep an eye on him. A few people had gathered around, and although my French was almost non-existent I gathered that some of the locals were unhappy with the *gendarme*. The Englishman looked out of the window but said nothing. Although I always smoked a pipe I had been given some small cigars the day before so I offered him one. For the first time he looked at me, took a cigar and, when I lit it for him, thanked me. He did not smile, but examined my uniform with steely eyes.

'Are you *Luftwaffe*?' he asked.

'Yes.'

He nodded, and although I may have misread the signs, he seemed to relax a little and the coldness went out of his eyes. I had to take him to *Oberst* Freisher, and I listened with interest as the *Oberst* asked him questions in very good English. I was pleased that I was able to follow most of what they had to say.

'We are sending you to one of our prison camps, but not before we have to talk to you,' the *Oberst* said.

'You mean interrogate,' the pilot replied.

'No, we're not the *Gestapo*.'

'No, they're too busy murdering people in the Polish forests.'

'I think you will find that was the Russians,' the *Oberst* replied.

'Yes, you would say that.'

I was surprised by his manner and the way he replied to the *Oberst*; he showed no deference for rank and no fear, although he was a prisoner.

'You will be collected in about ten minutes; would you like a small cognac before you go?'

'Thank you.'

'Sonn, pour them out, and one for yourself.'

I was surprised that he offered the pilot a drink and amazed that he should offer me one as well. When the Englishman raised his glass and proposed a toast to the total defeat of Germany, I was speechless. The *Oberst* smiled and said nothing.

When the Englishman had gone, accompanied by two *Luftwaffe* soldiers, the *Oberst* turned to me and said, 'You speak English, Sonn; I asked you to pour the drinks in English, and you responded. I knew you were listening.'

'I have been learning it for some time, sir.'

'You are an interesting man for a mechanic.'

'What did he mean, sir, by the Polish forests?' I asked.

The *Oberst* then told me that German troops had uncovered mass graves in a place called Katyn[19] and that Goebbels was letting the whole world know about the way the Soviets treated people.

'It's not just the Russians, is it, sir?' At first I thought I had overstepped the mark; the *Oberst* said nothing for a moment, then,

[19] German radio announced the Katyn discovery on 12 April 1943, enabling Goebbels to start an anti-Soviet campaign with full vigour. It took many years before the Soviet Union confessed to the deed.

lighting a cigarette he inhaled, blew his smoke over the desk and said, 'I was in the east as well Sonn, but the *Luftwaffe* has never been involved in such atrocities.'

I was dismissed, but as I was opening the door he called me back. 'Sonn, never say what you said to me to anyone else, and never quote me.'

'Of course not, sir.'

As I cycled back to my billet I realized that I should have kept my mouth shut. I would never normally have spoken my mind to any other officer, let alone an *Oberst*; I was fortunate that because we shared a love of chess some of the distinctions which normally occur between differing ranks had been put aside.

My billet was on the outskirts of Lille and as I rounded the corner I saw two *Wehrmacht* soldiers talking to my landlady. I was about to cycle by when I realized that they were not talking to her but demanding to look in her bags. I pulled over immediately, and one of the men came up to me.

'What do you want?' he said sharply.

'I know that lady,' I said, and thinking quickly, added, 'Do you know who she is?'

'No.'

'I will try to put it delicately,' I responded. 'But her closest friend, if you get my meaning, is a senior *Gestapo* officer.'

The soldier looked at me differently, and actually thanked me. He went over to the other soldier and they walked away as if they had received an electric shock. My landlady looked at me for a moment, then nodded and walked towards her house. We did not speak, but that evening I was given a better meal. A few Sundays later I saw her in church, and for the first time she managed to smile at me; progress at last.

I was almost beginning to enjoy my new life. I played chess with the *Oberst* nearly every day, and it was clear he was as fed up with the war as I was. It seemed to be taking place elsewhere. We were all conscious at the airfield that we were there for damage limitation, while the real war was being fought on the Eastern Front. We did not have sufficient planes because of the Russian front, nor sufficient airpower. The *Oberst* told me in June that over 250,000 troops had surrendered to the British in North

Africa;[20] he also told me that he had heard that there had been an armed revolt in the Jewish Ghetto in Warsaw. As we played chess in his office I realized we were no longer anywhere near a front line. We felt safe in France; there was the occasional scare about the Resistance, but they did not pose a threat like that of the partisans in the east. The *Oberst* began speaking English to me as we played chess; I was sharpening up his chess, as he improved my English. Nevertheless, it seemed strange to be forming a relationship with the top man when I was a mere office boy, and other people began to wonder who I really was, as I spent so much time with him. I had been sworn to secrecy about our mutual of love of chess, and in a childish way I quietly enjoyed this special but very unusual relationship.

I enjoyed going to the French church despite their refusal to accept me. Apart from the occasional smile from my landlady, most people ignored me. But I went because I found a deep and satisfying peace listening to the mass.

I was playing chess with the *Oberst* one evening when he told me that in a recent bombing raid over 5,000 people had been killed.[21]

'You remember that downed RAF pilot, Sonn?'

'Yes, sir.'

'He was confident of victory, wasn't he?'

I agreed that that he seemed aloof and that I was bemused by the fact that he had offered a toast to our defeat.

'That's the point, Sonn; he was aloof, because he was confident that we would lose.'

'Lose, sir?' I really did not expect defeatist talk from a senior officer.

'Look at this game,' he said. 'I am two pawns down; I hope to win but I know in my heart of hearts that I can't, not against you.'

'You still have a queen and a rook on the board, sir.'

'You have superior forces; I am only playing in the forlorn hope that you will make a mistake. The British are backed by their colonies, now they have the Americans on their side. And

---

[20] On 10 May 1943. The surrender was in Tunisia.
[21] Probably referring to a raid on Wuppertal on 21 June 1943.

they are fighters. On the other hand we have to fight the weight of the Russians first, and our Italian allies run away at the sight of a heavy gun.'

I decided it was safer not to answer him but nodded.

'Don't worry, Sonn,' he said sensing my uncertainty. 'No one can hear us and I trust you as I hope you do me.'

As the news of the battle of Kursk filtered back, the *Oberst* reckoned that the war had turned against us decisively. We had deployed over 2,000 new Panther and Tiger tanks in this battle, as well as over 2,000 aircraft, and the newly developed Ferdinand self-propelled guns, but we still lost. As usual Berlin took a long time to admit that there were problems. The British and Americans were rampaging through Sicily,[22] Berlin Radio actually announced that it seemed as if all Hamburg was on fire,[23] and Mussolini had fallen from power.[24]

Meanwhile, I was probably safer, and more content, than my poor parents in Berlin. When I had been injured, painful as it was, it had certainly turned out to be my lucky day. My arm was gaining strength, but it was not strong enough to do my job as a mechanic, and so I continued working in the office, mainly for the *Oberst*. The French people in Lille were more concerned about their ration books than anything else, but we did hear of the occasional skirmishes with the Resistance movement; somewhat cynically we believed this to be a forlorn hope by the French that the Allies might actually win. There were problems in Paris but there was little trouble in Lille, apart from the occasional industrial sabotage.

During my time in this backwater the war seemed to be moving at quite a pace. Berlin Radio announced that one million women, children and the infirm were being evacuated from Berlin, the city which Goering had promised would never be touched by enemy bombs.[25] It seemed to me that we were retreating in all areas

[22] By 22 July 1943 the Americans were in Palermo.
[23] On 24 July 1943.
[24] On 25 July 1943.
[25] On 8 August 1943.

especially, as I heard on that very day that Sicily had fallen,[26] and that Kharkov had eventually capitulated to the Russians.[27] I remember thinking that Poltava would soon fall, and wondered what had happened to my old friends Albert, Franz and Friedrich. For the first time I asked the *Oberst* a favour; I hoped he could find out where my friends were stationed. He said he would see what he could do, and two days later he told me they were still in Poltava; I knew then that they were in danger.

During August I saw, for the first time, the amazing sight of the huge American planes, which I later learnt were called Flying Fortresses.[28] Later I looked at photographs which the *Oberst* had in his office. 'It's not the size of the plane that worries us,' he told me. 'It's the fact that every time we shoot one down another ten appear. America is a gigantic factory and we can't reach it with our bombers.'

That week a few more planes and pilots, mainly fighters, appeared at our airfield, which was a clear indication that the High Command was becoming more and more concerned about the bombing raids. On one occasion I was filing in the office when three new pilots came in to report to the *Oberst*. They were fresh from the Eastern Front and they no longer looked like the young jubilant men I had seen in 1940. 'It's a waste of manpower and resources,' one of them said. My ears pricked up because I thought he was talking about being sent to Lille. But he continued, 'He's ordered the entire liquidation of all ghettos in Poland and the Soviet Union.'[29]

'Damned stupid,' another agreed. 'Thousands of potential front-line troops to clear up their mess.'

I was only an office boy, and knew better than to join in the conversation, but I was itching to know what they were talking about. By the time the *Oberst* invited them in I had worked out

[26] On 17 August 1943 Patton entered Messina at 10.15 a.m. It had taken the Allies only thirty-nine days to capture Sicily.

[27] Kharkov actually fell on 22 August 1943, but news was not always announced in the right sequence.

[28] B-17s.

[29] In June 1943 Himmler gave this order.

that they had been discussing the Jewish situation in the east.

A week later I was reminded of their conversation. I was standing in the front room of my landlady's house looking out of the window when three cars screeched to a halt outside, and two *Wehrmacht* soldiers and some *gendarmes* jumped out of the cars and, without knocking, ran into the house opposite. I went out into the small garden at the front of the house out of sheer curiosity. I saw my landlady walking up the street. A small truck appeared as the gendarmes brought out two women and four children, whom they bundled into the truck, leaving with the same sense of urgency, not even bothering to close the front door. My landlady went inside and I followed her like a recalcitrant schoolboy. She looked round at me in the passage and shook her head almost sadly. I opened my hands in an attempt to convey to her that I had no idea what was going on. She looked at me again and went out into the kitchen. As I followed her, she passed through the kitchen and out into her backyard. She talked to a neighbour, an elderly man whom I had often seen coming and going. When I appeared, they stopped talking and looked at me. Suddenly he spoke to me in faltering German, telling me that my landlady wanted to know whether I had caused the problem over the road.

I explained that I had no idea at all what was going on; I was only a *Luftwaffe* mechanic. As he talked to her in rapid French, she did not take her eyes off me. He then explained that the two elderly sisters opposite had been caring for four Jewish children, whose parents had been rounded up a year before, and that the sisters and the children would now be sent to a holding camp before leaving for the east. It was my turn to shake my head. I wanted to tell them I was a *mischling*, but I was still very cautious about revealing my status to anyone. I did, however, make it abundantly clear that I was very much against what was happening, and certainly had nothing to do with the raid. As he translated I was relieved that she nodded at me; I think she believed me. I then asked why the *gendarmes* were doing the *Gestapo*'s job. He told my landlady what I had asked, before he answered me himself. He said that some of the *gendarmes* could not be trusted, that there was an element amongst them that was pro-German and anti-Semitic, but not all of them were the same. He then looked at me as if he were weighing me up, before saying that after the war there would be reprisals.

That night, as I sat alone in the drawing room fiddling with my chess pieces, I reflected on the expression 'after the war'. It had never occurred to me that there would be an 'after the war'. All my adult life I had only known war and the only outcome I had anticipated was a German victory. I hated the Nazis but I found it difficult to contemplate a German defeat. Yet, as I ruminated, I began to think that a defeat was becoming more and more likely. Italy had surrendered[30] and our troops had been forced to occupy Rome,[31] while Mussolini had had to be rescued by German paratroopers.[32] Our army had retreated from the Dnieper, as well as Poltava and Smolensk.[33] With the fall of Poltava I pondered on the plight of my old friends Albert, Franz and Friedrich, and wondered if I would see them again.

Meanwhile, during the rest of 1943, as I safely wandered around the offices of the Lille airfield, the bombing raids intensified. I was able to read some of the reports as they passed through the office. There had been some very serious raids on Kassel, Bremen, Schweinfurt and Berlin, which had all been badly hit.[34] At the end of October I actually heard Berlin Radio admit that the Russians had broken through our main defences,[35] which meant that 1944 promised to be bleak. The *Oberst* told me that the bombing raids were very serious and were causing

[30] On 8 September 1943.

[31] On 10 September 1943.

[32] Otto Skorzeny's paratroopers brought Mussolini to Munich after a daring raid.

[33] The withdrawal from the Dnieper was on 19 September, Poltava fell on 23 September and Smolensk on 25 September 1943.

[34] Kassel on 3 October, Bremen on 8 October, Schweinfurt on 14 October and on 18 November when the RAF raided Berlin with 444 bombers and on 22 November, in the heaviest raid on Berlin, the RAF dropped 2,300 tons of bombs within thirty minutes.

[35] On 28 October 1943.

enormous numbers of civilian casualties. The industrial damage, however, was not as bad as they had feared. He also said that the large American planes were easy targets, despite the fact that they were armed 'like porcupines'.[36] He also told me that Kiev had fallen,[37] and that the *Führer* had sent out a directive to reinforce the defences in the west. The OKW believed that the British and Americans were preparing to invade France, probably at Calais, and therefore close to Lille. I also heard the rumour from my landlady's neighbour, to whom I now chatted, that the Danes had smuggled all their Jewish population into Sweden. I never questioned how he knew this, and it was only years later that I wondered whether he had been a member of the French Resistance, cultivating me in the hope of gaining some information.

Just after Christmas I received a letter from big Bruno, in which he told me that my parents and Aunt Ingrid had been killed in a bombing raid on 18 December. I sat down at my desk and wept silently for my parents who had been through so much, only to have been killed so cruelly in a bombing raid. The *Oberst* offered me leave, but as big Bruno had told me that the funerals had been conducted by the authorities, I decided to stay on the airfield, seeking comfort at the church and losing myself in my work and chess. I had no idea that big Bruno knew my parents, but he told me in his second letter that he and Marie, knowing I was away, had contacted them a few months earlier. I owed them so much, and although I had turned down the offer of returning to Berlin I looked forward to thanking them in person. As there was no way I could communicate with Ruth, I suddenly felt very much alone in the world. My friend Albert was somewhere in the east, big Bruno was working in his factory, which had been bombed twice, and my only local friend was a senior officer who had to keep his distance. My landlady could not speak German; it was only my Christian faith that kept

---

[36] On 14 October on the raid over Schweinfurt 300 bombers were involved, but sixty were shot down and 138 damaged.
[37] On 6 Nov 1943.

kept me going. I have to confess that at the end of 1943 I felt spiritually and mentally drained, and cared little for the fast-approaching New Year.

Chapter 12

1944 (January–June)

The *Oberst* gave me two weeks' compassionate local leave, but I felt lost in Lille. I went to the church on several occasions and lit candles for my family; I thought of my parents and prayed they were at peace. My mother used to say that there was no point in saying prayers for the dead because they were in the hands of God; my father's Catholic Church had no problems with such prayers, however, and they certainly brought me comfort.

During this time of mourning one of the French priests, for the first time ever, came and sat with me one Wednesday morning. He could speak no German and I no French, but he had a smattering of English. I told him about my parents, and after a few moments he left me but returned a few minutes later with an English prayer book, which I now know was called the *Book of Common Prayer*. He managed to explain to me that the morning and evening services could be said privately, and the Psalms were set out so that they could be read daily; he called it the Offices. I was very grateful to him, and I started to use the prayers more often, though the language in places completely baffled me. Later, looking through the small pocket edition, I saw that it had a stamp inside saying it was the property of Norwich Cathedral. How it came to be in the priest's vestry in Lille I shall never know; I still have it to this day.

I also discovered that when I prayed for my mother and my father I could visualize them sitting in front of me, looking at me. I also prayed for Josef but I could never really visualize him. I have no doubt that a modern psychotherapist would have a field day with me, but it has remained a very powerful spiritual force in my life.

Lille was not the most interesting place to be in and so on the last day of my leave I decided to wander back to my billet and practise some chess openings, using the English book I had been given years before. I knew my landlady was out because I had seen her in the market as I passed by. I had just sat down in the house when I heard somebody moving upstairs, in what I thought was my bedroom. I resisted the temptation to call out, and I quietly climbed the stairs. Whoever it was must have heard me because there was the sound of scurrying feet. When I arrived on the top landing of the three-storey house I saw a young girl disappearing into the attic; she pulled up a ladder and closed the loft door. I sat at the top of the stairs and thought about the fact that all the time I had been living here the landlady had been hiding a child in her loft; the only reason for that must have been because the child was Jewish.

I knew what to do at once. I guessed that the young girl would tell the landlady she had probably been seen by a German, and this would cause them to panic, putting everything at risk for them. I jumped on my bicycle and went to the market. With my superior spending power I purchased as much food as I could and arrived back at the house at the same time as my landlady. She left the door open for me and I took her by the elbow and asked her to come upstairs with me. She looked aghast and I realized what an ass I had made of myself suggesting this. I shook my head vigorously and still pointed up the stairs. Reluctantly she followed me, and when we reached the top landing I could see she was terrified. I gave her the bag of groceries and pointed up to the loft. At first she just stared at me and then, totally unexpectedly and completely out of character, she stepped forward and hugged me.

She took a nearby broom handle and knocked the trapdoor three times and then whistled. The loft opened and the ladder I had seen earlier was lowered. I was astonished to see not one but three faces looking down at me. When they saw my uniform they were petrified, but the landlady spoke to them in French and invited me to climb up the ladder. I saw three girls holding hands as they stood by three mattresses on the floor. The loft was gently lit by a red light and there were books and games spread all around the floor. I wanted to talk to her about the situation so I pointed towards her neighbour's house, but she shook her head. I nodded to indicate I understood that was not a good idea. I brought extra rations back from the airfield at every opportunity, and used my own resources to help her in her courageous effort to save the Jewish girls.

Two weeks later I returned to the billet with some bread and sausage, and found that my landlady had a woman guest; they were apparently waiting for me. It transpired that the other woman was the landlady's sister, and she had a smattering of German. She explained how grateful the landlady was, and how important it was that nobody knew about the children, not even her neighbour. I explained that I had fully understood the situation, and that she had nothing to fear from me, only help whenever there was an opportunity. Then the sister explained that my landlady could not sit near me at church, or be anything but hostile towards me outside the house because tongues would wag. Again, I said, I fully understood. I also said that when I was in the house the children could come down. However, she did not think this was advisable; if the police came I could at least plead ignorance. The landlady kept to her word; at church and in the streets she looked at me as if I were dirt, but in the house I started to feel part of her family.

When I returned to the airfield I found that there was a new set of problems. The *Gestapo* had informed the *Luftwaffe* that the British were dropping armaments to the French, Dutch and Belgium resistance movements, which seemed to be gathering strength.[1]

'I think,' the *Oberst* said to me as I was picking up some notes from his desk, 'that the British and Americans are close to invading us.'

'Are we not holding them in Italy?' I asked.

[1]The RAF and Americans started this operation, called 'Carpetbagger', on 4 January 1944.

'They've landed from the sea in Italy,[2] and I suspect from my lowly position that this is an exercise for them before crossing the Channel. And,' he added, 'their main forces are gathering in England.'

Because of this build-up across the Channel there was more activity in Lille, with planes detailed to look out for ground activity in England. This was now a dangerous mission. Gone were the days when we could fly over the Channel with impunity; there were British and American fighters in almost every part of our airspace. As an indirect result of this increased activity I found myself busier than usual. My arm was getting its strength back, but the *Oberst* was keen to keep me as his office assistant, and this meant that my twenty-fifth birthday was spent in the air, flying to Caen, in Normandy. He decided to make me his personal assistant and I certainly did not want to protest.

Early on that Thursday morning I found myself in the back seat of a Storch.[3] I was on my own as the *Oberst* always piloted his own plane. I had never looked out from an aeroplane before; on previous flights I had always been stuck in the back of a windowless Dornier. I should have enjoyed the experience, but he warned me that he would be flying low because this type of plane would be a sitting duck for any British fighters roaming the skies. I knew the Storch had a small 240 hp engine, and although it could take off and land on a 30 metre runway, and coast at a speed as low as 35 mph, its normal travelling speed was only about 100 mph. Sitting in the rear I felt vulnerable to say the least, and instead of enjoying the view, I spent most of the time looking around for British fighters.

It was a short journey and I was relieved when we landed at Caen airfield. My working situation had changed dramatically because as the *Oberst* talked with senior officers I sat behind him, taking notes. Fortunately I was always able to write quickly, but I could not help wishing I had learned shorthand; I had never thought I would become a secretary. After the main meeting I travelled with him, and two others, down to the Normandy coast to look at the fortifications. The general consensus was that the

[2]The Anzio Landing on 22 January 1944.
[3]Fiesler Fi 156 Storch.

anticipated invasion would come from the coast around Dover, straight into Calais. Others believed that the Normandy coast would be the preferred landing. When I saw the huge gun emplacements on the cliffs, and the construction of obstacles on the beach, I could not conceive how any enemy, however formidable, could possibly succeed in that area. The role of the *Luftwaffe* was to ensure that they stopped any form of landing craft getting as far as the beaches.

All day I sat with my mouth shut, listening intently. It was clear that the *Oberst* was held in great esteem by the others; but although their relationship was very respectful, there was humour and at times a lot of laughter. That night I stayed in a billet attached to the airfield because the *Oberst* was dining with his colleagues. I was just scrounging some blankets when a *Luftwaffe* soldier appeared at the door and called my name. I found that he had a couple of large bottles of beer for me, with the compliments of the *Oberst*. As I shared it with two others; I could not help but wonder how lucky I had been to serve this particular man. I had met some rats in my time, not least my own brother, but I had been lucky to meet a few very good friends, like Erik, big Bruno and Albert and now this senior officer.

The flight back the next morning was frightening because the *Oberst* and I saw a couple of British fighters overhead, but the *Oberst* was confident that we were flying too low and they were too fast to spot us. He was right once again and I breathed a sigh of relief as we landed safely in Lille. I spent the rest of the day trying to improve my skills on the typewriter, with which I was becoming more and more proficient.

That evening I played chess with the *Oberst*, who was delighted because he nearly won, but I forced a draw by creating a stalemate. 'It will certainly be a stalemate if they land on those beaches,' I said. 'Surely Calais is the obvious route.'

'I think,' he replied, 'that they will come over to Normandy, and our problem then will be insufficient aircraft. I know the British; they will treat the whole thing like a game of chess. They will make us think they're going north, and then go south, as they did in their bombing raids sending our planes in the wrong direction.'

'May I ask, sir, how you learned to speak English so well?'

215

'You're beginning to speak it just as well yourself, Sonn; I was lucky in having a good English education. My father was a businessman who lived in London for five years, and I was a boarder at a small prep school, a junior school, in Surrey, down the London road as you drive to Portsmouth. I know how they react, and have a good idea about the way they think.'

'Is it true that they torture our pilots?' I pursued.

'No – no more than the *Luftwaffe* would. They are civilized, but I don't know how they would react to the *Gestapo* or SS once they have heard about the atrocities you and I have discussed recently. I always found them fair, but not soft, even if they do manage to give you that impression at first.'

The next morning was a Saturday, and the *Oberst* had to fly to Berlin, so I had five days to myself. I tidied up all the notes and returned to my billet. The French were on very short food rations, and I used all my cunning and ingenuity to collect food from the airfield, in order to help my landlady feed the hidden Jewish children. It struck me as iniquitous that children had to hide from both the Germans and their own police. I felt guilty about spending time in my billet, knowing that when I was there the children could not emerge from their hideout. I found a café nearby and sat there for several mornings looking at chess openings and making sense of my English prayer book. One morning an old man, seeing my chess board, offered me a game. It was a hard game and I was lucky to escape with a draw. I would have liked to have met him again, but during the game somebody sneered at him and I never saw him again. I was aware that I might be able to sit in their cafés and go to their church, but I was an unwanted guest, an intruder.

By the end of February we knew that Germany was in trouble. The Russians were only a mile from the Estonian frontier,[4] but, more seriously, in the Korsun–Schevchenkosky area troops of the 1st and 2nd Ukraine Fronts had linked up enabling them to encircle two corps (ten divisions) of our 8th Army. In fact, the Russians were now at Brest Litovsk,[5] from where we had first

[4] On 1 February 1944.
[5] On 5 February 1944.

invaded the Soviet Union.

Nearly every day we were aware of bomber fleets in the skies, and our pilots had to turn around so quickly they had insufficient time for breaks. We started to lose both pilots and machines in great numbers and sometimes, although we had the planes, they were flown by our most junior pilots who were then confronted by experienced enemy aircrew. We were constantly expecting another raid on Lille once Limoges was badly hit; the enemy dropped a huge bomb which had reduced a large area of that city to rubble.[6]

I travelled with the *Oberst* in his Storch on quite a few occasions, and although I still worried about being spotted by enemy fighters I quite enjoyed the experience. I can remember trips to Amiens, Beauvais, Rouen and even Calais where we stood on the top of a gun battery outside the port, and without binoculars saw the white cliffs of England. I borrowed a pair of high-powered Zeiss naval binoculars and with them I could see Dover Castle clearly and some movement on the cliff tops.

At the end of February I had a very nasty scare. I had developed the habit of sitting in my local church to say my prayers and light candles in memory of my parents. There was always someone else there, and many of the faces were becoming familiar to me. The mass had just finished and I was sitting in my usual place at the back near the font when I felt a hand grasp my shoulder. I looked up into the faces of two undeniably *Gestapo* officers.

'Bruno Sonn?' one asked.

'That's me.'

'We'd like a chat with you.'

'Why?'

'We'll discuss that in our offices.'

Several members of the congregation who had stayed behind to meditate or pray, looked at me as they led me out to an old Citroen the *Gestapo* had obviously commandeered; I also saw one our pilots looking at me from the café opposite. I was not accustomed to being the centre of attention. They took me into

---

[6] Probably a reference to the first 12,000 lb bomb dropped by the RAF.

the town centre and into a building which appeared heavily armed. As I have stated before, I am not a particularly brave man and my heart was thumping. It soon became clear that they knew all about me and mentioned several times that my father was Jewish. 'Son of a Jewish rat,' one of them said.

'A Jewish rat who won a medal for Germany in the last war, a Jewish rat whose elder son died as an SS soldier on the Eastern Front, a Jewish rat whose youngest son, me, has spent all his working life in the *Luftwaffe*. Now he's dead because despite all the promises, Berlin is being bombed by the enemy,' I retorted. I was surprised by the anger which had welled up inside.

'Better than being gassed,' one replied. 'But we're interested in what you're up to.'

'I'm doing my job.' I replied curtly.

'We would like to think so, but you spend a lot of time making contacts with French people in that church.'

I laughed, but they did not. They emptied my small canvas bag, from which fell my chess set, my chess book of openings and my English prayer book. They examined each chess piece as if it contained a secret compartment; they flicked through the chess book and then opened the prayer book. The instant they saw it was in English all hell broke loose. Another man was called in who implied that I was English.

'How can I be the son of a Jewish rat from Berlin and be English?'

'I'm beginning to suspect,' the newcomer said, 'that you are a traitor because you resent what's happened to your Jewish father.'

'Rubbish,' I replied.

'Well, we'll see what's rubbish when we have interrogated the truth from you.'

I was then locked in a cell to contemplate the rumours I had heard regarding their idea of interrogation. I did not have to let my imagination run too wild, because I could hear someone screaming from the floor below. They were dreadful screams; whoever it was, they were in extreme agony. The cell was small with a bucket in which to relieve oneself: no chair, table or bed. Being early March it was cold, and I did not want to sit on the floor because it was smeared with excrement.

It must have been about seven in the evening when my door was opened. A huge man strode in and punched me straight in the face, knocking me down. I fell against the wretched bucket, and even though I was dazed I could smell the contents soaking my clothes. He was joined by two others who grabbed my feet and dragged me along the corridor, my shoulders kept catching on the door posts and the back of my head bouncing on the floor like a ball. I was dreading being dragged into a torture cell when my tormentors were stopped by another man, who ordered them to take me to the main office. This time they stood me up and frog-marched me to the room I had been in when I had arrived. I could feel blood running from my nose and I smelt quite disgusting because of the urine-soaked clothes. They virtually threw me into the office, where to my astonishment I saw my *Oberst* standing by the window. I could see that he was furious as soon as he looked at me.

'What in God's name is the problem?' He roared at the *Gestapo* officer behind the desk.

'He has an English book in his possession, he's always attending that church where we know the Resistance meet, and he's a *mischling*.'

The *Oberst* picked up my prayer book, which the *Gestapo* officer had pushed towards him, which he recognized immediately.

'Now you listen to me very carefully, and note my rank.' The *Oberst* was leaning across the desk, his face only a sheet of paper away from the somewhat flustered *Gestapo* officer. 'First of all Sonn goes to church to pray, I've known that since he arrived; secondly, this English book is a prayer book so that he can pray. It's in English because I taught Sonn to speak English for reasons you can never know; thirdly, I know his father was Jewish and that makes him a *mischling* but not an outlaw; fourthly, Sonn was wounded on the Eastern Front, where I am going to ensure you go unless you release him now, and swear you will not pester him anymore. Am I making myself clear?'

Although I had been with the *Oberst* in all kinds of situations I had never seen him angry before; he even frightened me, making me extremely grateful he was on my side. The *Gestapo* officer did not say a thing. The *Oberst* took the phone on the desk and demanded to be put through to the *Reichmarschall*'s office. The *Gestapo* officer snatched the phone away, countermanding the order, but apologizing profusely as he did so. I cannot recollect all that he said, but it amounted to mistaken identity and false information. The *Oberst* himself put my chess set and books back in my bag, and simply nodded at me to follow him.

Back at the airfield I was seen by the medical orderly, who packed my nose with gauze wadding, before I showered and scrubbed myself clean. In the *Oberst*'s office I thanked him for saving my skin.

'You knew I was a *mischling*, sir?'

'I had you thoroughly checked out from top to bottom when I appointed you as my aide; I couldn't care a damn that you're a *mischling* or even a full-blooded Jew, you're German as far as I am concerned, as much as I'm Prussian. They wanted *mischlings* out of the army, but sensible commanders turn a blind eye. I know about your church attendance. I even know about your radical friend big Bruno. We have our own investigation teams, but we don't use torture, my only interest is whether I can trust you, and I do.

A few weeks later the *Oberst* informed me that he had been ordered to Berlin and expected to be away for a fortnight. He offered me leave for the same period, suggesting that, given the unpleasant nature of the Lille *Gestapo*, it would be a good idea if I went with him in order to check my family home in the Hermannstrasse. Until he suggested this, it had never crossed my mind. We travelled together by train, first to Paris before going on to Berlin. We played chess all the way and when we arrived in Berlin we parted, I saluted him but he ignored it and shook my hand.

'Take care, Bruno; I'll see you back in Lille at the beginning of April.'

That was the first time he had called me by my first name; I then remembered my father saying that some officers were thorough gentleman of the old school, and they were instantly recognizable and respected by the men they commanded; my *Oberst* was one of them.

As I made my way through the city to my home I could barely believe my eyes. In places it seemed as if Berlin was just one great ruin. Some streets had simply disappeared in massive piles of rubble. The people looked gaunt and hungry, and at the railway and bus stations there were military guards checking everyone's passes. During my short journey I had my pass checked four times, and not just checked but scrutinized. I wondered whether the Nazi Party chiefs ever looked at this rubble and wondered what they had done. I sat next to a *Wehrmacht* soldier on the tram and he told me that earlier in the month there had been a major daylight air raid across the city but that all the American aircraft had been shot down.[7] I had heard that the bombing raids had become a regular occurrence, but I had not expected so much damage, even in the suburbs through which I was then travelling. I felt a deep hatred for the RAF bombers, but then I thought about the huge bomber fleets flying towards London from our bases, and knew that war was fundamentally wrong.

My house – because it had become my house after my parents' deaths – was untouched, but without them it looked desolate. I did not want to stay.

It was a bad day. When I arrived at big Bruno's house the door was opened by Marie, and I knew instantly that something was wrong.

'What's the matter, Marie?'

'Oh Bruno, come in, my brother is dead.'

I just slumped down on the wall, full of the same misery I had felt on hearing of my parents' deaths. All I could think was, 'This damned war, these damned people who started it.'

I stayed with Marie during that leave; she was now my only family. She wanted to speak about big Bruno and so did I. He had taught me my trade, educated me in the ways of men, trained me in chess, led me to my religious faith and made me question

---

[7] On 4 March 1944 600 Flying Fortresses and Liberators of the US 8th Army Air Force carried out its first daylight bombing of Berlin. They met powerful resistance and lost eighty planes.

political authority. He had been a friend and a father figure. Marie told me that at the beginning, when I first turned up at Daimler-Benz, he had come home and told her that I was a 'smarty' who was a fanatical Hitler Youth member whom he would never take a liking to. Within a month I was the best apprentice he had ever had, and soon he was regarding me as the son he had never had.

Big Bruno had been killed in a bombing raid because he had gone to the Erkner Ball Bearing factory for supplies; it appeared that the bombing raid that day concentrated on this one factory.[8] Nobody within the main factory, including big Bruno, had a chance. Thousands of people were dying in the cities, as well as in the major disasters at the front. We heard on the radio, that in one battle alone we had lost 10,000 soldiers and 4,000 others had been taken prisoner.[9]

Before I left I promised Marie that whatever happened I would try to stay in touch. She gave me a photograph of big Bruno and a hug that nearly took my breath away. This time I did not travel to Lille with the *Oberst*, but made my own way back, which proved to be a nightmare. When I was in the company of a senior officer I had become accustomed to being waved through the various barriers, and even now it was easier for me than civilians or the countless foreign workers, because I was wearing my uniform. I lost count of the number of times my pass and my credentials were checked and double-checked. Ironically, it was easier for me to travel in France, than in Germany. I arrived in Lille the same day as the *Oberst*, and we agreed that it was a holiday camp after Berlin.

Throughout April the *Oberst*, with me at his side, was busy going from one airfield to the next: I knew something important was happening but he said nothing until there was a major bombing raid on the heavy coastal guns in Normandy.[10]

'I think I was right, Sonn,' he said as we prepared to fly once

[8] On 8 March 1944.

[9] On 14 March 1944 on the Eastern Front at Nikolayer.

[10] On 13 April 1944 the US Tactical Air Force attacked Normandy's heavy gun emplacements.

more to Caen. 'They're going to land in Normandy. The trouble is everyone is convinced it will be Calais.'

The something 'big' was the expectation of an invasion by the British and Americans, and while the major fighting was taking place on the Eastern Front the last thing Germany needed was a serious invasion of France. The *Oberst* was not as confident as many other senior officers. I had overheard many of their views in the various meetings I had attended to take notes. Most thought the West, as we tended to call the British and Americans at this stage, would not be able to make it ashore. The *Oberst* pointed out that because of the Russian war, ninety per cent of our troops and, more to the point, most of our aircraft, were engaged elsewhere.

Near the end of April, I was leaving my billet in the early hours when there was a hammering at the door. There were two French policemen and a *Wehrmacht* soldier, demanding to search the house. I knew then that the children would be found. My landlady sat down at the table, looking as white as a sheet. I knew I had to do something; I could not turn my back on this problem. I raged at the soldier, saying that I had lived there for over a year, and if there were people hiding in the house I would know. Both the *gendarmes* understood my German, but they looked to the soldier for guidance. I further stressed my authority, exaggerating my importance and claiming to be the personal aide of *Oberst* Freisher. I noticed that this did have some effect upon the unwelcome visitors.

'Listen,' I said to the soldier, 'if you cross swords with the *Oberst* you may well land up on the Eastern Front; just take my word for it that this place is clean. I wouldn't wish that on you, and these Frenchmen will have to face the wrath of their own people one day.'

'All right,' the soldier replied. 'I don't like this business anyway. We'll take your word.'

I breathed a sigh of relief and hoped there would be no ramifications. I sat down opposite the landlady, and using pen and paper plus some sign language, suggested that she find another shelter for her Jewish guests. That evening, when I returned, she had obviously taken my advice. The attic was clear of any signs of habitation, and she indicated that the girls were somewhere down the street in another attic. It was with a great sigh of relief that I went to bed that night. During my stay she suffered no further intrusions from Germans or French *gendarmes*.

Some time in the middle of May, Lille came under further heavy bombardment. This time we were able to strike back. For some extraordinary reason we could see the bombers at a very high altitude, circling around the city. It gave our fighters time to clear the ground, and although the bombing was heavy, we reckoned we had shot down at least ten of the bombers.[11] It was quite clear to all of us that there was a build-up of activity in France. The Resistance was beginning to cause more problems and it did not go unnoticed that the bombing raids, which were now prolific, were mainly aimed at our communication lines, especially the railway junctions.

My wound had now completely healed, but the *Oberst* had decided that I should remain as his office boy, although he sometimes called me his aide, depending on what I was doing, where we were and the company we were in.

On the first weekend we were in Caen, after another flight in the *Oberst*'s Storch. I had the Sunday to myself and enjoyed wandering around the ancient city, although the weather was appalling for that time of year. We were due to fly back on the Monday, but there was a gale and the *Oberst* said the Storch would not cope in such conditions, but I suspect it was really so that he could look at Caen, and on the Monday night we had supper together in a small café and played several games of chess.

During the night there was a great deal of air activity, which kept me awake, and by 6 a.m. I put my uniform on in order to go and see what was happening. There had been a series of air strikes, and rumours were circulating that an Allied invasion was taking place in the Calais area. As I was walking over to the sheds I could hear the thunderous roar of low-flying planes and, looking

[11] On 10–11 May 1944 a large number of bombers circled Lille waiting for Mosquito marker planes to do their job. They circled for nearly an hour, and as a result lost twelve planes, four over the target area.

up, I saw what appeared at first sight to be a large swarm of enemy fighters heading straight for me, reminding me of the Yak on the Russian front. As I was near a sandbagged anti-aircraft site, I jumped over the wall to take cover. To say all hell broke loose is putting it mildly; I was deafened by explosions all around me, and it seemed to go on for hours. In fact, by the time I looked over the parapet only twenty minutes had passed, but the runway and many of our planes were on fire. They had targeted nearly every building, as well as the planes; I could see instantly that the runway was useless. People were running everywhere, some in panic, but most trying to help the many who had been wounded, and some to put out the fires. It was sheer bedlam and even two hours later, at 8 a.m. it felt as if the entire area was still on fire. During that time we were all very aware of the enemy planes crossing backwards and forwards in huge numbers.

I found the *Oberst* near the Storch. It had been tied down behind the one hangar that had escaped the attack.

'Sonn, jump in, I've got to get back to Lille; we must go now.'

'The runway's in a mess, sir,' I replied.

That did not bother him; he told me he could get the Storch airborne from a shed roof if necessary. Strangely enough, as I jumped into the rear seat, for the first time I did not feel nervous about flying, but I suspect that it was my adrenalin flowing. He taxied the plane towards a small access road, and although it seems impossible to believe, he was in the air after only about 100 metres. We knew now that the invasion had started, but at that time we thought there were two landings, one in Normandy and one in Calais.[12] In order to get airborne we faced a strong wind and for a moment we had to fly west towards the coast.

We had been in the air for about five minutes when, to my horror, the thing I had feared most on all my previous flights happened: an enemy fighter appeared behind us. I did not see what it was; I knew from the roundels that it was British, but all I can remember was the strange black-and-white striped wings[13] as it shot by so fast I thought we had stopped in midair. It circled

[12] 1944 June 6 Overlord started.

[13] All Allied aircraft had striped wings for ease of identification.

us and then returned; this time bullets and canon shells ripped though our wings. I could see the *Oberst* struggling to hold the plane steady, but it soon became clear to me that we were going down. The *Oberst* could only keep the plane airborne by trying to put more thrust through the failing engine; he could not turn it at all, so we were heading on a mainly downward westerly course. The enemy pilot did not return; he was either looking for bigger fish or thought we were done for. He was right; we were heading for a crash and I could see the *Oberst* trying to keep some height as he looked for a place to land. I was also concerned to see blood on the cockpit door which was not mine. There was absolutely nothing I could do except sit and pray, which I actually did. I was surprised that the plane stayed in the air as long as it did. We headed down to a small field; I was hoping for a soft landing, but because I did not know then that our undercarriage had been shot away, I am unable to recall the actual landing as I did not come to for nearly two hours.

At first I thought I was in bed suffering from a hangover, but as I opened my eyes the morning's dreadful events flashed before me; this explained why I was suspended in my harness upside down in the back of the Storch. The *Oberst* was in the same position and not moving. I mustered all my strength and managed to extricate myself from my harness before climbing out of the smashed fuselage. I went to the *Oberst* and was relieved to find a pulse; he was still alive but unconscious. He was bleeding from a wound in his leg. I managed after considerable effort to drag him out into the field. We were lucky that the plane had not burst into flames. I became conscious of some very heavy gunfire behind us: I remember thinking that it must be the rumble of naval guns, interspersed with light artillery and a lot of smallarms fire.

The field we were in was empty and strangely peaceful. I retrieved my bag and a first-aid box from the plane, and cut the *Oberst*'s trousers down the side in order to investigate his wound. His leg looked a mess, and I suspected that a fairly heavy-calibre bullet had shredded his lower leg muscles. There was blood everywhere, and after tying a tourniquet above the wound, I dressed it as we had once been taught in training. I knew he would need help so I pulled him away from the plane and put him in a nearby shed.

I could see some buildings in the distance and I walked along a lane towards a church spire. I was about to enter the village of Bieville when I saw a uniform I did not recognize. I froze and moved slowly into a hedge. I looked out cautiously, and realized that they were British soldiers, and that somehow I had managed to get behind enemy lines. I looked at my watch and realized that I must have been knocked out for some time, because it was very late afternoon. The situation meant that there was no point in going further forward, so I worked my way back to where I had left the *Oberst*.

He was showing the first signs of consciousness and I was able to give him something to drink. As soon as he was able to speak he asked me to retrieve his personal papers from the cockpit. I told him that the enemy was all around us and on hearing this he ordered me to fetch the papers at once and burn them. I could see he was very anxious and ran back to the plane. I found his case and dribbled some engine fuel over it before lighting it away from the plane. When I had done this the *Oberst* visibly relaxed: I did not ask him what was in his case but knew instinctively that they were top secret papers.

'You go, Sonn, on your own you can get through the troops ahead; they will be loosely spread out and that way you get back to our own people.'

'You can come with me,' I said. 'I can carry you.'

'You will not have a chance with me; just go, that's an order.'

'Sorry sir, you come with me or I stay; you can't be left on your own in this state.'

He did not answer, and I could see that the pain in his leg was becoming intense. There were planes overhead, but here in the field all seemed strangely quiet. We could still hear the continuous roar of guns to the west of us. I went back to the plane and rummaged through the contents. I found what I was looking for, a bottle of cognac. I took it back to the *Oberst* and after we had both taken a swig, I suggested that I put some on his wound to keep it clean. He agreed but promptly passed out with pain the moment I did so. Despite the fact that it was June we were frozen that night, so I covered us both with some hay and a tarpaulin and waited, hoping that some *Wehrmacht* soldiers would soon appear so we could get him to hospital.

As soon as it was light we woke up with a start, not because of the light, but because of a noise outside the shed. Cautiously, I looked towards the plane and could see a group of heavily armed British soldiers examining the wreck. I pulled the tarpaulin over us but I was too late to keep us hidden. Two soldiers had walked into the shed and were pointing sten-guns at us; my only hope was that they were not trigger happy.

'Up you get, Jerry,' one said.

I had never been called a Jerry before, but it was a term I was to become all too familiar with as the years passed.

'My leg's been shattered by a bullet and I can't move,' the *Oberst* replied.

'You English?' The British soldier was taken aback by the *Oberst*'s clear English voice.

'No, I am German.'

'You would have made a bloody good spy then,' said the soldier smiling; that smile was something I shall never forget.

'I'm not a spy; we're both *Luftwaffe*, that's our plane over there.'

'I'll speak to the Sarge. Johnny, keep an eye on them.'

They soon relieved us of our service pistols; the *Oberst*'s Luger seemed of significant interest to them. I was feeling more and more confident that they were not going to shoot us.

Soon other troops gathered in the field, quite a few of whom came to look at us as if we were unusual. Some of them did not look as pleasant as our original captor but I never felt threatened. Then a medical orderly appeared to look at the *Oberst*'s leg. He was very gentle as he did so, and shook his head. He gave him some morphine which helped relieve the pain. I can remember reflecting that had it been the Russian Front no prisoners would have been taken, and no German would have given precious morphine to a Russian; nor for that matter would a Russian have helped a German. As I sat next to the *Oberst* I took my pipe out in order to smoke, and they left me alone to do so. I had half-expected to be ordered to stand with my hands in the air, but these troops seemed very confident and casual compared to the

Wehrmacht. I did not deceive myself though; I had no intention of making a run for it because they also looked very professional.

Mid-morning a stretcher arrived and I was detailed to carry one end while a British soldier took the other. We walked about 2 miles west until we reached a busy tented area. They took the *Oberst* into a large tent and I was packed off to a fenced area where there were about forty other German prisoners, all *Wehrmacht*; I was the only *Luftwaffe* man in that compound.

Later I was to learn that this was the second day which the West called D-Day. On reflection I was fortunate to be captured early on. As we sat in the compound we became aware of different soldiers coming to view the spectacle. One or two spat at us, some glared, but most just looked out of sheer curiosity, and one or two even smiled. We were stuck there for three days. I will not mention the primitive and embarrassing sanitary arrangements, but we were after all virtually at the front line. However, we were fed and, after what we had experienced in France, fed quite well. What amazed all of us was the number of troops, tanks and guns passing us. Later we were moved to a larger compound, where there must have been at least 300 prisoners, this time under armed guard. The further we moved away from the front the less relaxed our guards became; it was probably because there were so many of us.

'Any of you speak English?' The voice was just behind me and made me jump. A British officer was standing there, and I responded that I did to a certain extent. No one else volunteered, so I was pulled out of the compound and taken to a house that had been badly shelled.

'We're shipping you Jerry lads to England, but we need to talk to you before we load you up. There's a British officer on the way who speaks German, but you will do until he gets here. Sit there please.'

My job was simple; all I had to do was to take the name of the prisoner, his unit and his number. One man, Heinrich Dürmer if my memory is correct, caused the British to sit up and take some interest. I had to ask him where he had been before he arrived in Normandy and I saw them marking their papers, but I had no idea what was going on apart from the fact that they were registering us after their own fashion in a hurried way.

They say that life is full of coincidences and I have experienced a few in my time, but I was totally taken aback when the German-speaking British officer eventually appeared; it was my old school friend Erik Lobb. We recognized one another immediately.

I stood up and Erik, suddenly smiling, shook my hand.

'Steady on, Lobb,' the other officer said. 'These are Germans you are listing, not bloody friends.'

Erik did not look at all embarrassed, but turned to the other officer and told him that we were old school friends and, more to the point, that I was *mischling*. He then had to explain what he meant and, as he did so I noted that the other officer started to look more relaxed at the strange situation.

I answered a few of Erik's questions about name and rank, and was about to be taken back to the compound when the other officer called me back. 'I gather you have felt persecuted in Germany because you are half Jewish, but I must warn you that you will feel just the same in England, because in our book you're a German.'

I nodded and went off with the soldier back to the others. Just before nightfall Erik came to see me again. He took me aside and I told him as quickly as I could all that had happened in the last few years, including the deaths of my family, big Bruno and my brother Josef. He was interested in the Rossenstrasse incident, as well as my experiences on the Eastern Front, and especially the atrocities I had witnessed. He also wanted to know how I had learned to speak English so well; I had not realized how proficient I had become, and was quite pleased. In return he told me that Ruth was living in California, and that Hans was with the American troops, attached to a parachute infantry group as a translator, as Erik was to the British. He explained that he could not stay long because they were moving out the next day, but said that he and the other officer had written a long report on me, pointing out that I did not have to go to a special de-Nazifying camp, whatever that was, which meant I would be classified as a 'safe prisoner'. I asked him if he could find out about the *Oberst* and he said he would try. He returned later that evening to say the *Oberst* was fine, and that we would probably be on the same shipment to England. Before he left he slipped me some chocolate and a large bag of pipe tobacco. One or two of the other prisoners wanted me to tell them why I had been singled out, and I was frank with them saying that Erik was an old friend; I did not tell them he had once been a German Jew.

A week later we had to walk about 10 miles down to the coast. We were all astonished to see the amount of equipment coming ashore. There were British troops everywhere, and above us enemy planes were zooming over without interruption. When we got to the beach we were totally amazed at the number of ships offshore. It felt as if every ship in the world was berthed in the Channel.

'We've lost this war,' one man said to me. 'It looks as if the whole world is fighting us.'

I did not reply, simply nodding, because it was crystal clear that we had bitten off more than we could chew. I saw little else because we were shipped out on a landing craft that had just brought fresh troops ashore, and then were herded below decks into an area that stank of vomit. I looked out for the *Oberst* but there was no sign of him. Finding a corner near a fresh air vent I sat down and checked that my bag was still intact. I was well and truly a prisoner, but for some reason I did not feel concerned about the future. I have often wondered why this was; was it my youth, or that our reception by the enemy was civilised by Eastern Front standards, or was it because I could no longer cared what happened to me? I have never been able to answer this question satisfactorily.

Part 3

Prisoner and Citizen of England: from Being Disliked to Being Loved

Chapter 13

1944 June–December

The journey across the Channel was debilitating and disorientating. It took all day and our vessel corkscrewed its way through the water. It was the first time I had been on a ship and I think it was the same for most of the prisoners. We were so seasick most of us wished we could die. We did not even try to communicate; we just became filthy with one another's vomit. When at last we reached calmer waters the relief was overwhelming and I started to wonder what would happen next. It was late evening and I had no idea what the name of the port was where we landed. We were herded out onto gangplanks and ordered down on to the quayside; our guards were few in number, but they were well armed. There were people standing around watching us and I remember feeling like an exhibition at the zoo, a feeling which would stay with me for some time. Someone shouted abuse like 'Huns and bastards', but I could not fathom what he was actually saying. Most of the onlookers just stared, mesmerized by what must have appeared a pitiful sight. We were put into columns of four and marched off the quay to a railway platform.

I looked for the cattle trucks I assumed would be our mode of transport, and I think we were all surprised when we were put into ordinary railway carriages with soft seats. I was in a compartment with eight others; they were *Wehrmacht* soldiers, but three of them were Russians who had opted to fight for us. There were soldiers up and down the platform. Suddenly our door opened and a box was put inside; as it was nearest to me I opened it, and found that it was full of food. There were sandwiches made from white bread – we had not seen that for years. There were also biscuits and some bottles of drink. I shared it out with the others, and as most of us were famished we ate it all very quickly. As the train pulled out of the station I was as surprised that we were able to look out at the passing scenery as I had been that they had fed us and put us into ordinary passenger carriages. The town, which I now believe must have been Portsmouth, had been bombed, but not as severely as my home city before I left. There were vehicles on the streets, but it seemed strange that they all drove on the 'wrong' side of the road. Apart from the Russians we were all curious about the views: had it not been for the small fields it could have been Germany. As the sky darkened we all fell asleep.

I remember that journey vividly, particularly the silence of my fellow travellers; never had a group of men been more lost in their own thoughts. The train stopped several times in sidings, and I could see that when it did so there were soldiers on the tracks outside. However, I for one had no intention of trying to escape; the white bread was the best food I had eaten since childhood, and since the *Oberst* had told me that the British did not torture or execute prisoners I was beginning to relax, and accept whatever lay ahead. When I looked around the carriage I had the distinct impression we were all feeling equally resigned, with the possible exception of the Russians.

In the early hours of the morning we stopped at a station and were ordered out. A German-speaking British officer, informed us that we were at a temporary reception camp to be identified and sorted out for transport to other camps. Looking around I realized that we were on a racecourse; years later I learnt that it was Kempton Park racecourse at Sunbury-on-Thames.[1] It was full of huts and tents, and we were led to an enclosure. By this time there were about 200 of us, but still no sign of the *Oberst*. Some of my fellow prisoners seemed distinctly frightened about the future, but I was feeling quite relaxed; here my *mischling* status might even prove to be beneficial rather than a danger.

---

[1] Used as a holding camp for screening and interrogation if necessary.

We were given postcards on which was inscribed in large black letters, *'DURCHGANGSLAGER SCHREIBEN SIE NICHT BEVOR DER KREIGSGEFANGENE SEINE ENFGILTIGE LAGERANSCHRIFT BEKANNT GIBT'* ('Transit camp. Do not write before the prisoner of war has informed you of his valid camp address') and told we could write to our families reporting that we were alive. I saw one of the Russians merely screw the card up and drop it on the floor, but most of the prisoners were borrowing the proffered pencils. I was not going to bother until I remembered Marie. I only hoped she would survive the war, as I now believed I would. Then I saw the *Oberst*; he was sitting on a chair by the gate and I made my way over to him at once.

'Morning sir,' I said. 'How do you feel?'

'Bruno.' He addressed me by my first name again. 'I owe you my leg. They told me that if you had not taken immediate action I would have had to have it amputated, and without the tourniquet I may well have lost my life. So, Bruno, I am indebted to you.' With that he used a stick to stand up and shook my hand. After all he had done for me I felt humbled by his gratitude.

'It's the irony of life,' he continued, 'that my role in Lille was to help organize aerial defence in the event of an invasion. We were only in Caen because the senior army staff said there could be no invasion because of the weather, and you and I end up being captured on the second day of their arrival. But that's war, my friend.'

He too had seen the thousands of ships in the Channel and, like me, knew that Germany would be lost. The Russians in the east were almost on our doorstep, and the industrial might of America and tenacity of the British were now coming at us from the west.

'Will I be able to stay with you, sir?'

'Bruno, my friend, I have no idea.'

He had, however, found out a great deal in the previous twenty-four hours. Because he spoke English like an Englishman and was a senior officer, he had been able to elicit quite a bit of information. He was able to tell me that we were in what was called a holding cage whilst they screened us all. They would want to know whether any of the senior officers had information they needed, whether we were strong Nazi supporters or not and, he added, 'They have a list of people they are very keen to find.'

The *Oberst* then told me there would be some screening after which we would be given one of three colours: white, grey or black. Black meant a prison camp in the north, or even Canada, because that indicated a fanatical Nazi who could not be trusted. Grey meant a degree of uncertainty. White was for those prisoners who had no affiliation with the Nazi Party at all. White was also called 'A' category, 'B' was grey and so forth.

'You will be white, Bruno. Fortunately I had no party affiliation; I have always been just a military professional, but because of my rank they may well put me in the grey category. Tell them about your father's Jewish background, but keep it from your fellow prisoners; many of them have been bred to automatically hate Jews.'

We talked for nearly two hours before we were lined up again to be fed. We were given tin plates, mugs and spoons and served a stew made from meat, as well as vegetables and more white bread. There was not a man there who was not surprised at the amount and quality of the food. It was as good as the food our family enjoyed before the war started. By 1941 ordinary Germans were starving in comparison with this feast. The man in front of me turned to me on receiving his and said he would have surrendered in 1939 if they had explained that he would be looked after like this.

The *Oberst* was a mine of information: he said that prisoners were given the same rations as British troops,[2] which struck me as incredible. My mind went back to the Russian prisoners I had first seen at Poltava airfield, being thrown scraps of brown bread and dying from starvation and the cold. Whilst we were eating and generally relaxing, another train-load of prisoners arrived and were taken to a different part of the racecourse.[3]

---

[2] POWs received the same weekly rations as British soldiers: 42oz of meat, 8oz of bacon, 5½lb of bread, 10½oz of margarine as well as vegetables, cheese, cake, jam and tea. These amounts were slightly increased in June 1945.

[3] There were 208,000 German POWs held in the UK by November 1945; 19,448 were screened as white, 85,380 as grey, and 50,205 as black. About 53,000 were still waiting to be screened.

'They've heard about the white bread,' someone said, and several of us laughed for the first time in a long time.

'What happens to those in the white category?' I asked the *Oberst* as he was dipping his bread into his stew.

'I wish I knew, but I gather from the medical people I chatted to, that they can work for money!'[4]

I did not say anything, but I was beginning to agree with the soldier who cracked the joke earlier, and it struck me that some of us, especially me, a *mischling*, would have been better off as prisoners of the English than fighting for Nazi Germany.

That night we slept under canvas and my camp bed was next to the *Oberst* and five others who had been captured on the beaches. We did not talk much, but the *Oberst* was pleased that my chess set had survived, as we settled down for a game of chess. Next morning he was taken to the medical tent, and that was the last I saw of him for many years. He had just been helped away by an English medical orderly when the rest of us were lined up for some rapid interviews.

When it was my turn I knew instantly that Erik had been of great assistance. The British officer seemed to know all about me. He was curious to know why I should be fighting for a regime that would have executed my father. I realized that he was fishing to see if I was one of those sons that had turned against his family. I explained that I had chosen a different course from my brother Josef, and I had trained as a mechanic and joined the *Luftwaffe* as the safest bet. I also told him how the Nazis had treated my beloved father because of his Jewish background. He seemed to accept this, and once he knew I could speak English he told me to stay with him to assist in the monitoring of the other prisoners.

This gave me quite an insight into some of my fellow interns. Most of them were relieved to be away from the fighting and not one of them claimed to be a member of the Nazi Party. I knew this could not be true and so did the British officer who, when he smelt

[4] In fact white and grey were allowed to work with pay (*lagergeld*), which could be spent within the camp. By 1946, 22,000 prisoners were involved in construction work in Britain and around 169,000 were involved in agricultural work.

a rat, asked more questions; then I saw him write down statements followed by question marks. He never once asked me what I thought, for which I was grateful. One or two proudly admitted to being Party members and appeared confident that we would still win the war. One of the worst people interviewed that morning was a foreign Waffen-SS soldier; I think he was Dutch and his arrogance was unbelievable. I could see the contempt on the British officer's face, and I wondered whether he might be handed back to his own nation, where he would be treated as a traitor.

The officer thanked me for helping him and gave me a small packet of biscuits. Many of the soldiers were being deloused in special showers, but I was not at all dirty compared with the soldiers, so I was allowed to have an ordinary shower and clean my tunic. I had only just finished when I was picked out along with two other *Luftwaffe* men and taken to another tent. This time I was questioned about the nature of my work; as a mechanic they seemed very interested in where I had been working. They kept pressing me about recent engine development, and for the first time I heard about jet planes and rockets. To me these were in the realms of science fiction, but it became clear that they suspected Germany of developing such weapons. I explained that I was an expert on the DB601 engines and serviced most ordinary internal combustion engines, but knew nothing about new inventions. I pointed out my lowly rank and reiterated my situation as a *mischling*. At this stage I do not think they fully understood the nature of my problem as a *mischling*, apart from one officer who asked me how my father had been set free and why. Before the interview concluded I was told that I was going to a camp in the east of England, from where I would be allowed to write to any members of my family.[5]

I kept myself to myself during those days of waiting. I wandered around our allotted area and looked at the buildings; I

[5] Under the Geneva Convention it was agreed that prisoners of war of other ranks would be allowed two letters per month, officers three. Everyone could also send four postcards a month on stationery provided. They would also be allowed to receive letters and relief parcels.

worked out that we were in the middle of an old racecourse. The soldiers who patrolled on the other side of the wire were older men, but every now and then I noticed that there were a few well-armed younger guards. I think the older men were there because of the number of men in France, but they were backed up by fighting troops in case the prisoners caused problems as we grew in numbers.

I found a place at the back of the racecourse where I could sit and recite my prayers, still using my English prayer book from Norwich Cathedral. As I recalled my parents and big Bruno I could almost see them standing before me; even in those alien circumstances I could feel their presence. I can still remember reading Psalm 22 that morning, 'But as for me, I am a worm, and no man: a very scorn of men, and the outcast of people.' As a matter of spiritual discipline I tried never to feel sorry for myself. However, having once been an ardent member of the Hitler Youth, I had lived all my young adult life in fear because of my *mischling* status; from admiring the Nazis I had quickly grown to despise them. I had continued to work for victory because I still felt German, but when my father had been arrested as a Jew and then killed by a bombing raid, I had become indifferent to the war's outcome. Now I was in a British prisoner of war holding camp, despised, not because I was half Jewish but because I was German. It seemed to be my destiny to be always in the wrong racial class. As I pondered this I began to fall into the trap of self-pity. So I taught myself to laugh at myself, pick myself up and see what each new day brought.

We were told nothing about the war, and the new arrivals told us nothing more than that there was fierce fighting in Normandy. We all realized that the Allied troops had not been thrown back into the sea as anticipated. After two weeks I was called for another interview. This time they asked me about Hans and Erik, not least because through Ruth I had a brother-in-law fighting with the Americans. I detected that the interviewer was a little more sympathetic to my position, and at the end of the interview I was told to sew a white patch on my uniform. 'Better than a yellow star' the elderly officer said as he directed me to another area of the compound.

That evening a small group of us, all wearing white patches, boarded a train. Once again it was an ordinary passenger train, with comfortable seats, and we were given more delicious white bread with chunks of cheese. We were being treated as fellow human beings, and I felt quite excited about where we might be going. We saw very little as we travelled through the night; we stopped several times but most of us slept after a few hours.

When I awoke in the early morning I could see that we were travelling through some very flat agricultural land. There was not a cloud in the blue sky and I could see acres of corn and narrow roads with small hedges. It all looked very beautiful and peaceful. It reminded me, once again, of the Germany I had enjoyed in my early childhood. At the station we were ordered out onto the platform and then into buses. In Germany our main transport had always been the back of trucks, so we felt more like guests than prisoners. There were a few civilians around and they looked at us with obvious curiosity. One of them shouted something, but I did not hear what he said, and I noted that one of our guards shouted at him to be quiet. When we eventually arrived at the prison camp we were lined up and a British commandant, a lieutenant-colonel, addressed us. He told us that we were in Victoria Camp in a place called Mildenhall,[6] and that if we tried to escape we would be shot without hesitation. He said they wanted to trust us because we were all category 'A' prisoners. The war would soon be over and if we behaved ourselves we would soon be repatriated. Apparently we were the third group to arrive, more were expected. As long as we followed the rules of the camp there should be no problems. He then introduced us to our German Camp Leader, *Stabsoffizier* Heinz Hausen.

I managed to find a bunk in one of the huts close to the fire. It was not that I was cold, as it was a warm summer, but I thought that when winter came I would need the warmth after Poltava. There were paintings on the hut walls, and we gathered that the

[6] Victoria Camp, Brandon Hall, Mildenhall (now demolished) was classified as a standard-type German working camp, having been used for Italians until the 1943 Armistice. Prisoner accommodation was standard Ministry of War Production huts of pre-cast concrete panels, 18ft 6in wide and 65ft in length.

previous occupants had been artistic Italian prisoners. I would not call it a holiday camp, but it was better than all of us had expected, and few of us complained about the food.

I wandered around the camp looking at its layout and trying to see beyond the wire fences to the fields and houses beyond. Out there was another life and one which I really wanted to see for myself.

On Sundays church services were organized, one for Protestants and one for Roman Catholics. Although I had attended Roman Catholic churches in Germany, Sicily and France I was not Catholic, so I went to the Protestant service. The first time it was taken by a British officer and was what I would call today a hymn-sandwich. I did not feel comfortable with this form of worship because there was no sense of the sacred, but the following Sunday an Anglican priest, who spoke excellent German, took the service with candles. He wore the priestly vestments of the chasuble, stole and maniple, and celebrated the mass, which he called the Eucharist. I made my communion with a dozen others, and it was a life-changing experience, because here I found within the Protestant Church that sense of the sacred and of mystery I yearned for in the mass. The priest, who was called Father Michael, asked if anyone would help in future to set the room up each Sunday and act as a server at the altar. In military life I had learned that it was not good to volunteer, but for once I ignored the rule and raised my hand instantly. Father Michael came three times a week, every Sunday and then on Tuesdays and Thursdays, when he took English classes and taught us about England. His classes were popular because he had a tremendous sense of humour, which several people took time to understand.

I soon learned how to set up the altar and to serve. I would give him the wafers first, followed by the wine, held out the water for him to bless, which he then added to the wine – in the chalice; I would put the lavabo towel over my wrist so that he could cleanse his fingers. I would ring the sanctuary bells during the consecration, and after the last communicant had left the altar I would pour water into the chalice, onto the paten and then over his fingers, before holding the prayer book up for him to give the blessing. He was bemused by my ownership of the Norwich Cathedral prayer book, and was interested in the fact I had acquired it from a French priest in Lille.

I found his English lessons fascinating, and he spent some time helping me to sound 'more English and less mechanical,' as he put it.

'I tell you, Bruno,' he said, 'most English people can tell you are a German the minute you open your mouth. We pronounce our letters differently and there is a flow to our language which takes years to understand, but give me a few months and I will make sure you can pass as an Englishman, as long as you do not then apply to become a spy.'

I laughed but gained the courage to confide in him about my peculiar circumstances; I could sense he was genuinely interested. After a few hours I soon learned to pronounce the English 'W' properly; when I look back I wonder why I had a problem with this in the first place. I grew very fond of him, and owe him a great deal for introducing me to a form of worship which I valued, for improving my English, but above all for always treating me as a valuable human being.

My greatest disappointment was the lack of a good chess partner. I had a few games with those in my hut, but they were all social players, and once they lost a game they lost interest, and I could not bring myself to lose a game unless it was genuine. I saw very little of the British Camp Commandant or of the German leader. My life now revolved around English lessons and attending the Eucharist, and I was, on the whole, very happy to be there. I was sometimes a little bored but then I would resort to my chess book and study an opening. During my stay in the camp I began writing notes in code about my early years, and it is these notes that form the basis of this account. We were not told about what was happening in France or Germany and I never tested my relationship with Father Michael by asking for information. I kept to my promise to live each day and be grateful.

I think it was about October when I was called in to see a senior British officer, who was waiting with Father Michael. 'Sonn,' he said, 'I gather from the Padre here that you can be trusted.'

'Yes, sir,' I replied 'so long as it does not mean betraying my country.' I did not want to be his spy in the camp.

'I think your country betrayed you,' he replied, 'The Padre has told me about your father.'

'That was the Nazi Party, sir, not my country.'

He looked at me for a few moments without replying. Eventually he simply nodded his head as if he had taken in what I had said, weighed it in the balance and finally agreed.

He then asked me if I would be prepared to work on a local farm which I agreed to without hesitation. I was told to report at the main gate next morning at 7 a.m., from where a soldier would escort me to the farm. They would provide me with food during the day, and the money I was paid could be spent in the camp, on things such as tobacco and toiletries. I would be brought back to the camp at 6 p.m. If I tried to escape I would be given category 'C' status and sent to a secure camp in the north. I had no such intentions and happily signed the form of agreement. As I was about to leave I made a point of turning back and thanking them. Father Michael smiled but the officer just nodded.

The next morning I was up and at the gate bright and early, and I was watched by my fellow prisoners as I wandered through the gates, feeling like a free man. I was met by a corporal who was pushing a bicycle, as we walked off down the road. It was a wonderful sensation just walking through the countryside; it was better than a cold glass of beer and I felt a real sense of exhilaration.

'The locals will not like you,' the corporal suddenly said.

'They haven't met me yet,' I replied.

'You speak good English,' he said, 'but you're German and you started the bloody war. Many of them have lost family in this war, or they have family members away fighting, which is why you're needed on the farm.'

'I understand,' I said, and I did understand. There was no point in trying to explain myself or defend my situation.

Two miles later I was delivered to the farm and a huge elderly man and his wife came out of the thatched farmhouse to look at me. They did just that, simply stood and looked. I felt like an alien being scrutinized.

'You have him until 5.30 George,' the Corporal said, and then, turning to me, said, 'George is the farmer, and he runs the village garage. You do whatever he wants, understand?' I nodded, beginning to feel more and more uneasy about being in such a strange world with foreigners.

The corporal cycled off and the farmer asked me if I spoke English. I replied that I had been learning it but that I was 'not entirely confident.'

'Not entirely confident,' he repeated. 'Sounds bloody good to me, especially for a Jerry.'

'Jerry' became my name for some considerable time. I was set to work in the barn, cleaning it out, and then I was asked to drive an old tractor hauling bales of straw to the barn. It was not difficult work, and I enjoyed the morning. I was called by George's wife for lunch, which she gave me at a table outside in their porch. It was an incredible lunch, a whole pork chop with potatoes and runner beans as well as cabbage. Afterwards I had apple pie and a small glass of beer. I believed I had fallen on my feet once more. In the afternoon two middle-aged men came and helped in the fields. They both looked at me with what I can best describe as sneering curiosity.

'Bloody Hun,' one said to me. 'I hope you all rot in hell.'

I looked at him but did not reply. 'Ignorant bastard,' he continued, 'can't even speak English.' I still resisted replying and continued to work. They returned to their work.

An hour later Farmer George came into the barn and called out to me 'Jerry, do you know anything about cows?'

'No,' I replied, 'but I can soon learn if you show me what you want done.'

'Well,' said one of the other workers, 'the Hun does speak English; he's just too scared to answer us.'

'I am not scared,' I replied, 'but I did not know how to answer your insults.'

'Jew killer,' he retorted.

'My father was Jewish.' For the first time I revealed my background, more out of anger than reasoning.

'And my father was Adolf Hitler.'

'That wouldn't surprise me,' I replied.

Both Farmer George and the man's companion roared with laughter, but the man, who I later heard was called Frank, was not amused. I was glad to leave the group to learn how to milk cows. I was a qualified *Luftwaffe* mechanic who had become an office boy and was now a milkmaid; I was happy despite Frank.

When I walked back that evening the corporal told me that I ought to keep an eye on Frank; his son had been killed in North Africa and he hated Germans. Back in the camp I was pestered all evening about what had happened during the day, and I told my companions everything, including Frank.

'There will be a number of Franks out there,' someone by the door said. We all nodded and were silent for a moment until another added that at least we would not be lynched in this country. One or two said they would not work for the enemy but I detected that the vast majority were keen, which, given that we were all category 'A', was not surprising. As a matter of interest one of the most vociferous against working on the outside was amongst the first to volunteer to join a construction team on a road-widening gang.

One Sunday we heard from Father Michael that Paris and the whole of France had been liberated,[7] and that British troops were on the Rhine.[8] He did not say it with any sense of victory, and he followed it by saying a prayer for our families. This was the kind of man he was; he really understood us as human beings. My parents were dead, Aunt Ingrid had died with them and big Bruno had also gone to his Maker. I only had Marie to think of, and I prayed for Albert and my old friends Franz and Friedrich, but apart from them Germany was not the country of my youth, and seemed to be another world.

As winter drew on I was grateful that I had grabbed a bunk near the fire, not that it ever became as cold as Poltava. The nature of the work on the farm changed with the season, but I was still kept busy. When the weather changed Farmer George

[7] Paris actually fell as early as 25 August 1944.
[8] He was probably he was referring to 'Market Garden' and the battle for Arnhem in September 1944.

247

invited me into their house to eat lunch at their table. This was progress, but neither he nor his wife spoke to me much, not out of malice but from habit.

In December a young lady appeared on the farm to help with the cows. I thought she was the most beautiful woman I had ever seen. She was small and looked somewhat fragile, but she had long brown hair and fierce blue eyes. Whenever I could I would sneak a look at her, but although she was for me beauty personified, she was beyond my reach; she was Frank's daughter, and it was her brother who had been killed by Germans in North Africa. She looked at me occasionally but only with the same venom as her father. I also gathered from Farmer George that she had a boyfriend who was serving in the Royal Navy. It was the first time in years that I had looked at a woman with such interest, and with a real sense of desire.

I was working in the yard, cleaning up some horse muck when I heard Farmer George having trouble starting his tractor. I knew instantly that the problem was fuel starvation; something was blocking the diesel leads. I walked over and asked if I could have a look. He looked at me quizzically, as if to question what a labourer could know about such things. I asked if he had any tools and he opened the tractor's box, where there was a complete set. I set to at once, stripping the fuel system down and cleaning it through. It was an easy job, a large engine with no cowling making access easy. The girl, who I learnt was called Ann, came and stood by Farmer George to watch me. As I worked my way through the fuel feeds, which stank of old diesel, I was conscious of her standing close to me. When I had finished I asked him to start the tractor, which fired immediately. I smiled and he clapped me on the back, but Ann just walked away.

'Where did you learn about engines?' he asked me.

'I was a *Luftwaffe* mechanic,' I replied, 'and before that I built engines for Daimler-Benz.'

'Well I'll be blowed.' I had never heard that expression before.

Before I went back to the camp that evening Farmer George's wife gave me an apple pie. It had taken months, but I thought I detected a slight change in the atmosphere as they adjusted to having an enemy working for them. It was from about that time that they stopped calling me Jerry and called me Bruno. Frank, his daughter Ann, and the other worker, called Colin, still never spoke to me unless they were obliged to. Over time I had become friendly with the corporal and as we walked to and from the camp we talked a great deal. On two occasions he was late so I walked up the road to meet him, but never as far as the camp, in case he got into trouble. His name was Fred; he was not local, but came from Hackney in London. I gathered he had been a member of the Territorial Army but was considered too old for front-line duties. As I got to know him I liked him; he was blunt, with a crude sense of humour, but he seemed to have little malice in him. I gave him a slice of the apple pie that evening, and it was as if I had given him a gold bar.

Although the camp was filling up, many of us now worked on the outside and during the day the camp was half empty. Most travelled by truck and trailer, but as I worked locally I enjoyed my stroll down the road with Fred each day. I always had Sundays to myself, and I continued to serve in the chapel for Father Michael and improve my understanding of English, as well as the English people. It was one of the newcomers who told us about our victory at Arnhem, but the forecast for Germany was still very gloomy.

One Saturday near Christmas that year, Fred was late, which was becoming a habit, so I wandered slowly up the icy lane towards the camp. I was lost in thought. I had written to Marie as well as to Hans and Erik, but I had heard nothing. I was not very surprised; very little post was coming to the camps, mainly owing to the disruption caused by the war. It was dark now and very cold, and ice was forming on the fields. Behind me I heard Farmer George's tractor coming down the road; I recognized the sound of the engine. I looked round and saw Frank driving it very fast. I stood to one side by the ditch, but then I saw that he could see me and was driving the tractor directly at me. I jumped across the ditch at the last moment but the tractor skidded and started to topple into the ditch I had just jumped. My initial response was, 'That would teach him,' but then I noticed that Frank was trapped between the tractor and the water in the ditch. If I did nothing the tractor would push him down into the water and either crush him or drown him. I was angry with him but I could not let him die. I jumped down and tried to pull him free, but he was well and truly stuck, and looked panic stricken; he too realized exactly what was happening.

I shut the engine down and squeezed myself between the tractor and the firmer bank of the ditch. The tractor weighed a ton but because of the angle I thought I might be able to gain some purchase. I can remember, as I was struggling to do this, hearing an owl in the tree nearby. I moved the tractor slightly, just enough for Frank to pull himself clear, but just as he did so the tractor slid in the mud and pinned me to the bank by my left shoulder. It hurt badly because it was the same area where I had been wounded. In fact, the pain was excruciating and at times I knew I was passing out. The sheer weight of the tractor seemed to be squeezing all the air out of my body. Then I became oblivious to anything except the hoot of the owl; I remembered the old saying that the owl is a sign of death. Then, I think, I just passed out.

When I came to I was in what I thought was an army van, but it was an ambulance and I was on my way to hospital. It was yet another Christmas I would be spending in hospital. They stitched up my old wound, which had reopened, and told me that I was to spend the next few days under observation. I found it too uncomfortable to sit up so I lay down on the bed and hoped no permanent damage had been done. I was thrilled when Father Michael visited me, bringing with him my bag, my chess set, the prayer book, as well as my carefully preserved photographs of my parents and big Bruno. He also told me that they were not going to put a guard at the bed because I was trusted. In the afternoon my guard Fred turned up with what looked like a *Gestapo* officer but was a British policeman who was very pleasant to me. It transpired that as I was walking along the road Fred had seen Frank drive the tractor straight at me, as a result of which Frank was at the police station on a charge of attempted murder. I was totally amazed that they would arrest one of their own because of an attack on me.

'No no,' I said. 'The tractor slid on the ice; his mistake was travelling too fast in those conditions.'

'My dear boy,' the policeman sounded like a kindly uncle, 'Frank has confessed to trying to hurt you by making you jump in the ditch.'

'He was trying to kill you.' Fred said.

'I was closest,' I said. 'I tell you it was an accident at the best or at worst just a silly joke.'

'So you do not want to press charges?'

I said I did not; it was just a silly accident. The policeman told me his son was a pilot who was in a German POW camp. I said I hoped he would return home safely.

The next day I was able to sit up in bed despite the terrible pain. Farmer George and his wife came in to see me, and then, to my astonishment, Frank and his daughter Ann.

'I got you wrong, Jerry,' he said. 'You saved my life, then you saved me from prison. I'm sorry and anything I can do for you I will; just ask.'

'There is one thing,' I replied. 'Call me Bruno.'

'OK Jerry, Bruno it is, and I'll belt anyone who calls you Jerry in future.'

He actually did look repentant, twisting his cap in his hands and looking at the floor. I was more interested in Ann. She said nothing but smiled at me in such a way that I hoped she would have reason to do so again one day.

The ward sister soon chased everyone out, and when they had gone I put my chess board on the cover in front of me.

'Why did they call you Jerry?' the man in the next bed asked.

'I'm German.'

'Did you come over before the war?'

'No, I'm a prisoner.'

'Bloody hell, a real German. You don't sound German. I'm not supposed to like you, but everyone else seems OK with you.'

I looked at him; he was very old and I just smiled. He was right, Frank had inadvertently helped me to become part of their social fabric and I was beginning to feel at home in this small town.

I was studying the Ruy Lopez opening when an elderly doctor came to see me. He told me that all seemed well, but I was to stay in hospital until the 28th to make sure I was properly fit.

'I see you play chess,' he said.

'All the time, when I can.'

'You play at the camp?' he asked.

'Not much, there are no real chess players there.'

'I know a good chess player locally, who is in need of a real challenge. And when I say a challenge it will not just be chess, would you be interested?'

Although I wondered what he meant, I agreed immediately.

Chapter 14

1945

When I returned to the camp there was some confusion about the overall situation regarding the war, and I never knew how reliable any news was, where it came from, or whom to trust. There was a small group of so-called category 'A' or white prisoners who were more like dark grey or even black whom the interrogation centre had misjudged. They were rejoicing in the fact that the German army had once again pushed the Western Allies back into the sea, and they were keen on escaping, or making life at the camp difficult. They also believed that the *Führer* would still win the war by using secret weapons. Most of us, indeed the great majority, had come to the conclusion that the war was lost and we were happy to be out of the fighting. A few of us, most especially me, had good reason to hope that the Nazis were totally crushed, but I had some concerns about the survival of Germany; after all it was my home. Or was it? They had persecuted my father and made me feel subhuman. Had I been in the *Wehrmacht* and not the *Luftwaffe*, I think more people would have been made aware of my peculiar racial situation, and life would have become untenable.

Just before my twenty-sixth birthday I had an opportunity to speak to Father Michael and I asked him about the rumours. He listened carefully: I did not tell him about the few restless Nazis amongst us, because I felt that to do so would have been wrong. He told me that the Germans had broken through the Ardennes again during the previous December but that the Allies had counter-attacked[1] and were still heading for the Rhine. He had also heard that the Russians were on the River Oder itself.[2] He then told me that prisoners would eventually be given more news, but in the meantime I should keep my source of information to myself. I promised him that I would say nothing. He then warned me, 'You Germans are not popular in the outside community at the moment, because London is being heavily damaged by rockets.'

'Rockets?' I asked. 'They asked me about them when they found I was a *Luftwaffe* mechanic, but I didn't know what they meant.'

'They're faster than planes and their explosives are killing thousands of people in London.'[3]

I was keen to go back to work on the farm, but I was told that would not be possible until February, as there was not enough for me to do in January. I played a few social games of chess, attended English classes, helped in the chapel and kept myself very much to myself. My birthday fell on a Saturday, not that anyone knew. So you can imagine my surprise on finding that the doctor who had treated me in hospital had come to see me. He was with a senior British officer, and I was called to the gate to meet him. He had come because he knew someone who played chess well, and wondered whether I could go out for a game. My record showed that I had been reliable during the previous year and so the officer said he was happy for me to go if the doctor was prepared to take responsibility for me. A soldier would be detailed to collect me at a given time. Naturally, I was pleased to be able to meet another chess player, and also to leave the confines of the camp, and so I agreed at once.

[1] On 16 December 1944 the Germany army surprised the Allies by breaking once more through the lines in the Ardennes, but this offensive had lost its strength and, by 16 January 1945 the Allies were on the advance again; this is commonly known as the Battle of the Bulge.

[2] On 1 January 1945.

[3] First the V1s then the V2s, fired from the Netherlands. It is believed that 1,100 V2 rockets were launched on London, killing 2,750 people and injuring 6,500.

'There's one ticklish problem,' the doctor said. 'The person I'm speaking about is my brother, and he was a pilot until he was badly injured and burnt. He's not a pretty sight to look at, and he hates Germans.'

'I'll do my best,' I said.

'I saw you in the hospital with some of the locals, and I think with your English it will be OK, but his manner is fairly blunt and confrontational.'

The doctor drove me a short distance in his very small car to a thatched cottage which I had seen before, as it was not far from Farmer George's farmhouse. He was right about his brother being blunt; while I was standing in the hall I could clearly hear his brother shouting, 'I'm not playing chess with any bloody German. I'd rather shoot the bastard.'

The door was then closed on me, and I could detect the rise and fall of a heated argument. The hall I was standing in had a picture of deer, very similar to my mother's favourite painting, and a huge grandfather clock took up most of the space. Eventually the doctor emerged looking red in the face and apologetic, but I told him not to worry. When I entered the room I saw that the man was the same build as the doctor, but there the similarity ended. His face was seriously disfigured, and was as smooth as glass; the wounds from his burns were horrific, and I also noticed that his left arm was missing and the remaining arm looked as burnt as his face.

'No need to stare at me, Jerry,' he barked.

'Peter!' the doctor exclaimed.

'My name's Bruno,' I said sitting down opposite him, and looking at the pleasantly familiar sight of the chess board. He muttered under his breath, but I was already setting the pieces out. He was a good player, but I maintained a small edge; we played in silence for nearly three hours.

'Were you a pilot?' he asked suddenly.

'Mechanic,' I replied with the same brevity.

'Your friends did this to me over Berlin,' he said.

'My parents were killed by bombs dropped on Berlin,' I replied tartly.

'You started the bloody war.'

255

'Do you want to start another game?' I replied.

'Pour me a whisky first.'

I saw the bottle on the table so I poured him a large one and put it by his side. 'Pour yourself one.'

I did, and discovered that this golden liquid went down my throat like fire water: my eyes watered, and as he noticed the impact of the drink on me his eyes twinkled with delight. The last game was a draw, and then Fred the corporal arrived on his bike to walk me back to camp. I said goodbye to my opponent, but he did not reply.

'You're mixing with the high and mighty, Bruno,' Fred said as we strolled past Farmer George's house.

'Only chess,' I replied.

'Cards and darts would be more in my line.' He laughed and we walked on until Fred saw a woman by the post office who he wanted to speak to. It was a very odd situation because he left me holding his bike and rifle while he chatted to the woman over a cigarette. One or two people looked bemused seeing me in my tatty German uniform, holding the rifle for my guard, as he merrily flirted over the road. I still smile when I think of that moment; a little cameo of humour in an otherwise strange world.

I did not think I would be invited back to the small thatched cottage again; the occupant's attitude towards Germans was very clear. However, the following Saturday the doctor collected me again, and I was happy to go, not only for the break from camp life but also for a good game of chess. The game was played in the usual sullen atmosphere; a feeling of deep if not bitter resentment pervaded the room.

We played for another three hours, this time drawing. There was no sign of Fred by the time I was due to leave, so I said farewell; again he did not reply.

I started to walk back along the lane and then saw Fred's bike against a hedge. Looking around I found him below the hedge. At first I thought he had been hit by a car, but on taking a closer look I realized he was drunk. It took me some time to get him on to his feet. I slung his rifle over my shoulder and, pulling his arm around me, helped him along the road. It dawned on me that if I returned to the camp with a drunken guard, carrying his rifle, he would be in very serious trouble. I knocked on Farmer George's door and explained the situation to the startled farmer. He wondered what I was doing there, because I was not expected until Monday morning, and certainly not armed. When he eventually fully understood the problem he rushed in to speak to his wife while I propped George up in the porch. It was the farmer's wife who solved the problem by stating that a strong cup of tea and one hour should get him upright.

'I was due back half an hour ago,' I said.

'I'll walk back with you,' Farmer George said, 'and tell them that Fred came off his bike and is nursing his wounds in the farm kitchen. Hopefully they'll believe us.'

By the time I returned, two or three soldiers were being gathered together to form a search party, but Farmer George told them all was well, and that I had helped Fred to the farm. The officer in charge looked at me for a moment, then nodded and thanked the farmer. I waved goodbye and started to wander off to my hut when the officer called me back. 'You're Sonn, correct?'

'Yes, sir.'

'Did you carry the corporal's rifle?'

'No sir, he wouldn't let go of it.'

The officer looked at me long and hard, and then nodded, indicating that I should return to the hut.

On the Monday morning when I walked out to be taken to the farm Fred was waiting for me. We walked out through the gates silently, and when the camp was some distance away, Fred thanked me for covering for him. 'Would have been a bloody court martial,' he said, 'letting a German prisoner have my rifle when I was pickled.'

'That's all right, Fred, I don't see you as the enemy.'

Fred stopped and looked at me. 'That's what we bloody are, enemies; bloody silly really, at home you'd be just another one of the lads, larking around with the rest of us. I've got this for you.' He handed me a pouch of pipe tobacco, for which I thanked him profusely.

We walked down the lane, one British soldier and one German prisoner strolling together like old friends.

Fred dropped me off at the farm, but that was the last of my farming days; Farmer George had another way of making a living at the local garage. He asked me if I would be prepared to work there for him, in the back of a long shed, where he serviced and repaired the few cars still on the road. I was only too happy, especially when, on arrival, I saw that Ann worked there on the petrol pumps, and she also did the accounts. I also found it gratifying when she smiled at me as I walked in.

I spent the whole day working on an old tractor; by completely stripping it down, working on the piston heads and putting it back together I managed to restore it to excellent working order despite the lack of spare parts.

The whole situation did not make sense to me; I was a prisoner in the land of my enemies, I played chess with a man who might have dropped the very bombs that had killed my father, I was in love with a woman I dared not approach, and yet for the first time for a long time I was feeling happy. I was not liked as I was a German but even that was preferable to being a *mischling* in Nazi Germany. Sometimes I was aware of local people looking at me as if I were some kind of alien, and occasional unpleasant remarks were made, but on the whole I have to say I was treated very fairly.

I had to face one major disappointment when one week, some time in early March, Ann's boyfriend turned up. He was in a sailor's uniform and I felt a deep sense of distaste when I saw him hugging and kissing Ann in the office. It really was none of my business, but for the first time ever in my life I was in love with a woman who was beyond my grasp. Ann introduced him to me. His name was Keith and I had to make every effort to be polite to him.

'Best Germans are dead Germans,' he said as he refused to shake my proffered hand.

I did not hang around, but giving a slight bow, which I knew the British hated, I returned to work on yet another tractor I was endeavouring to repair.

Every Saturday afternoon I played chess with Peter. On one occasion near the middle of March I entered his inner sanctum to find he had poured a whisky for me, and he began to call me

Bruno. It had taken weeks for our relationship to get this far, the longest thaw I had ever known. Normally I would not have been willing to persevere, but we were of similar strength in chess and the matches were always interesting.

'I gather from that high church priest that you serve at his altar?' he said suddenly, and then added, 'do you believe all that?'

'Yes to both,' I replied. 'I serve at the altar and I believe all that. What do you mean by high church?'

'Bloody funny a Nazi being a Christian.'

'I was never a Nazi. What is a high church?'

'Never a Nazi?'

'Never.'

'Why did you join up?'

I put the piece I was about to move back on its original square.

'Do you want to hear?'

'Tell me,' he replied.

It took half an hour, but I told him about the Hitler Youth, about my father being declared a Jew, about what being a *mischling* meant, even about Josef. Finally I pointed out that one did not 'join up' in Nazi Germany, one was ordered.

'You realize that it might have been my bombs that killed your parents?' he said.

'That thought had crossed my mind,' I replied.

'Well?' He looked at me almost quizzically, though his burnt face made expressions difficult to interpret.

'That's war. What is high church?'

Having asked this I studied his face, looking past the scars, and I discerned a smile. He educated me, in his abrupt and forceful manner, into the ups and downs of the Church of England. I shall never forget the description he gave when he said 'Low-church people are frustrated Methodists, high-church people are frustrated Catholics, and the rest of us are just frustrated.' By the time Fred collected me we had not finished the game, having discussed all these issues, and as I left he called out, 'Goodnight, Bruno'. They say the English are reserved and difficult to get to know, but it is even more difficult when you are a prisoner of war from a country they hate; I think, when I look back, that once again chess had been the catalyst.

We got back on time, but the camp was in uproar. One of the British soldiers had been found, behind one of our huts, unconscious. Everyone had been lined up, which meant I had to find the place where I normally stood in for roll calls. I was immediately suspicious of the vociferous few category 'C' prisoners, but having decided it was best to keep a low profile I kept my opinions to myself. For the first time the British soldiers looked menacing, and we were kept standing until ten that night. There was plenty of activity as our huts were searched, and our Commandant was arguing with a group of British officers.

Once back in our hut we could talk of nothing else, but it remained a mystery to all of us. The only interesting factor was that one of my fellow inmates knew the soldier in question, called Bert, because he had been selling the prisoners cheap tobacco. Next day we were ordered out again at 6 a.m.; it was cold and dark, and we were kept standing until nine, when we were released for breakfast and chapel.

The real disappointment came when on Monday morning none of us were allowed out of camp. I saw Farmer George turn up at the gates with one or two others; I guess that our labour was missed by some of the locals. There was a distinct sense of hostility in the place. We never did find out what had actually happened, but by Thursday those of us who worked outside were allowed to do so again. It was several months later that Father Michael hinted to me that the soldier, Bert, had probably had a run in with someone; he was certainly saying nothing and blaming no one. All the talk of escape was that of the small minority who were ardent Nazis, and who had somehow managed to talk themselves into the 'A' category; they were very much on the periphery of camp life.

I soon discovered that Farmer George had been looking for me; his tractor was in need of repair again, and although he was an amateur mechanic he had no idea how to resolve the latest problem. When I stripped the engine I found that it needed a spare part which was unobtainable, but I managed to overcome the situation by a make-do repair; in fact, it lasted for the rest of that tractor's working life. I was somewhat proud that the locals were beginning to see me as a genius when it came to engines. I also learned a great deal about British car engines, which I had never seen before. I always used big Bruno's method of dismantling an engine back to square one before rebuilding once more. In those days it was impossible to get parts from the manufacturers because they had to concentrate on the war effort, so I became an expert in either making the parts or adapting other bits and pieces. I also set up a spare parts system in the shed by stripping defunct engines and cars, and never throwing away anything which might be useful at a later date.

During April we were given a news-sheet which not only gave information about the various courses one could attend in the camp, but was sprinkled with news about the war. It was becoming abundantly clear that the last days were approaching. We read that the Russians were not only in Pomerania[4] but had taken Vienna.[5]

My chess opponent, Peter, asked me whether I had heard the news and I told him what I knew. He had heard on the grapevine that the Russians were fighting in Berlin[6] and wondered whether I had any family left. I had already told him about my parents and Josef but now I told him about Ruth. One evening he invited me to share some cold chicken and salad; it was one of the best meals I had eaten for a long time – not that any of us complained about our rations. Those who did moan about the food had not seen the realities of war on the Eastern Front. When I walked home that evening with Fred I saw Ann's boyfriend sauntering ahead of us with his arm around another girl's shoulder. I knew it was not Ann by the colour of her hair. As we passed him he looked at me with some venom, but I looked the other way and talked to Fred.

'Do you know sailor boy?' Fred asked.

'He's the boyfriend of Ann, who works at the garage.'

'That's a pity.'

'Why?' I asked.

'He's down my local pub most nights, supposed to be on extended

[4] On 1 March 1945.

[5] On 13 April 1945.

[6] On 18 April 1945 Zhukov crossed the Spree and by 25 April Berlin was encircled.

leave, but we reckon he's got girls all around the place. He's a right bigmouth.'

As we passed the last field before reaching the camp I saw a plover rise from a nearby track so I asked Fred to wait for two minutes. I ran over the field and found the nest, in which was just one egg. When I got back Fred asked me what I had been up to and when I told him he roared with laughter.

'Where's the egg then?'

'I left it.'

'You left it! Get it and eat it, people pay money for plovers' eggs.'

'Leave it Fred, it's too small.'

' 'Ere, grab my rifle.'

I held his bike and rifle for the third time since he had started guarding me, while he dashed over the field. I knew he would not find the nest; my only fear was that he would tread on it, because its brown mottled colour merges perfectly with the earth.

Our five minutes of madness caused problems. Unbeknown to Fred, and me, Ann's boyfriend had walked past us and having seen me holding Fred's bike and rifle, and he later reported Fred for dereliction of duty. That evening I was called to the Commandant's office. I was worried about the reason for my summons and even more worried when I saw Fred standing to attention between two military policemen.

'Padre Michael tells me, Sonn, that you are a faithful servant to the chapel, is that correct?'

'I hope so, sir.'

'So if I ask you a question you will answer me truthfully?'

I just looked at him, and as he turned his back to me to go and sit behind his desk, I took a swift glance at Fred, who very gently shook his head at me.

'You must tell me the truth,' he repeated.

'Yes sir,' I said.

'We have had a report that a serving member of the Royal Navy saw you holding the corporal's rifle while he went to relieve himself in a field.'

'No sir.'

'Are you certain?'

'Certainly sir.'

Next day Father Michael took me aside, and said he was surprised I had lied, because he had passed by in the car and seen the same incident.

'Did you report it, Father?'

'Of course not.'

'Well I did not lie.' I went on to explain that the commandant had asked me if I had held the rifle while Fred went for a pee; I had only held it while he looked for a bird's egg. 'I was not pressed any further by the Commandant.'

Father Michael smiled. 'You would make a good lawyer, Bruno, that was quick thinking. They're still not sure you're telling the truth, but the Commandant is not overly worried. He thinks you like Fred, and did not want him to go before a court martial.'

'That, Father, is perceptive of the Commandant.'

Fred could have faced a court martial, lost his stripes or had his pay docked. None of this happened, and I received another packet of pipe tobacco and a friendship that was to last for many years.

That spring was not all fun and games. Ann's boyfriend was at the garage a few days later, and looking for a fight. I knew that if I became involved in a brawl I would not be allowed out of camp, and so I stood there like a weak-kneed boy while he shoved me around the workshop.

During May the news came in thick and fast. First we heard that the German army had surrendered in Italy,[7] which was not as much of a shock as the news that the *Führer* had committed suicide.[8] There was some debate about the validity of this information, but as our German Commandant told us, there was no reason for the Western Allies to lie about it. One or two people looked downcast at this, but most of us no longer gave it much thought. We had seen the damage done to Germany by the war, and most of us were more worried about our families and friends than about the *Führer*. This sense of concern grew when

[7] On 29 April 1945.

[8] On 30 April 1945 Hitler shot himself in his bunker.

we heard that Berlin was in the hands of the Soviets.[9] Then we were told the war had ended.[10] The British thought the Soviets were great allies and talked of Stalin as Uncle Joe; I could understand why, but Peter, my chess opponent, had other views: 'Bedfellows with the Nazis,' he used to say.

While we worried about Germany, and thought about our eventual release, we had no idea that the greatest nightmare of all was about to hit us. We were all ordered into the largest hut for what we thought was a film show. I suspected that something else was about to happen when I saw that our guards were fully armed. The British Commandant stood up, and in his well-rehearsed German informed us that we were about to watch a newsreel about Belsen[11] and Dachau.[12] I wondered why they were going to show us a film about prison camps, and thought it might be to show us how lucky we had been.

'I want you all to know that the rest of the world is disgusted at the unbelievable evil perpetrated by your Nazi so-called leaders. This is not propaganda, it is real. We all know that when a war starts there can be cruelty on both sides, but your leaders have dragged the name of Germany into the sewers.' There was a brief murmur of dissent from some, but most of us were stunned by the sudden ferocity of a man who was generally liked for his calmness. 'We have uncovered atrocities that seem unbelievable in the modern world, perpetrated by your Nazi leaders as they attempted to liquidate every Jew, Gypsy, homosexual, even Jehovah's Witnesses, or anyone else they did not like. They have committed a series of acts so savage that we are showing the world these films so that you can see exactly what has happened: this, I repeat, is not propaganda but reality, the reality of your own Nazi leaders. Show the film.'

Since then we have seen a great deal more, but in that hut that evening we sat in stunned silence. I believe that none of us in that

[9] On 2 May 1945 Berlin surrendered.

[10] At one minute past midnight on 9 May 1945.

[11] The British Army discovered Belsen on 15 April. They found 10,000 unburied dead, 40,000 sick and dying; 28,000 died even after liberation.

[12] On 29 April the XV Corps of the 7th US Army came upon Dachau.

particular camp had any idea of the bestiality of the camps. Some, like me, had heard rumours; I had even heard that some people had been gassed, but I had no concept of the scale of the industrialized slaughter that took place. One person next to me mumbled that it had to be anti-German propaganda, but that line of thinking we all knew was a flimsy argument dreamed up out of desperation. I do not think anyone spoke after the film; we filed back to our huts in silence. I spoke to Father Michael next day, but even he seemed a little remote; it had shaken him as well. He wanted to know how it was possible for Germans to plead ignorance of such slaughter on such a massive scale. I was as honest as I could be, pointing out that I had seen some atrocities in Poltava, that I had heard rumours, but never realized that it was so widespread.

'How could you support such a regime?' he asked me.

I explained to him the nature of the Hitler Youth, but I did not go on to reiterate my fears as a *mischling*; I had already explained this to him. Instead I tried to make him understand what a hypnotic effect the *Führer* had had on the wider population. It was an impossible mission, and I decided I had to accept that in embracing Hitler we had made a terrible choice. I do not want to dwell on the subject of German guilt, but I have felt frustrated all my life because I have felt guilty about being involved, yet my father was amongst the persecuted, and I, as a *mischling*, always lived in fear.

We soon gathered that the wider population had been exposed to the same or similar films, and several locals refused to have us working for them any more, including Farmer George. They also showed us a film in early or mid-June, about the end of the war, including pictures of Berlin after the bombing, and the Russian artillery attacks. I thought of Marie, because I could not see how anyone could possibly have survived such prolonged explosive onslaughts.

I was, however, allowed out to play chess with Peter and, to give him his due, he behaved in a way quite uncharacteristic for him by never mentioning the camps or the atrocities, which still filled the papers that we were now allowed to read. If anything we seemed to be getting on better than we had, and I was pleased when his doctor brother called in one day with a bottle of whisky for me. He believed that my companionship, and games of chess, had done more for Peter than he had dared to hope for. 'He can even say "German" now without having a fit or spitting on the floor.'

I was disappointed that they did not want me at the garage any more, just as I was becoming used to it as a way of life. Then my problem was solved by Father Michael. He had been to see Farmer George and had explained that as a *Luftwaffe* mechanic I would not have known the full extent of the atrocities; he also explained about my father and the nature of being a *mischling* under the Nuremberg racial laws. I was back at work on Monday morning and Farmer George was waiting for me.

'I keep getting you wrong, Bruno,' he said. 'But when we saw what those Nazis had done I hated all Germans, really hated them. But I know you're OK and that vicar bloke has confirmed it. Friends?'

He held out his hand and I shook it. It felt like being back at school, making things right after a squabble. Nevertheless, the knowledge of the existence of those camps had a marked effect on many Germans for the rest of their lives, even though they had not been involved; it left deep scars on the German psyche.

There was talk about repatriation, but we were told that it would be some time yet, not least because of the sheer destruction and confusion in mainland Europe, with millions of displaced people trying to find their way home. We were also told that any dedicated Nazis would be kept until they had been 'de-Nazified'.

I was pleased to be working again in the garage, as it was for me the most natural environment. One good thing that had happened was that Keith reported back to his ship, which I was told was off to fight Japan in the Far East. I was pleased I would not have to watch my back, and Frank seemed to be pleased he had gone; it was clear that he did not want him as a son-in-law.

Frank was only an amateur at the work in the garage but he had sufficient experience to be a great help, and after a few weeks I noticed that he was keen to learn from me some of the intricacies of the tasks.

At the end of July I had another major change in my life, which was totally unexpected. Unbeknown to me Farmer George, Father Michael, Peter and his doctor brother had met the Commandant saying they were prepared to back me for what I gathered was called parole. It was explained to me that I could now live outside the camp, reporting back every six months until my repatriation papers were ready. I was delighted but wondered where I would live. Apparently, there were rooms above the garage that could be converted into a bedsit, and that was to become my home. I said goodbye to my hut mates, not that I had come to know many of them very well, and I was off to my new room that very day. I think the most remarkable memory of that month was walking out of the camp on my own; no Fred and no check at the gates. I walked down through the small town unaccompanied, and felt like a free man. I felt more independent than I had in Germany because not a single person asked me for my pass. I carried my *Luftwaffe* overcoat and uniform in my bag, and wore my garage overalls so that no one looked at me, not even the locals.

I discovered that Ann had cleaned the flat for my arrival and put some food, real coffee and tea, which I now enjoyed, in the small kitchen. I had my own lavatory and a small tub for a bath; I was happier than I had been for a very long time. I was doing the work I enjoyed most, and I had my own accommodation. That evening I walked up to Peter for a game of chess by myself and I did not have to hurry the game because Fred was no longer waiting to collect me. As I walked back later I realized that for me the war had well and truly ended, and although I was in a foreign land, I could speak their language and with my mechanical knowledge and skills I felt at home.

The war had finished for me but not for my neighbours. In early August news came through of the atomic bomb explosions in Hiroshima and Nagasaki.[13] It was difficult for all of us to understand the enormity of such power; there was just a sense of relief that the war had now completely ceased. Peter said that although a great number of lives had been lost, the death toll would have been greater had it been necessary to invade Japan.

[13] On August 1945 a uranium bomb exploded over Hiroshima and on 9 August a plutonium bomb over Nagasaki.

I knew I had made some progress in my relationships because when we first heard the news in the garage Frank blurted out that it was a pity 'they hadn't dropped the same bomb on Berlin,' then looked at me and apologized, adding, 'Well a small one just to take Adolf out.' I nodded and smiled, because if the *Führer* had not existed life might have been very different for the whole world. I also reflected on the fact that the *Führer* had not hesitated to do something evil to achieve his desired end.

I was now earning money I could spend in the local shops – not a great amount but as much as most locals. I purchased a paraffin heater for my rooms because I thought it would be cold in the winter, although not Poltava cold. I also put the photographs of my parents and big Bruno in photo frames on the wall; they were creased, but like me they had at least survived. I was lucky because I had managed to hang on to my few belongings: my chess set and book, my prayer book and my photographs. Many of my comrades in the huts had arrived with only the clothes they stood up in. I though about throwing my *Luftwaffe* uniform away, but decided to keep it in a trunk and used my greatcoat as an additional bed cover. I attended the local church; it was not where Father Michael worked, and the worship was more what I would today call 'middle of the road', but I was made to feel very welcome and I was soon serving at the altar once again for the 8 a.m. communion. My English was rapidly sounding more natural, and new people I met did not automatically assume I was German. I did not enlighten them but if asked, as I was from time to time, I told the truth. When this happened it raised a few eyebrows and the occasional grunt, but apart from one man, who turned his back on me, nothing unpleasant ever happened. In fact, I was learning a sharp lesson: that it was easier to be a German in England than a Jew or a *mischling* in Germany.

One day in October I was finishing the work I was doing on an old coach engine when, looking up from the pit, I saw two people in uniform. I climbed out cautiously hoping this was not trouble, only to find Erik and Hans standing there. Erik was in a British uniform and Hans was wearing an American one. Ann and Frank looked surprised when they saw us hug one another. We closed the garage and, inviting Frank to join us, walked down to the local pub, the Green Man. I had never been there alone but I had been once before with Frank. Since there was no more black-out, the pub looked warm and welcoming. It was full of the usual locals, as it was about 7 p.m. There were curious looks as people wondered why their local German was so obviously friendly with a British officer and an American paratrooper. Frank actually looked pleased to be part of this mystery group.

Hans had been dropped on D-Day and had then fought in the Battle of the Bulge, after which he fought his way all through Germany. He sounded American and no longer considered himself German. He had been decorated twice, and now that the Japanese war was over, he was looking forward to returning home to Ruth in California. I gathered that she was working as a nurse and later, I read in her letter, that she wanted me to join them in America. Erik had eventually been attached to XXX Corps and had been caught up in Operation Market Garden which culminated in the Battle of Arnhem. He had decided to try to stay on as a professional soldier, and because the Allies were now occupying part of Germany the fact that he was bilingual assured him of a future. In return I told them all that had happened to me, and how much I was enjoying my life in Mildenhall and my new job.

I was sorry to hear that Erik and Hans could find no trace of their parents, and hoped they would soon have news; they were still trying to find out what had happened. It certainly did my local reputation no harm being seen in the company of Hans and Erik, and in a strange sort of English way, this gave me permission to go to the pub and feel more at home; in today's modern teenage parlance it would be called 'street-cred'.

We swapped addresses; Frank and I waved goodbye to them as they drove off in Hans's jeep. It was all a very remarkable experience, and I was thrilled that they had both survived the war. It seemed another world when I remembered Erik and I going birds'-nesting, and then later worrying about them as they fled Nazi Germany. They were both strong characters and I admired the way they had had the courage to take up arms against their own country, which had turned against them.

That Christmas turned out to be excellent. To my joy and

surprise Frank invited me to his house for the day, and at lunch I sat next to Ann. In the evening Farmer George and his wife joined us for a cold meat supper, and we played cards all the evening. It was the first time I had eaten turkey! Frank's house was a small terraced cottage with a large open fire that reminded me of my own home. All day I wished that Ann would forget Keith and look favourably on me; I knew, however, that it was a lost cause, and that she would not want to come back with me to Germany or go to America.

Chapter 15

1946–49

When I look back I realize that the immediate post-war period was a time of great adjustment for me personally. It was during those years that I first became aware that events happened to me and around me, and that I was never really master of any of the circumstances that governed my life. In Nazi Germany I had been under orders; in England I started life as a prisoner and later as a prisoner on parole, an object of suspicion. Living and working within a community of people who had once been my enemy was testing for all of us.

The late forties may have been a time of peace, but it was also a time of considerable austerity. I no longer feared for my life, or the lives of those I knew and loved, but spiritually and psychologically I was beginning to feel, if not damaged, then somewhat frayed. The new year started badly for me, as I had a series of nightmares, revisiting in my sleep the scenes of Frau Goldblatt being beaten into the gutter, the SS troops shooting the family of Jews at Poltava, the partisan woman I had killed. I have always wondered why those memories should have haunted me at that point in time. Father Michael thought that after the turmoil of the previous five or six years it was my mind trying to deal with its own wounds. These memories and nightmares have never quite left me, and I can remember them now fifty years after the war, but in the immediate post-war years they were almost destructive, sending me into a spiritual wilderness. It was pointless saying that 'in war these things happen', and it did not help when I read of far worse atrocities. I shall always feel guilty for having stood and watched the attack on Frau Goldblatt, making no effort to help the old shopkeeper who had always been kind to me as a boy. Apart from Father Michael, I kept this problem to myself, but Peter was astute enough to know that something was troubling me, and he speculated that, as with him, it was a laying to rest of the traumas of my own personal war.

It struck me that the amount of food available seemed to decrease in the post-war years; there was certainly less than during 1944 and 1945, when I had lived in the prison camp. A complex ration system was established, which limited everything right down to the amount of margarine or cooking fat a person could purchase.[1] I suspect that having Farmer George as an employer meant I was better off, along with many of the neighbours, than people living in large towns and cities. Nevertheless, it was only because Frank, Ann and I shared our ration coupons that we did not suffer too much. I had only to cast my mind back to the situation in Europe before I was captured to realize how lucky I was; it put food rationing into context for me. The locals were especially annoyed when bread was difficult to purchase,[2] but what amused me more was hearing them discussing the fact that television broadcasts had been resumed,[3] but only for a limited number of southerners. 'It's the establishment looking after their own,' was the key phrase amongst the local gossips. I have to confess that I had heard little about television until that point, and Peter had to explain to me the English notion of 'the establishment'.

During 1946 my English improved considerably, and I listened carefully to the local people speaking to help me pronounce words correctly. Peter was a great help and made me say words until I sounded 'English', though I noticed that his English was more

[1] On 7 February 1946 a world shortage led to cuts in rations of butter, margarine and cooking fats from 8oz to 7oz a week.
[2] On 21 July 1946 bread and flour rationing were introduced.
[3] On 7 June 1946 TV resumed for the south-east only, and then only for an estimated 11,500 viewers.

precise than the locals. He also started educating me in English habits and, more importantly, English humour, which sometimes took me by surprise. I had to watch a person's face and eyes to make sure they were not 'pulling my leg'.

Frank and I worked more and more closely together in the garage, and a real friendship started to develop between us. He was intrigued by Erik and Hans, and when Erik sent me a letter from Germany I was confident enough to read out the contents to him. The sad news was that, as we had thought, Erik had discovered that his parents had been killed in a concentration camp we had never heard of somewhere in Poland.

The newspapers were full of German war crimes, especially at the Auschwitz-Birkenau[4] complex where people had been systematically gassed. Those who knew me and my story did not mention these atrocities, but quite a few others made a point of glaring or staring at me. I read the papers myself and felt disgusted with what had happened and ashamed that the Nazis had allowed Germany and German people to be smeared with this downright evil.

I spent an afternoon talking to Father Michael about the situation, and although he understood my depression, he felt that by allowing the Nazis to take power there was a sense of corporate responsibility.

'There's nothing you can do about it, Bruno,' he said. 'It's now a matter of Germany rebuilding itself and its reputation. You have a troubled conscience, but you were not involved in massacres in or out of camps, so you have to live each day as it comes and do your best.'

'But I saw a massacre and I heard of others,' I replied, 'and I hate myself for being weak, standing by as a frightened onlooker.'

'Had you protested in Poltava,' he answered, 'what would have happened to you?'

'I would probably have been arrested and sent to a camp as a Jew-lover.'

'That would have taken a good deal of real courage.'

'That's why I am ashamed, I lacked the courage.'

---

[4] Relieved by the Russians on 27 January 1945.

This is the gist of a conversation that lasted all afternoon, and although it helped ease my mind that evening, my personal doubts returned in my dreams and in my thoughts as I worked in the garage during the day. I was wrestling with my own sense of guilt and cowardice, as well as the shame of what Germans had done, which was revealed in the daily newspaper reports of the Nuremberg trials. When I heard that the Nazi commandant of Belsen was called Josef Kramer I found myself wondering about my SS brother Josef. German children born after the war should have no sense of guilt, but my generation, though we seldom talk about it openly, have the memory of the camps lurking like dark shadows in our background.

A local coach firm took their work away from us at the beginning of the year because Farmer George was employing a German. I felt very bad about this, but when the garage in the next town could not cope with the work, they soon returned, and Farmer George, to use an English expression, made them come to me 'cap in hand'.

During the summer of 1946 we were visited by two sets of military personnel at the garage, neither of whom were welcome. The first were two senior officers wanting to speak to me. I took them upstairs to my bedsit and offered them a cup of tea, which they declined.

'We need to know that you are actually Bruno Sonn,' the taller one said.

'Who else could I possibly be?'

'In the aftermath of the war we are coming upon people who have swapped identities.'

'Why?' I was quite innocent of the post-war situation and had no idea why they were questioning me.

'You had a brother called Josef?'

'Yes, he was killed earlier in the war.'

'How do we know you are not Josef?'

For a moment I was at a complete loss. I had photographs of my parents but none of Ruth or Josef. 'Why are you asking after Josef?'

'He's a minor war criminal who had been indicted for war crimes when he was a guard in one of the camps.'

I shook my head, not so much in disbelief but as at the news, which made me glad that my parents were not alive. I explained, as quickly as I was able, something of my family background.

'So you and your brother were never close?'

'We were never close even as youngsters, and when he turned on my father, my mother also rejected him. Because of their pain I wanted nothing more to do with him.' I could see them scrutinizing me closely, trying to establish whether I was telling the truth.

'What was the age gap between the two of you?'

'Josef was born on 1 April 1915 and I was born on 27 January 1919. Listen,' I said, 'Josef was an SS soldier, I was, and still am, a mechanic. You can check with my sister Ruth who is a naturalized American, or with my last commander, *Oberst* Georg Freisher.'

I had no idea where the *Oberst* was, but I guessed they would know, and I also gave them Ruth's address as well as Erik's, who was still serving in the British army somewhere in Berlin. I gave them so much information that I think I convinced them before they left that I was not Josef. When they left I sat on the chair by my window watching them walk up the road to the pub. The very thought that Josef had committed such acts, that he was being pursued as a war criminal, brought on a sudden bout of depression.

Outside the garage I found two military policemen wandering around the petrol pump. My heart fell, so I ignored them and walked in to find Frank.

'What's going on?' Frank asked.

'They were checking that I really am Bruno Sonn and not someone else.' I had never mentioned Josef to anyone except Father Michael and Peter.

'No, I mean those two outside.'

'I have no idea.'

We soon found out because, having looked around the pump, they wandered into the workshop.

'Can I help you?' Frank asked.

I was relieved to hear that it was not me they were after, but Ann's boyfriend, Keith Green. It transpired that when he had left us, to sail for the Far East, he had failed to report for duty. He was absent without leave, they said.

'He left here months ago.' Frank said.

'And we've been looking for him for months. Both he and his wife have disappeared.'

'His wife?' Frank sat on the tractor's footplate.

'You have the wrong man,' I said. 'The Keith we know is engaged to this man's daughter.'

'He married a girl in Portsmouth the day before he was due to sail, and that was the last we saw of him.'

'Why are you looking here?' Frank asked.

'He's a local lad, we gather.'

They could see from Frank's face that it would be unsafe for Keith to return to this town, and after taking a few more details they left.

I knew exactly how Frank felt, but dared not say a word as I still loved Ann which I knew would be totally unacceptable. Frank was not a man who thought long and hard about anything, as I knew from the time he had tried to kill me with a tractor; he walked straight into the small office, where Ann was preparing bills and paying invoices. I busied myself with the tractor waiting for her to cry out, but it did not happen. When Frank came out he said simply, 'She wasn't bothered.' We worked on in silence, stunned by two sets of military visitors in one day bearing extraordinary news; I was pleased with the last visitors especially since Ann was not upset. I wondered whether she had found someone else because I never saw her in the evenings; once the day was over I tended to keep myself to myself.

The next day I reported back to the camp to fulfil my parole obligations. The place was barely occupied. Many of my old comrades had been sent to transit camps, returned to Germany, or were out working. I signed a book, had a quick chat with the supervising officer and left: as I was going back out through the gates I heard a call. 'Bruno, how's it going?'

I stopped and turned and saw Fred strolling from the canteen, 'I'm fine, Fred, busy in the garage every day.'

'You're never in the pub?'

'I went there once, but I don't like to go there alone

because . . .' I paused, 'because Germans are hardly popular at the moment.'

'You're OK, mate, people like you, and most forget you're German because your English is posher than mine. Hang on, I'll walk back with you, I'm going to see a man about a dog.'

It took me years to find out what 'seeing a man about a dog' was all about. We walked down the road together, no rifle, no longer a guard and his prisoner, just two friends. Fred insisted on buying me a drink in the pub, which I accepted as I did not want to offend him. No one said anything or even looked at me in that crowded bar, and as I left I felt Fred had done me a favour; I began to feel more confident about the future.

That Saturday evening I talked to Peter about this experience between our games of chess.

'I'm not surprised,' he said. 'People around here are used to you now, and strangers would have no idea you're German. Did those military police looking for that Keith scallywag, ask who you were?'

'No.'

'I know military police, had they thought for one moment you were a Jerry they would have said something, and probably searched you just for the hell of it.'

'Fred said I speak posher than he does. What does that mean?'

'You know, Bruno, for a Jerry you're bright in some things, but slow in others. Remember my talking to you about the English class system? It's all to do with the way you speak, it's nothing to do with money, that's the American class system. Fred, bless him, is a Cockney and he murders the English language. I told you to copy me or Father Michael. We're not Cockney; in fact, you sound like a public school boy already, perhaps one who has been on holiday in Germany. You pass as an Englishman, which for a Jerry is amazing.'

'My *Oberst* spoke like you do because he went to an English school.'

'Are you going back to Germany?' he suddenly asked.

'I don't know what to do.'

We started another game, which we both enjoyed, because we were now virtually equal, and our games tended to be long and interesting. I was lucky to draw that particular one, as Peter's question had set me thinking. I had heard from Fred that many prisoners were going home, and only the hard nuts, as he called them, were being kept back. Soon I would have to come to a decision, which would not be easy. I had already ruled out any idea of joining Ruth and Hans in America, even if it could be arranged. Technically, I was still a prisoner of the British, who happened to be allowed to live outside the camp, and work for my living. I think, when I look back, that Fred played a major part in my thinking because as we walked down the road together I felt at home and welcome. I decided not to jump the gun but to wait and see how life worked out during the next few months. It was something of a relief when the Western Allies executed some of the Nazi criminals,[5] because the papers stopped being so full of the horrors perpetrated during the war. The locals were now more interested in their local football team,[6] some supporting teams who played as far away as London. I had not realized how fanatical the English were about the game. Peter preferred rugby, which until then I had never even heard about.

During the winter of 1946 he asked me to drive his old car for him, as he had no left arm which meant he very rarely left the house, and he wanted to watch a rugby game. Although I had learned to drive in the *Luftwaffe*, I had no idea whether it was legal for me to do so here in England. Peter convinced me saying that there was nothing to worry about, but the car would not start. As it had been left in a large garden shed, unused for over two years, I spent the next day, Sunday, working on it, cleaning out the rusted carburettors and fuel lines, clearing the air intakes and recharging the battery. It was a small sports car, and when at last it did fire, I could tell that it had quite a powerful engine. We went out for a drive and I quickly became used to changing gear with my left hand and driving on the left – a strange quirk of the British. The following Saturday I took him to a local rugby match, and I was amazed at the ferocity of the game. What fascinated me most was the politeness of the players towards the referee; they

[5] On 16 October 1946 eleven leading Nazis were hanged at Nuremberg.
[6] On 31 August 1946 league football resumed after stopping in 1939.

almost bowed to him when they were reprimanded. On the way home Peter told me that 'rugby was a hooligan's game played by gentlemen and football a gentleman's game played by hooligans'. I have never understood why rugby never caught on in Germany; I think most of us would have relished the physicality of the game, as I did by watching it over the years after that first encounter.

As 1946 drew to a close, the local vicar preached a sermon based on what the Archbishop of Canterbury had been saying earlier in the year, that there should be full communion between the churches.[7] Remembering that my mother was Lutheran and my father Roman Catholic, this seemed to make eminent sense to me. I had been received by the Bishop of Norwich into the Church of England at a service arranged by Father Michael, but I was conscious that in the small town in which I now lived, there was the Church of England Parish Church, a Roman Catholic church, a Methodist, a Baptist and a Congregational Chapel. Then, as now, I thought it tragic that Christians cannot worship together.

Father Michael was very ill at this time, and when I went to see him I realized he was dying. He could only have been in his sixties, but his face was pallid and drawn, and when he coughed there was blood in his spittle. There was definitely something seriously wrong with him. From then on I made a point of calling on him once a week, to do his shopping and take his washing home to do. I owed him a great deal and I was sad to see him suffering so much. He did not seem to mind that he was dying, simply saying that all he wanted was *de bono mortis*, apparently Latin for 'a good death'.

'What's a good death?' I asked.

'Well, Bruno, although I'm scared of the actual process of dying, and I have many things on my conscience, for me a good death would be meeting my Lord, and putting my hand in His.'

He died at the beginning of the week preceding Christmas and I lit a candle for him in my local church. One of his church wardens

[7] On 3 November 1946 Archbishop Fisher preached on the need for full communion between the churches in a sermon at Cambridge.

came to see me and said that Father Michael wanted me to read the lesson at his funeral service. This was most unusual in those days, and I felt deeply honoured. As I went towards the lectern I felt more nervous than I had expected. I could see people looking at me, as if I were some distant relative they had never met. I was surprised that there was no eulogy, which was the practice in Germany, but it was many years before the Church of England saw the funeral service as a more personal farewell. In his will, Father Michael had left me some books, his large desk crucifix and, of all things, his bicycle. It was a marvellous old machine, what we would call today a 'sit-up-and-beg' bike with a wicker basket attached to the handlebars. It certainly gave me more freedom.

Once again I spent Christmas with Frank, who had become a close friend. I was disappointed that Ann was not there; she had gone to see her aunt in a place called Ormesby, near Great Yarmouth. We put our rations together and with the help of Farmer George we enjoyed a traditional feast, but I could never get Frank to come to church!

Business at the garage increased month by month, with men returning home from the armed forces, now that the war was over, and getting back to their normal lives. However, we did have a sudden drop in trade over the New Year of 1947, when it was extremely cold by English standards, and everyone stayed at home as much as possible in order to keep warm. Having endured a bitter winter in Poltava I did not think it was too bad, but Frank assured me it was very unusual for England.[8] Coal was in such short supply that it had to be rationed and because of the reduced power the daily newspapers were reduced in size. I helped Frank collect wood for his fire, but as my room was heated by a paraffin heater and I had sealed up all the gaps, I was as warm as, if not warmer, than most of those who lived in houses.

My twenty-eighth birthday fell on a Monday, and I invited Frank and Ann, along with Farmer George and his wife, to share a few beers with me in my room. I cooked a stew for us all by

[8] In 1947 coal was rationed during the coldest weather since 1883. On 6 March blizzards cut off fifteen towns, and were followed by serious flooding.

saving my food coupons each week in order to buy the ingredients. I also invited Peter, but I did not think he would come. I was just serving out the stew when Peter arrived, bringing with him some extra beer and a new chess set as a present. I noticed that as soon as he appeared Frank and Farmer George fell silent, and Ann and Farmer George's wife almost ceased their endless chatter. I thought at first it was the embarrassment of seeing Peter's scars, which, although I had become used to seeing them, still looked frightful to anyone seeing them for the first time. However, using his one good arm Peter poured the beer out liberally and we were soon relaxed and talkative again. They all said they would like to swap my garage attic for their houses, because it was the warmest place in town.

The next day Frank and I were tidying up the garage by putting spares into an itemized box system, when he suddenly asked me how I knew Peter. I had assumed that everyone in this small town knew that I played chess with him for a long time. I explained that following the tractor injury the doctor who treated me had asked me to play with his brother Peter, which I had done every Saturday evening since that time.

'That must be a one-off,' Frank said.

'Why? Because I am what you used to call a Jerry?'

'No, nothing to do with the war. He's one of the toffs.'

'Toffs?' I asked.

'His father was the local squire, and he and his brother went to Eton, the poshest school in the country; they wouldn't normally mix with the likes of us.'

The following Saturday I recounted this conversation to a bemused Peter who said it was all true. He told me that he did come from the privileged class and that Eton was what people like Frank called a 'posh school'; he showed me photographs of it so that I could understand why it was seen as unusual by those who did not go there. The uniform was unique; the boys wore striped trousers, tailcoats, starched winged collars with tabs or bow ties. I had never seen anything like it before.

'The war changed all that,' he said. 'My best friend was a pilot who was killed on the same raid on Berlin in which I was injured. He was a brilliant pilot, highly educated, with all the social skills and amusing, but we were not allowed to drink in the same mess because I was a pilot officer, and he was a sergeant pilot, all so bloody stupid.'

'So some of your pilots were not officers?' I asked.

'Only in this country could the class system permeate war; but this war has started to change all that, because this war demanded skills; the way you spoke or where you were educated was not important.'

I sat and listened as he explained yet more about the class system in England: I learned a great deal about the country I was hoping I would be allowed to stay in. There seemed no point in returning to Germany; I had no family there, just bad memories, and the only person I cared for was Marie, from whom I had not heard, despite sending her several letters and the enquiries made by Erik after I had asked him to do so.

During March we put the garage on hold as trade was poor, leaving Ann to fill the occasional car that pulled in. Farmer George needed all the help he could get on the farm because the snow had caused him problems with his livestock, followed by serious floods. By pulling together and through sheer hard work we helped Farmer George through this difficult period, and by April, Frank and I were back in the garage, where business was beginning to pick up again.

That summer I went to the camp in order to report and see how much longer I needed to be on parole, but I found the place entirely deserted; I had been completely forgotten. I decided to speak to Peter about the situation, as I had come to trust him. His advice was that, as I wanted to stay in England, I should continue to keep a low profile and hope that I would eventually fall off the official radar. 'Marry that young girl in the office,' he said.

'What? Ann! I would love to, but she wouldn't marry a German, her brother was killed in North Africa.'

'I lost my best friend over Berlin and I am damaged for life by you lot, but I like you; I don't like the Nazis, but we all know you're normal. Anyway, I could see by the way she was looking at you that she loves you.'

'Frank wouldn't like it.'

'Bruno, stop being a daft arse: Frank has forgotten you're a

German, he actually admires your skills and he's obviously treating you like the son he lost.'

In emotional matters I have never been hasty: at the age of twenty-eight I had only kissed a girl once. My life had consisted of school, war, prison, parole and survival. I pushed all that Peter had said to the back of my mind and decided to watch and wait.

I was surprised to read in the papers that there were anti-Jewish demonstrations in Lancashire, but Frank explained it was not so much anti-Jew as anti the situation in Palestine, where some Jewish terrorists had killed British soldiers.[9] I knew that thousands of displaced Jews were trying to establish a new homeland, but as I had developed the tendency to read only what I wanted to in the newspapers I knew no more. I had, for example, read with pleasure that conscription had been reduced from eighteen to twelve months, which seemed to indicate that peace was here to stay, but I rarely read about the problems in the Holy Land.

At the beginning of November I had a letter from my old *Oberst*. My letter had found its way to him just before he was repatriated to Germany. He had returned to his home in Munich, and discovered that not only had his parents survived, but so had their home. He wrote a long paragraph about the fact that most of the German countryside he had travelled through was completely ruined. I was touched by the fact that he had appreciated what he called my 'comradeship', and promised to stay in touch. He never asked me whether I would return to Germany, and I assumed he had rightly speculated that it was my intention to try to stay here. He also asked me to address him as Georg, and not as *Oberst* because, he wrote, 'the damned war is over now, and you and I were already good friends before we were taken prisoner, luckily by the British and not the Russians'.

It was late November when I made a serious breakthrough as regards a happier future. I was making some tea at the back of the garage and Frank was reading aloud from a newspaper about the marriage of Princess Elizabeth.[10] He was telling me that the royal family had been German, and during the First World War they had

[9] On 1 August 1947.
[10] On 20 November 1947.

anglicized their German names. Just as a joke I said perhaps I should do the same thing and to my surprise Frank said that was not a bad idea and it could be arranged. 'Most people,' he said, 'do not realize you are German, but your name is a dead giveaway.'

'I would like to stay in this country,' I said, 'but I am German.'

'I hope you do stay, this garage won't bloody work without you. We've never been so busy.'

For a minute we said nothing more as I poured out the tea, and Frank perused the pictures of the happy couple.

'I wish my Ann would marry,' he said.

'If I weren't German I would love to marry her.' I suddenly realized what I had blurted out, and nearly spilt the tea, half expecting Frank to snarl and put an end to our friendship because of my audacity.

'Bruno, you are such a fool, why don't you court her?'

I was not sure what Frank was actually saying, but I felt that he meant I was slowly becoming part of their community. Could it be that the man who had once tried to kill me as an act of revenge for his lost son was now happy for me to court his only daughter?

'I am not sure what Ann will feel,' I said.

'Find out, you bloody twerp.'

'Twerp? What's that?'

'A fool.'

That concluded the conversation because a man appeared at the door seeking help with his old Morris, which he had pushed to the front of our garage.

Later that afternoon, with my heart beating so loudly I thought Ann might hear it, I asked her if she would like to go for a drink in the pub that evening.

'What, just the two of us?'

'Is that OK?'

'I was going out, but I can soon cancel that.'

After work, as I washed and got ready to go out, I felt so happy I could not believe it would last. That evening, while Ann and I were sitting in the lounge bar, her old boyfriend Keith walked in. Ann saw him first, and it was only because she flinched that I looked up and saw him approaching us.

'Going out with a Jerry now?' he sneered.

'At least Bruno's not married,' she retorted.

'That was a misunderstanding,' he replied. 'Come on Ann, let the Jerry drown in his own beer and come out with one of your own kind.'

Ann stood up, and for a ghastly moment I thought she was going to leave me sitting there. I was wrong. She stood up in order to throw her cider over Keith. He stepped back and roared at her saying that she was a traitor, being with a Jerry. 'They killed your brother, didn't they?'

'At least my brother was killed doing his duty; he wasn't shirking like you did.'

'Bloody whore,' he shouted.

That was more than I could stand, I rose to my feet and before he knew what had happened I dealt with him in the way we had been taught in our unarmed combat sessions in the *Luftwaffe* training school. I hit him hard, straight on the nose, which has the immediate effect of making the victim shut their eyes; then I punched him hard in the solar plexus, doubling him up. I avoided the third stage of giving him a chop on the back of the neck because that can kill a person. Instead I grabbed him by his hair and after dragging him to the door of the pub, I kicked him out into the street.

When I returned to the snug I realized that I might have made myself deeply unpopular by dealing with the situation in a quasi-military fashion, but instead I was cheered by all and the barman, Ted, offered me a job as a minder for him and his property. It appeared that Keith was universally disliked. Having removed him I did not have to buy another drink that evening. But that was a memorable day for something much more important: I kissed Ann for the first time and she responded in a way that gave me hope for the future. We never saw Keith again that evening, or for several years, but he did turn up once more in 1953.

I do not want to detail too much of my domestic life; thousands of ordinary people have had the same experiences. In fact, I had wondered whether these reflections were worth pursuing, but I have been persuaded that because of what happened to me, as a German prisoner of war in England, it is worth continuing, at least to explain why I feel I must remain totally anonymous, even to this day.

Ann and I were married on Saturday 31 January 1948, four days after my twenty-ninth birthday, and from that date to this I have never regretted marrying her. Frank gave Ann away and Peter was my best man. We were married in the local church and most of the members of the congregation were there, along with Farmer George and many of the farmhands, as well as some of the locals from the pub. I received telegrams from Ruth and Hans as well as Erik. The *Oberst* wrote later, and I was thrilled to have received so much support from past and present friends. In those days we could not begin to contemplate something as expensive as a honeymoon, and the reception consisted of sandwiches and a few beers at the pub. Frank offered to live above the garage so that Ann and I could have his house, but neither of us would allow him to make such a sacrifice. When we did eventually return to my rooms, later that day, we discovered that Peter had left us a bottle of champagne and a wedding present – a crystal decanter which I am looking at as I write.

The international scene that year started to take on a sinister look; we heard that Ghandi had been assassinated[11] but, more seriously for Europe, Berlin seemed to be the centre of attraction once again. This time the enemy was the Russians and we watched with amazement the Berlin airlift,[12] when food and resources were flown in by the Western Allies to relieve the Berliners. It struck me as odd that a few years earlier the same planes had been bombing my home city, yet now they were trying to save it. I also read about the breach between Stalin and Tito,[13] and as the British conscription period was raised by another six months[14] I began to wonder whether the world really was at peace. I suppose that I had been born into a world preparing for war, and had survived that war, and I was now almost paranoid about repeating the same cycle once again. I need not have worried, but I did.

[11] On 20 January 1948.

[12] On 24 June 1948 the Berlin airlifts started.

[13] On 29 June 1948.

[14] On 1 December 1948 conscription was raised again from twelve to eighteen months.

I told Ann all about my life, in the same detail as I am writing about it now, including the events surrounding Josef. She asked me a great number of questions, most of which I could answer. One Saturday morning I received a letter from Albert, which I translated for Ann. It was highly informative and helped her get some sense of my past. I lost the original letter long ago but strangely I have the English version which I copied for Ann.

My Dear Bruno,
I was so pleased to hear that you survived the war. We had no idea what happened to you after Berlin, because we were sent back to Poltava and instead of your returning there to join us, they sent a new chap who was not really very good. A British officer, a Major Lobb, found me and told me all about your adventures from beginning to end. I gather he was an old school friend of yours: I could tell he was once German because he spoke so fluently.

When the Russians eventually broke through there were no planes to transport us back to Germany so we walked, grabbing lifts when we could, for what seemed thousands of miles over endless months. I know you once had a brush on the front line, Franz told us all about it when we walked back, but we seemed to move with the front line as it retreated, and we were treated not as *Luftwaffe* mechanics but as front-line soldiers. We saw some very unpleasant fighting and I consider myself lucky to be alive.

Poor old Friedrich was killed in April in the battle around Berlin. I don't know what happened to him but I heard that he had been killed outright in a shell blast; at least that was merciful. Both Franz and I landed up in the final street-fighting for Berlin. We knew from the start that we would never win, and I think both of us were just preparing to die as suddenly as Friedrich had done. There was no choice in the matter; one of our small squad decided to go home and see if his family was safe, but we found his body next day hanging by the neck from a lamp post. He had run into some SS security guards, who treated him as a traitor for fleeing from the front line. He was not running away, he had just nipped out of the way to check his family, who were supposed to be living only two streets away from where we were positioned.

When the surrender came Franz and I decided not to hand ourselves over to the Russians. We had seen what happened to Russian prisoners at the hands of the SS and we had little doubt that they would not be merciful to us. There was no way we could break out of Berlin and move west, so we found a cellar in a bombed-out suburb and hid for months, going out at night to forage for food. We both lost so much weight that when we did eventually fall into British hands they thought we were concentration camp prisoners. I am glad we did this, because I hear that all those who surrendered to the Russians were taken back to the Soviet Union, and most people doubt that they will ever return.

I cannot begin to tell you what a terrible time the women had after the fall of Berlin. For nights Franz and I just tried to shut our ears to the screaming. They raped old women and children: it was unbelievable. Once the Allies entered Berlin we surrendered to the British, and then we managed to wangle our way out of Berlin. I don't know if you have seen any photographs of the old city, but it is totally wrecked. People live in cellars and single rooms: I don't think a single house survived without serious damage. The total lack of food and fresh water, let alone power supplies has reduced the city to the most primitive state you can imagine. The horrors of what we saw in the fighting and the terrible raping of women and children had a strange effect on Franz. Do you remember how keen he was on the Nazi regime and how he started to change after the massacre in Poltava; he's changed even more now. I hope you are sitting down as you read this, because it will come as an astounding shock when I tell you that the last time I heard from him he was in a seminary training to be a Roman Catholic priest. I get the occasional letter from him and, with your permission, will give him your address. As for me I was lucky, and have found myself in Wolfsburg working on the production of Käfers, the Beetle Volkswagen, making them for the British Army.[15] One of my ambitions is to do what I gather you are doing, open my own garage. In the meantime I am just grateful to still be alive, having found work, food and shelter. I sincerely hope that one day we will be able to meet again and enjoy a game of chess. I am told by your old friend that you have married an English girl called Ann; please convey my best wishes to her.

Your old comrade,
Albert.

This letter was a sharp reminder of a previous life and it certainly made Ann ask me even more questions. I was thrilled to hear from Albert and wrote back at once, promising that one day we would meet again.

Ann and I went to the cinema to watch a film about the Olympics in London,[16] and I was able to tell her about the one held in Berlin which was noted for its extravagance. Life was beginning to feel more settled, especially when the bread rationing came to an end,[17] and with Farmer George's permission I managed to extend my accommodation by building another room on stilts. Frank did most of the work, and this time I was his labourer. In fact, when I look back it was an exceedingly happy time; we were incredibly poor but the future always felt exciting. I continued to play chess with Peter, and near the end of the year he lent me a book by Winston Churchill all about the start of the war.[18] I was fascinated by the author's clarity; he put the whole situation into perspective for me, although with an obvious bias towards the British actions.

[15] The Volkswagen factory at Wolfsburg was handed over by the Americans to British control. No British car industry was interested in the car! The reopening of the factory is mainly accredited to a Major Hirst. He persuaded the British military to use these cars and by 1946 the factory was producing 1,000 cars a month.

[16] April 1948 – the austere XII Olympiad at Wembley.

[17] On 25 July 1948.

[18] In 1948 Churchill published Volume 1, *The Gathering Storm*.

I was a little concerned about Peter because of his own frustrations; his face was about as distorted as it could be and he knew that most women would find it revolting. His loss of an arm stopped him from doing the simplest of things, and apart from chess, reading and the occasional ride in his old sports car, when I drove him, he seemed to be drifting into a state of apathy. His brother, the doctor who had treated me, had moved to America and Peter, despite his wealth, was very lonely, as he had no other family. He would only go down to the local pub if I went with him, and he would become quite aggressive if anyone looked at his face for any length of time.

It was at about this time that two new cars were built: the Morris Minor and the Land Rover. In time I was to become something of an expert on both these cars, especially the Land Rover, which was much used and loved by the local farmers. I also liked the Morris Minor, with its monocoque body (unitary construction – no separate chassis) and accessible low-slung forward engine. I always claimed that it was a car with built-in obsolescence because it was so simple and easy to maintain. I made my first ever trip to London, to visit the Motor Show with Peter,[19] who, despite the fact that he could no longer drive, loved looking at cars. In fact, it had been an RAF friend[20] of his who had named the prototype of the Morris Minor, the Mosquito, after the RAF plane. London was a very different city from Berlin, but I found it fascinating, and spent most of my time looking at some of the famous buildings I had only seen in picture books, especially Buckingham Palace and Nelson's Column in Trafalgar Square.

The new year, 1949, started well for us with the birth of our son whom we called Edward Frank; he was actually due on my birthday, but as he was a little late his birthday was on 29 January. He was baptized a week later in the local church, and my only sadness that day was that my parents and big Bruno were not there; I felt, however, that they were there in spirit. As a consequence

[19] The London Motor Show in October 1948, when the Morris Minor and Land Rover made their first appearance.
[20] Probably Miles Thomas, an ex-fighter pilot.

of the baptism Ann started to come to church with me, and even Frank, the proud grandfather, put in the occasional appearance.

However, life was not always straightforward. One Monday morning in February I had yet another visit from two army officers. They did not want to check my parole or see what I was up to, but once again asked about Josef.

'The war ended nearly four years ago, and he's long dead; why are you so interested in him?'

'You've never heard from him?'

'How could I? He's dead,' I replied.

'Well, that's the problem. One of his victims who survived claims he has been seen.'

'He's definitely dead. What did he do to keep this interest alive?'

'He was a particularly vicious guard; he was part of a group of SS who murdered nearly a hundred Jews and also hundreds of Russian prisoners; there's a real interest in his whereabouts.'

'I'm not lying; I believe he's dead.'

'We've done a background check on you. All we needed to do was hear it from your own lips.'

Before they left I asked if there was any news about my repatriation papers, not because I wanted to return to Germany but because technically I was still a prisoner of war. They just laughed and said I should be sensible and leave it alone, not get tied up in red tape.

I thought about Josef for a day or two, but decided it was all nonsense and spent the weekend shopping with Ann for some clothes, since the clothes rationing had finished.[21]

Although the garage was doing well, which meant Frank and I were always busy, Farmer George was having trouble with his farm. The weather had caused problems and some sort of disease had hit his livestock. He came to see Frank and me one Saturday early in 1949 and told us that he had no choice but to try to sell the garage. We were both thunderstruck and pointed out that the garage was beginning to make real money. He was very upset, and although he agreed with us, he said he was a farmer first and

[21] On 15 March 1949.

foremost; the garage had to go. He was going to try to sell it as it stood: as a working garage with staff and one living, as it were, over the shop. If the worst came to the worst he would employ us on the farm, and he would find a cottage for Ann and me. Nothing could have been more generous and yet at the same time devastating; I was a mechanic, not a farm labourer.

I discussed the issue with Ann but we could not see any way through the problem. The garage occupied quite a large property in the centre of town, and Farmer George was expecting to raise £1,500 from the sale. As we never had more than £20 in the bank at any one time and Frank was only a little better off, the situation seemed hopeless. I felt under enormous pressure, with a wife and a young son to support, and had an extremely restless night worrying about the future. I had a recurrence of some of my nightmares. Frau Goldblatt dominated my mind most of the night, and when I was woken suddenly by a crash of thunder I could have sworn I saw her standing by the bedroom door. I actually sat up in bed and tried to focus on the apparition, but as I came to Frau Goldblatt turned into my old *Luftwaffe* coat, which I used as a dressing gown at night, hanging on the back of the door. As I sat there in a daze, with Ann sleeping beside me, I slowly remembered the diamonds that Frau Goldblatt had given me, which my mother had carefully sewn behind my *Luftwaffe* badge. I had forgotten all about them; indeed only the year before I had nearly sold my coat to a person collecting clothing, but decided to keep it as a dressing gown, the lavatory being downstairs in the cold.

Before Ann woke from her sleep I quickly unstitched the badge and there, to my relief and delight was the bag of four diamonds, dirty but safe. The next question was how I could sell them, or even begin to explain their sudden appearance. While Ann was giving Edward his breakfast I told her the whole story, including why Frau Goldblatt had given them to me in the first place.

'How much do you think they are worth?' she asked.

'I have no idea. I know that lots of people in Germany, especially Jews, put all their savings into gold or diamonds, as it was supposed to be safer. They may be worthless, as many were cheated in the exchange.'

'Ask Peter, he knows all sorts of people.'

That was a simply brilliant idea, and asking Frank to excuse me that morning I left the garage and pedalled up to Peter's house on Father Michael's old bike. For the second time that morning I explained how I had come by the diamonds. Peter said he knew someone who worked in diamonds in a place called Hatton Garden. I explained that the money the stones might raise could make it possible to buy a small stake in the garage business. Peter agreed to help me, and took a train to London, something he rarely did because his disfigurement drew too much embarrassing attention to him.

The next day Frank and I were having a tea break with Ann when Peter walked into the garage. He explained that the diamonds were large and valuable; he could sell them for £800. I suggested that we bought half the garage from Farmer George while encouraging him to keep the other half. However, Peter came up with a better idea, which he had been ruminating over during his train journey back. He said he would like to purchase a fifty per cent share with Frank and me, but on two conditions: first, he wanted to do the books and advise us on business matters; and secondly he wanted to start a car sales business, with him as manager. He said, 'I am fed up with nursing my wounds and feeling sorry for myself. I need an interest, and as I have always loved cars this would be ideal. Do you agree?' He continued, 'As the war recedes the good times will come again and every Tom, Dick and Harry will want to own a car of their own.'

I said nothing, just stood up and shook his hand, while Frank looked on dumbstruck. I have often wondered whether Frau Goldblatt merging into my old *Luftwaffe* coat was in fact a dream or an apparition.

Chapter 16

1950–2000

To write about the rest of my life year by year would be too boring even for my own family. So, in order to tie up the loose ends, I have decided to summarize the next fifty years. I have always insisted both to my family and my friend Andrew that I must remain anonymous, but I must delay explaining the reason for this for a few more paragraphs.

The garage worked well; Frank and I continued to service and repair cars, and we remained firm friends until his death from cancer in 1969. He lived just long enough to enjoy the company of three of his grandchildren as they were growing up. Peter expanded the garage to include the sale of second-hand cars, and through his connections managed to persuade someone at Rover to grant us a franchise to sell new models. Through a strange twist of fate, I read in a car magazine that Volkswagens were being sold in this country, through an agent in Sheffield called Jack Gilder, and at the same time my old friend the *Oberst*, Georg Freisher, visited me for the first time.

We had stayed in touch, even playing a few games of correspondent chess, but never meeting until early one morning in 1953 a knock on the front door announced his arrival. Ann and I now lived in a small house almost next door to our garage. When I opened the front door and saw him, I almost saluted him, which amused us both. Ann adored him, and although I had a few misgivings about Peter meeting a German pilot, they were soon chatting about the old days and very quickly became close friends. I say close friends because Georg, as I now called him, stayed in close contact with us all until his death in a car accident in 1987.

Georg was a senior manager at the developing Volkswagen works, and he was proposing to grant us a franchise to sell the new Beetle. Both Peter and I were very keen, not least because in our opinion, the air-cooled, fuel-economic, yet fast car would do as well as, if not better than many of the British models, including my favourite, the Morris Minor. We were right, and because of an increase in business we sold our garage a few years later and bought a new place in a larger town, which Peter decided had too few garages and was ripe for development. Two years later we bought another garage that sold small sports cars, which had always been Peter's main interest.

It was in this new town that I bumped into Ann's first boyfriend, Keith. I could hardly believe it was him; he was now a policeman. We met in the High Street, and it was immediately clear that he was still antagonistic towards me. I looked him straight in the eye and asked if the authorities knew he had been on the run from the Royal Navy. His look told me that was not the case, so I pointed out that it was probably best that our paths never crossed again. I heard some time later that he had requested a transfer to a police force on the other side of the country. I suspect, apart from Keith, that I am the only person alive who knows why he moved so quickly. Many years later I read that he had been in trouble with the law himself, and had landed in prison; apart from reading this in a Sunday newspaper I never heard anything else about him.

Very soon we were employing quite a large staff, but, although I was one of the owners, I still worked with Frank as a mechanic. Peter did all the upfront work, but always consulted me on any changes he thought were necessary. As I worked in the workshop many new employees thought I was just another fellow worker; they had never known a boss roll up his sleeves and work in the oil and grime – it led to several amusing incidents.

During this period of expansion I had a letter from a Jewish council in Israel asking me if I was the Bruno Sonn who had worked in Lille during the war. I at once thought that the case of my brother Josef was still being pursued, and consulted Georg about the matter. But he and Peter both agreed that I had nothing to hide, and so I answered in the affirmative. Nothing happened for a year, and I had all but forgotten about this enquiry when I received a letter that acknowledged that when I was billeted with a Claire Champeaux, I had been extremely helpful in saving the lives of some Jewish girls hidden in the lady's attic. I had all but forgotten this incident, and it came as a bolt from the blue to revisit this scene. I was invited, with Ann and one other guest, to a reception in London. We decided to invite Peter, and the three of us set off in one of the new Beetles. Along with mainly French people, we were wined and dined at a club near Pall Mall. I met Claire Champeaux, who still spoke no English, but Peter spoke French and he told me how much she had hated me until I had saved the girls' lives. She said that it was the only time during the war that she saw Germans as human beings. Then, to my astonishment, I met one of the girls; she was now a French doctor. Another was working in a kibbutz in Israel as a teacher. I have to confess I was somewhat embarrassed and a little overcome; I was not used to being praised for what had happened during the war. I had never mentioned this incident to Ann or Peter, and my greatest pleasure was seeing their faces glow with pleasure as they realized that I really was as human as they had always hoped. As in the old days I shook hands formally and politely with my old landlady, and was delighted that both she, and the young woman doctor, gave me a hug which meant more to me than words. I never heard from Claire Champeaux again, but the doctor, who was called Naomi, wrote to me, and we have stayed in touch ever since. I have even visited her in her home just outside Paris.

In another coincidence I bumped into Fred, my old prison guard, at a motor show in Earls Court. He had not changed a bit, and, true to form, was running a pub somewhere in Hackney. He came to stay with us on a few occasions, but one day he suddenly left England to live in Wanganui, New Zealand. I always suspected that he had run foul either of the law or of some local gangsters; he was a good man, but he always sailed close to the wind.

In 1960, when Georg invited me to visit him in Germany, I realized I was still technically a prisoner of war; I was still on parole. Fortunately Peter, who was a great administrator and knew all sorts of people, managed to untangle the situation. It took nearly six months, but I was soon a free man again and I chose to become a British citizen. As I looked at my new British passport I wondered what my father or big Bruno would have thought.

Ann stayed at home because of the children, but Peter and I travelled together to see the Volkswagen works in Wolfsburg. Georg entertained us as if we were royalty, and we could see that VW was going places. I also managed to catch up with Albert, who to my amusement was running his own garage selling Beetles, just like me. We talked and played chess, just as we always had, but I was sorry that Albert had never met a woman to marry. I often wondered if he was lonely because he remained a firm bachelor to the day he died in 1990. He visited Ann and me many times in England, and it was he who advised Peter to take a long serious look at the BMW, as he believed it would one day be a best seller in our market.

Peter liked him very much, and it was now my turn to pull his leg about how once he would not play chess with a Jerry, and now he played with me, Albert and Georg. It did not stop him grumbling about the fact that although Germany had lost the war they built the best cars. It was all very good-natured banter, and I found it fascinating that a British bomber pilot had become firm friends with a *Luftwaffe Oberst* and two *Luftwaffe* mechanics. The end of the war had stripped away any consideration of rank or nationality. I am grateful that I learned to play chess, as it was this that brought us all together in the first place. It is a game that crosses boundaries of nationality, rank, class and even religion.

Berlin was the not the easiest of places to visit in those days, but Georg did manage to come with Peter and me to visit my old city once more. I think we were all shocked, not just at the division of the city by the Soviets, but by the bombed-out buildings everywhere we went. My old friend Erik met us and looked after us for four days. He had many things he wanted to tell me, and tried several times to talk to me alone, but as Peter was in a strange ex-enemy city, which he had once bombed, I could sense he was interested but uncomfortable, and so needed my company.

On the final day of our visit Georg went off by himself to meet some old friends, and Erik told me about big Bruno's sister, Marie, whom I had been asking about. It appeared that she could still be alive, but there was no way of knowing because she lived in the Soviet sector of the city; the war was still dividing us. A year later Erik eventually found out that Marie had been killed during the battle for Berlin. I found this very sad and hard to come to terms with because I had always hoped to meet her again, although I had suspected the worst because of the lack of response to my many letters. After hearing this I lit four candles in any church I visited, or in which I worshipped.

It transpired that it was not Marie that Erik wanted to speak to me about, but my brother Josef, and as time was running out he spoke to me in German. I replied in German that Peter was well aware of Josef, what he had done, what he had been and the fact that he was dead. We were sitting at a coffee shop table on the pavement. I was enjoying my pipe and Peter one of his favourite American cigarettes, when Erik pushed a photograph towards me and asked if I thought the man in the background could be Josef. My pipe fell out my mouth and onto the table: it was Josef, or his perfect double, older but little changed. I said it had to be someone who was very like him, because Josef had been killed in the east years ago. Erik explained that he believed that Josef had been involved in a battle in which he was the sole survivor, and had taken the opportunity to switch identities with another man who had been killed. I asked how this could happen, since the family would know the difference, but Erik pointed out that many families had been completely obliterated.

At this stage Peter asked Erik the point of this enquiry; he was surprised that war criminals were still being hunted. He pointed out that it would be unfair to expect me to turn my own brother in. To my surprise he then told Erik about the French landlady and the Jewish girls I had helped, suggesting that that may redress the balance. I thought Erik was about to explode, but he managed to restrain himself, and simply asked me whether I would be prepared to see if the man in the photograph was actually Josef. Then, as an act of friendship, he would ask my permission before he informed his superiors. I agreed, and that evening Peter and I went to a rebuilt office block and watched a door through which Josef was due to pass at about 6 p.m. At precisely that time Josef came out. I walked up beside him and greeted him by name; he stopped dead in his tracks and looked at me, and I knew beyond any doubt it was him.

'I thought you were dead,' he said, and even as he spoke he was looking around to see if we were being watched.

'More to the point, I was told by the authorities that you were dead, so why are you using a different name?'

'How did you find me?' he responded.

'I saw your photograph.'

'Where?'

'In a newspaper.'

I can hardly recall that fraught conversation. He made it clear that he had changed his name as a precaution, and I told him he was being hunted as a war criminal. He made a sour reference to my father being a Jew, and indicated what he believed the Jews had done to Germany by sweeping his hand around, pointing at some derelict buildings. I looked at him with disgust and told him we had met by accident, and would not be meeting again. He looked relieved at that, and I walked straight back to Peter, who was watching from a distance.

I told Erik I did not care if he exposed Josef, but perhaps he would be kind enough to wait until I was back in England. I shared this incident with Georg, and on the way back to England, Peter suggested that if this news got out it might be wise to consider changing my name by deed poll, 'Anglicise it like the royal family,' he said. For the sake of the children Ann agreed, and I changed my name to an English version. Bruno remained my middle name so that there was no confusion amongst my oldest and closest friends. My new passport was issued within three months of our Berlin visit, and when Peter and I purchased our third garage, a BMW dealership, we changed the name of the firm to my new name, alongside Peter's.

A few years later, when Erik stayed with us for a week, I heard that Josef, using his new identity and image, was an up-and-coming politician in the new West Germany, but very much under the control of British intelligence, who had made it clear to him that his future depended on their goodwill. I found it all rather distasteful, but I was glad that I had kept everything to myself, because although Josef died in the 1980s his son became a German politician, and I felt the sins of the fathers should not taint their sons. I never saw or spoke to Josef again.

Erik died in a mysterious accident in the late 1970s; although nothing was said I am sure it was to do with the Cold War. I attended his funeral and that was the last time I saw Ruth and Hans. I did not tell Ruth about Josef, but I gather that Erik told Hans, who told Ruth, and she resented my silence. I wrote and apologized, but she did not reply, and it has always been a source of deep regret that Ruth cut me off so completely. I have no idea what happened to her and Hans; when I saw them at Erik's funeral they had no family, and although Hans was polite, Ruth ignored me. Josef had much to answer for in the wider world, but he also certainly tore our family to shreds.

In 1980 I turned sixty, but I had no intention of retiring, even though Peter and I were very wealthy. Nobody knew I was German. I was a member of the local chamber of commerce and, despite my mistrust of politics, I became a member of the town council and remained so for fifteen years. I was about to announce my retirement from the council when they elected me Mayor. I was bemused by the fact that I was travelling around in a chauffeur-driven car, opening fêtes, attending school events, and even opening a new hospital wing. When I opened the new hospital wing I visited the patients, and found a lady called Mrs Goldblatt. It was not Frau Goldblatt, of course, but she had come to England in the 1930s, and I wished my Frau Goldblatt had done the same. When Peter and I shared a whisky over a game of chess, he would frequently pull my leg about my being the Mayor. He knew that had anyone bothered to ask about my origins I would have told them the truth; but nobody did – they all assumed that I was as English as the next person. When a town councillor asked Peter whether I had been his colleague in the wartime RAF he said, 'Yes, in a funny sort of way.' A fellow member of the Rotary club also assumed that Peter and I had been friends during the war, and asked me to do an after lunch speech; I declined and persuaded Peter to do so. He spoke with great authority, but with a gentleness that I would not have recognized when I first met him as a prisoner of war to play chess. We both joined the local chess club, and Peter was chairman for many years. We played in a few tournaments, but our best chess, our favourite games, were personal, with a glass of whisky at our side. Ann was always brilliant about such evenings, never resenting the two us disappearing into another room.

I was a church warden for five years, a position which does not appeal to many people, but which is vital to any Church. I continued to serve at the altar, finding great spiritual value in worshipping in the old-fashioned Anglo-Catholic style. Not because, as Peter claimed, the incense reminds me of my pipe, but because it brings in the element of awe and mystery, as there is a sense of mystery in life, and there is also a sense of awe in that style of worship which appeals to me. Sometimes I sit alone in the church and remember the dead, especially my parents, big Bruno and Marie, and I can almost feel a sense of the numinous as I light candles in their memory. I still read my daily offices but from a more up-to-date prayer book; and I confess that I smoke my pipe at the same time. I was once told that I should not smoke when I pray, but that I could pray when I smoke; so I smoke first then pray.

Before Albert died he discovered that Franz had indeed been ordained a priest and was now a bishop. Albert had managed to contact him briefly, and he had explained that the experience of the war had forced him to question why man was on the earth in the first place. The Battle of Berlin had been a turning point for him; the senseless brutality and cruelty had darkened his soul, and he had vowed to himself, and to God, that if he should survive he would devote the rest of his life to God's service. This was excellent news for me, because I had seen aspects of my brother in Franz, as well as reminders of Adolf Bier and Big Dick, but he had changed completely.

Then Peter died, which was a dreadful shock to Ann and me. He did not turn up to play chess one Saturday evening, and when he failed to answer the phone I walked round to his house, let myself in and found him dead in his chair from a heart attack. As his only brother lived in the USA he had left all his belongings and holdings to Ann and me. I now light another candle when in church.

Ann died four years ago, a devastating loss which made me sell everything and move to a flat in Bromley to be near my daughter. Ann and I had three children: Edward, followed a year later by William, and finally Ann, named after her mother. I left a garage to William, my son who, like me, was a mechanic, but sold the other four. We had sufficient funds to send them all to good schools, Edward, who was very bright, went to Cambridge to study law, William did not like school, and left as soon as he could to work with me in the garage, and Ann became a doctor, and married a fellow doctor whom she had met at King's College, London. Edward did not remain a lawyer for long, but entered politics, despite my protestations that it often led to a corrupt way of life. At the time of writing he is now an MP, and does not know that his uncle was a war criminal, and that the German politician he frequently meets in Brussels, is in fact his cousin. For better or worse I decided that Josef did not exist, which is why I have kept this account anonymous.

Having reached the age that I am now, I am very much on my own as I have outlived my own generation. In my prayers I often see Ann sitting beside me, and Peter sometimes feels present when I am looking at a chess problem. At times it also feels as if big Bruno is sitting on the other side of the room waiting for me. I wait, I simply wait for God to call me to Him, and spend my remaining time smoking my pipe, playing chess and saying my daily prayers. Now that this account has been completed it is time for me to lay to rest the dark times, and focus on the memories of the good times.

Bruno died in 2007.